# MAKING
# SPACE FOR
# INDIGENOUS
# FEMINISM

# MAKING SPACE FOR INDIGENOUS FEMINISM

edited by
JOYCE GREEN

Fernwood Publishing • Zed Books

Editing: Brenda Conroy
Cover image: Christi Belcourt
Cover design: John van der Woude
Printed and bound in Canada by Hignell Book Printing

Published in Canada by Fernwood Publishing
Site 2A, Box 5, 32 Oceanvista Lane
Black Point, Nova Scotia, B0J 1B0
and 324 Clare Avenue, Winnipeg, Manitoba, R3L 1S3
www.fernwoodpublishing.ca

Published in the rest of the world by Zed Books Ltd.
7 Cynthia Street, London NI 9JF, UK
and Room 400, 175 Fifth Avenue, New York, 10010, USA
Distributed in the USA exclusively by Palgrave Macmillan,
a division of St. Martins Press, LLC, 175 Fifth Ave., New York, 10010, USA.
www.zedbooks.co.uk

Zed Books ISBN 978-1-84277-929-3 hb; ISBN 978-1-84277-940-8 pb
British CIP available from the British Library.
American CIP has been applied for.

Fernwood Publishing Company Limited gratefully acknowledges the financial support
of the Government of Canada through the Book Publishing Industry Development
Program (BPDIP), the Canada Council for the Arts and the Nova Scotia
Department of Tourism and Culture for our publishing program.

  Canadian Patrimoine
Heritage canadien  The Canada Council for the Arts
Le Conseil des Arts du Canada  NOVA SCOTIA
Tourism and Culture

Library and Archives Canada Cataloguing in Publication

Making space for indigenous feminism / Joyce Green, editor.

Includes bibliographical references.
ISBN 978-1-55266-220-5

1. Indigenous women—Political activities. 2. Indigenous women—Social conditions.
3. Feminism. 4. Women political activists. I. Green, Joyce A. (Joyce Audry), 1956-

HQ1161.M34 2006      305.48'8      C2006-906208-0

# CONTENTS

*This book is dedicated to
the search for authenticity and justice
that define feminism.*

# ACKNOWLEDGEMENTS

Special thanks to:

• Alyssa Peel, Rauna Kuokkanen, Gunhild Hoogensen and Makere Stewart-Harawira for acts of editing and translation that made it possible to meet deadlines;

• Lorraine Cameron and Dena Klashinsky, Status of Women Canada, B.C.–Yukon Region, for feminist solidarity and faith in the project of the Aboriginal Feminism Symposium;

• the contributors to this book, whose brilliance sheds light on the reality and power of Aboriginal feminism and who, in their lives, put their politics into practice and demonstrate that "the personal is political" and the political is the responsibility of all;

• Christi Belcourt, Métis artist, for the image on the cover;

• all the women who attended the Aboriginal Feminism Symposium and all who are part of the growing network of Aboriginal feminists;

• feminist elders Shirley Bear and Shirley Green, who offered constancy and support from the Symposium through the process of book making;

• the non-Aboriginal feminists who supported the Symposium and my efforts to bring this book into being. Among them, Darlene Juschka, professor of Women's Studies, University of Regina and member of the Kitchen Table Collective, deserves particular thanks;

• the Kitchen Table Collective, for its feminist solidarity and sustaining support for this project. KTC members Sheila Roberts, Darlene Juschka, Carmen Gill, Pat Gallagher, Adriane Paavo and Kathleen McNutt warrant particular mention; and

• the Fernwood Publishing people, Wayne Antony, Brenda Conroy, Beverley Rach and Debbie Mathers.

# THE CONTRIBUTORS

TINA BEADS is an Aboriginal feminist of Ojibway and Finnish descent. She began her activism while working at the Native Brotherhood of British Columbia with an interest in Aboriginal fishing rights. After having two daughters, Beads shifted her focus to the anti-violence movement and joined the collectives of Vancouver Rape Relief and Women's Shelter and the Aboriginal Women's Action Network. Beads is currently working at Status of Women Canada but still dreams with her activist heart that one day all of the struggles by feminists past, present and future will make the world a safer place for all women.

SHIRLEY BEAR is a Maliseet artist, traditional healer and political activist best known for her opposition to the sexist membership sections of the *Indian Act*. She was born on the Negootkook First Nations, New Brunswick, which she describes as, "a deceptively peaceful community nestled between two rivers, Wulustookoqw and Tobec, a traditional food-gathering place. I grew up weaving baskets and drawing pictures whenever and wherever I could. My first introduction to petroglyphs in the 1960s was a revelation. I found, in these images, a history, and an ancient story which continues to be my strength and a sense of foreverness on this continent. It's this fortitude that has been a lifeline for me throughout the battle to change the discriminatory set of laws in the Canadian *Indian Act*."

JORUNN EIKJOK is a Sami social anthropologist, feminist and Sami rights activist from Varanger, the north-eastern part of Norway. She is working on documentaries about Sami society and has run programs about Indigenous community development in Russia and Norway. Her professional activities include free-lance journalist, teacher, social scientist, senior official in Sami affairs in the regional county administration, and she headed and established the Sami department at University Hospital of Tromsø. She has been a member of the steering committee for the International Indigenous Women's Network.

COLLEEN GLENN is a Métis woman, a mother and grandmother, and a life-long political activist. Glenn has worked in organizations ranging from Planned Parenthood, to the Métis Association of Alberta, the Alberta Status of Women Action Committee, Indian Rights for Indian Women and the New Democratic Party, for which she was a candidate in the 1993 federal election.

JOYCE GREEN is associate professor of political science at the University of Regina. Green's work focuses on the politics of decolonization in Canada; on identity, human rights and citizenship; and on the way in which sexism, racism and race privilege is encoded in Canadian political culture. She is is of English, Ktunaxa and Cree-Scots Métis descent.

SHIRLEY GREEN is of English, Ktunaxa and Cree-Scots Métis descent. Green was born and raised in Ktunaxa territory. She is a mother and grandmother, elder and senior. She is exploring the relationship between experience, identity and sex in the context of her family and community. She currently lives in Cranbrook, B.C.

DENISE K. HENNING is President and Vice-Chancellor of the University College of the North. A Cherokee/Choctaw originating from Creek County in Oklahoma, she has committed her life, work and research to inclusion and equity in higher education in North America. Henning has worked to develop and implement programs that will reduce the disparity in education attainment of Indigenous peoples in Canada and the United States.

GUNHILD HOOGENSEN is a non-Indigenous woman of Norwegian ancestry in solidarity with Indigenous feminists. She is a political scientist at the University of Tromsø and mother of three children. Her research focuses on the application and relevance of the human security concept to the Arctic region and peoples. She generously translated Jorunn Eikjok's article from Norwegian to English as a contribution to this book.

KATHIE IRWIN is descended from Ngati Porou, Ngati Kahungunu, Scots, Orkney Island and Irish forebearers. Mother of two teenage children, Irwin is the Director, Academic Programs at the Wellington Campus of the tribal university Te Whare Wananga o Awanuiarangi. She has served over twenty years as an academic in New Zealand universities. Irwin specializes in Maori research and development, and has a particular interest in the issues facing Maori women.

RAUNA KUOKKANEN is a Sami woman from the Finnish side of the Deatnu Valley. She completed her Ph.d. at the University of British Columbia. She has edited an anthology on contemporary Sami literature (*Juoga mii geasuha*, 2001), nominated for the Sami Council Literary Prize in 2002. She has published articles on Sami literature, oral tradition and issues related to Indigenous research paradigms. Currently, she holds a post-doctoral fellowship with a collaborative research project on Globalization and Autonomy at McMaster University, where her research focuses on Indigenous women and alterNative economic models.

EMMA LAROCQUE is professor of Native Studies at the University of Manitoba, where she specializes in historiography, contemporary Aboriginal writing, post-colonial criticism and popular cultural productions/representation, gender roles, identity and Métis history. LaRocque is both a published scholar and poet. She is a Métis woman, originally from a Métis community in northeastern Alberta. In 2005 LaRocque received a Lifetime Achievement Award in the National Aboriginal Awards.

SHARON MCIVOR served the Native Women's Association of Canada as vice-president in the turbulent time of the late 1980s and early 1990s. She is a prominent activist for Aboriginal women's human rights. She is on the board of FAFIA (Feminist Alliance for International Action), which advocates for women's human rights. She is Nle?kepmxcin, from Merritt, British Columbia.

ALYSSA PEEL is a non-Indigenous woman in solidarity with Indigenous people and a scholar of Aboriginal governments, politics and decolonization efforts in Canada. She assisted in editing several chapters in this collection.

ANDREA SMITH is Cherokee, assistant professor of American Culture (Native American Studies) and Women's Studies, University of Michigan; the author of *Conquest: Sexual Violence and American Indian Genocide* (South End Press, 2005); the co-coordinator of the Boarding School Healing Project; and a co-founder of Incite! Women of Color Against Violence. Her forthcoming manuscript with Duke University Press is tentatively titled *Unlikely Alliances: American Indian and Christian Right Organizing*.

VERNA ST. DENIS is associate professor of Education in the College of Education, University of Saskatchewan, specializing in teaching anti-oppressive education. She was born into a Métis road allowance community on the southwest border of the Prince Albert National Park and is also a member of Beardy's and Okemasis First Nation. She is both a graduate and former faculty of Aboriginal Teacher Education programs in Saskatchewan. Her research includes promoting a critical race analysis in Aboriginal education.

MAKERE STEWART-HARAWIRA is of Maori-Scots descent and is an assistant professor in the Department of Education Policy Studies and Director of the International Centre for Indigenous Research Project at the University of Alberta and the author of *The New Imperial Order: Indigenous Responses to Globalization* (London: Zed Books; New Zealand and Australia: Huai Books, 2005). She is also a mother and grandmother.

CHRISTI BELCOURT created the beautiful artwork for the cover of this collection. She is Métis, feminist, mother and wife, and artist. Born in 1966 and raised in Ottawa, she now lives in Whitefish Falls, Ontario. Her art has been shown across Canada, including the Canadian Museum of Civilization and The Thunder Bay Art Gallery, and has been reviewed in *Canadian Dimension* magazine. Her work may be viewed at <www.christibelcourt. com>. It is also on permanent display within the Canadian Museum of Civilization, Hull, QC. Belcourt provided the art for the cover of this book as a gesture of solidarity. These are her words:

> Like generations of Aboriginal beadworkers before me, my art celebrates the beauty of flowers and plants while exploring their symbolic properties. I follow the tradition of Métis floral art, inspired by the traditional beadwork patterns of Métis and First Nation women, and use the subject matter of plants as a metaphor for our own lives to relay a variety of meanings which include concerns for the environment, biodiversity, spirituality and awareness of Métis culture. This journey has led me on an exploration into traditional Métis art, Métis history, traditional medicines and contemporary issues that face the Métis in modern times.
>
> Although not apparent to me at the outset, I would now define my artwork as unabashedly feminine. The subject matter may speak to the universal in all — but it is clearly from a woman's standpoint. This is because of the strong women in my life who have propped me up, who have inspired me, and whose own artwork has had an indelible influence on my artwork. The women I've been blessed to know have been the backbone and the centre of their families, their communities and their Nations. When women share with each other, when we give to one another, or set ourselves out to work together it is a powerful force. I am thankful to be included in the company of the fine women in this publication.

# INDIGENOUS FEMINISM
## From Symposium to Book

### *Joyce Green*

Over the years that I've been studying Indian[1] women's political organizing, I noticed that Aboriginal women who organized on apparently feminist issues rarely identified as feminist. Yet, I knew Aboriginal[2] women who had dedicated a large part of their lives to political activism who deployed an explicit or implicit feminist analysis. These women sought to claim rights for Aboriginal women. None sought to destroy their communities, their identities or their cultures: quite the contrary. All had witnessed or experienced patriarchal and colonial oppression in both the settler society and in their own communities. None were blind to the effects of colonialism and racism on Aboriginal men. They took gender seriously in the context of understanding the life experiences of Aboriginal men and women, and understood Aboriginal women to suffer from the particular ways in which racist and sexist oppression are brought to bear on that inalterably unified category.

Nor was this Indigenous feminism limited to Canada. A number of women from Indigenous communities in the U.S., Sápmi (Samiland), Aotearoa/New Zealand and Australia also seemed to be using a feminist analysis, or drawing on feminist theories or organizing principles, in political and community activism and in their writings. Some of this work was carefully qualified as deriving from traditional Indigenous cultural values concerning women, but much of it melded an interpretation of traditions, or a critique of traditions and contemporary practices, with approaches that were clearly feminist in orientation.

The slim literature base on Aboriginal women contains virtually nothing by Aboriginal authors claiming to be feminists or to write about Aboriginal feminism. A number of writers unequivocally reject feminism for Aboriginal women. Some Aboriginal women activists and scholars privately identify as feminist but are cautious not to do so in their political statements and written work. Some of these women relate stories of being harassed and persecuted for their political positions. Despite this, these women were also catalysts for some very powerful and interesting political movements and for original and insightful academic work. It was obvious that this small but powerful critique deserved to be taken seriously as a valid political stance.

In Canada, since the 1970s, the academic literature has been strengthened by the emergence of a cadre of Aboriginal intellectuals, most of whom were gender-blind or hostile to gendered analysis. Non-Indigenous scholars began reading these contributions and uncritically accepting the proposition that feminism was inauthentic, un-Aboriginal and in other ways deeply problematic for Indigenous peoples. This led to a consensus in the thinking of scholars and others that feminism was an alien ideology inimical to the political and cultural objectives of Aboriginal women in particular and Aboriginal peoples in general.

In 2002, my interest in Aboriginal feminism and the opportunity to focus on it came together. I was spending a year at the Saskatchewan Institute of Public Policy (SIPP) and had time to devote to organizing, research and writing. The conditions were right for me to organize a symposium by and for Aboriginal feminists. It seemed important to bring some of these women together to talk about being Aboriginal feminists. The Canadian federal government agency Status of Women Canada had funds available to community groups to pursue research activities, community building and similar kinds of tasks. I belonged to a feminist affinity group, the Kitchen Table Collective (KTC), and we decided to apply for funds to bring some Aboriginal feminists to Regina for the symposium.

With the sterling support of Lorraine Cameron, Director of the B.C.-Yukon regional office of Status of Women Canada; the technical support and assistance of one of her officials, Dena Klashinsky (herself an Aboriginal woman); and the support of the Alberta-Saskatchewan regional office of Status of Women Canada, the KTC submitted a successful proposal and grant application to hold the Aboriginal Feminism Symposium in Regina. Cameron and Klashinsky epitomized the best of feminist solidarity, in this case making it possible for the KTC to do what we may not otherwise have been able to. Thus, the organizing (and then the Symposium) was a good example of activists, a community group, a government agency and the university working together to make possible an event that involved political theory, public policy, feminist activism, empowerment, community building and exploration of citizenship capacity.

Some of the contributions to the symposium helped me to understand the parameters of and context for Aboriginal feminism better. Virtually all participants expressed the view that coming together was therapeutic, politically significant and interesting — and further, that we should make an effort to build on the Symposium. This book is part of that, and its purpose is to stake out some discursive space and to provide evidence that, for some Aboriginal women, feminism has some theoretical and political utility.

The Aboriginal Feminism Symposium, August 21–22, 2002, was comprised of self-designated Aboriginal feminists, who I had invited based on either my own familiarity with their political and intellectual positions and activism, or based on references from other feminist Aboriginal women. The number of invitees was kept small, in keeping with a tentative first initiative. Thus, the participant list at the first symposium was not a result of representative or systematic invitations; rather it was developed from networking with the Aboriginal feminists I knew.

The symposium brought together twenty-four participants for a program that included panel presentations and round-table discussions on particular topics. This was a diverse group: participants included Inuit, Métis, First Nations and non-status Indian women; some women were firmly located in Aboriginal communities and cultures, others had more urban or hybrid identities. It included women whose first language was their Aboriginal language, and who continued to speak it, and women who spoke only English. It included women with graduate and professional education, and women with basic in-school education. Clearly, then, the shared interest in feminism transcended these other characteristics and was not alien or hostile to any of them. And yet, most of the women had endured much criticism and some had suffered direct physical abuse and political attacks by Aboriginal men and women as a result of defending Aboriginal women's interests. Some women had endured snide comments about their sexuality, about their authenticity as culturally located people, about their political integrity and about their motives.

The symposium opened and closed with prayer offered by Maliseet elder and Tobique Women's Group activist Shirley Bear, who was also a participant. This helped to focus us on the importance of treating each other, and our discussions, with respect and kindness. Some women had been asked to make presentations using their feminist analysis; the topics had to be relevant to Aboriginal feminism. Within those broad parameters, a number of issues relevant to identity, security and community emerged. The range of papers included children and self-government and treaty negotiations; the *Indian Act*; women and violence and psychological trauma; elder perspectives of race and racism; teaching in the racist, sexist academy; Aboriginal feminist activism; First Nations and Inuit constitution and political development; Aboriginal identity politics; Aboriginal and human rights; and racist and sexist misconstructions of Aboriginal mythology. Throughout, it became clear that these women experience a profound lack of security in their professional, political and personal lives as Aboriginal women and as self-conscious feminists; as racialized Others in a racist society; and as Indigenous persons located in (and sometimes, excluded from) colonized Indigenous communities. The very label "Aboriginal feminist" was fraught for symposium participants.

Speaking at the symposium about the pressures exerted against Aboriginal feminists, Sharon McIvor said once Aboriginal women identify publicly as feminist,

You don't have a place anymore because there's no one else around like you… so it is a very, very lonely place to be…. Even those women and men who support you can't do it publicly because it's not safe…. Even in the academic arena (when) you're presenting papers, it's unusual to do a presentation and not have an Aboriginal woman academic get up and challenge what you've said and invariably it will be "You're not traditional. You're destroying the foundations of our nations because you are saying what you're saying."

The few Aboriginal women who do identify as feminist are very cautious about claiming the label and about publicly invoking the analysis. This reality had impelled the decision to frame the symposium as a closed space, limited to the invited participants, to ensure that women would feel safe to talk to each other about being feminist, absent the disciplinary effect of having to justify their self-designation or their Aboriginal authenticity. The lack of intellectual and political space for the vigorous and free exchange of ideas, including critical and oppositional ideas such as feminism, suggests that Aboriginal feminists do not enjoy enough security to participate routinely in the freedoms of speech, thought and association that are considered minimums for expression of citizenship in contemporary Canada.

As the 2002 Aboriginal Feminism Symposium was closing, it became apparent to many of us that it had been important to come together to share views in a safe space with others of like mind, and the wish was expressed that this could happen again. The symposium participants agreed that the presentations should be collected into a book, and I offered to coordinate that project. However, over time it became apparent that life is too complicated and too busy for many women to find time for writing and editing. If the book was to be written, it would have to include authors who were Indigenous feminists but who were not necessarily at the symposium. Thus, this book includes both authors who were at the original symposium and authors who were not. It demonstrates that there are more Aboriginal feminists "out there" than those few who attended the symposium and that their intellectual contribution is powerful and original. The book also shows that Indigenous feminism exists throughout the settler states: our contributors are primarily from Canada, but they are also from the U.S., from Sápmi (Samiland) and Aotearoa/New Zealand. Had we more time and space, we could have included many more women from the international Indigenous community; the perspectives here are evidence that they exist.

Two non-Indigenous contributors participated in this book as acts of solidarity with Indigenous feminists. Gunhild Hoogensen, a political scientist at the University of Tromsø in Norway, translated Jorunn Eikjok's chapter from Norwegian to English. Alyssa Peel, a graduate student at the University of Regina, served as an able editorial assistant, editing prose, fact checking, confirming references, providing technological support and otherwise making it possible for chapters to proceed to publication with as few copyediting problems as possible.

Readers will notice that not all contributors to this collection agree with each other on all matters. This diversity of opinion and perspective does not mean that there is no agreement — most authors are in general agreement on many issues. The differences do suggest that Indigenous feminism is a body of work, a set of theoretical perspectives and a set of political positions and practices whose practitioners take a general approach, and then make it specific. The contributors to this book deploy their feminism carefully, specifically — and differently — drawing on political, historical and cultural contexts and their own particular ideologies to form their feminism. Thus, each has a particular "take" on the topic, and this collection reflects that diversity.

The chapters in the book are divided into three parts: (1) the theory of Indigenous feminism; (2) particular political eras and issues where Indigenous feminism and feminists played a role; and (3) individual Indigenous feminists who talk both about their particular political struggles and about their feminism. Authors also consider issues using feminist analysis, or they explore what Aboriginal feminism is and what its strengths are. Joyce Green addresses the question of what Aboriginal feminism is. Verna St. Denis uses post-structural theory to reveal and condemn colonialism in education. Emma LaRocque writes about the ethical foundation for decolonization and feminism; LaRocque also contributes a powerful poem that has a manifestly feminist and post-colonial sensibility. Rauna Kuokkanen explores the transformational power of Sami feminism. Andrea Smith shows the lie in the proposition that Aboriginal women do not and should not use feminist analysis, by showing that patriarchal oppression isn't only a colonial imposition. Jorunn Eikjok writes of the power and peril of feminism for Sami women, thus also demonstrating the international power of patriarchy and colonialism. Makere Stewart-Harawira considers how Indigenous feminist analysis may be used to fight contemporary imperialism. Joyce Green documents the activism of Canadian Aboriginal women's organizations seeking justice, equality and participation in the process of defining constitutional change and constitutional rights in Canada. Shirley Green raises the vexed question of identity and racism in the Canadian context for those of us descended from both Aboriginal and settler forbearers, and shows how a healthy identity must include all of one's cultural inheritances. Kathie Irwin documents some of the powerful Maori women leaders and role models she has known. Denise Henning brings together her cultural experience as a Cherokee woman; her feminism, which is rooted in her matriarchal culture; and the need to teach her daughters how to be powerful contemporary Cherokee women. Shirley Bear demonstrates the powerful nexus between politics and culture through her poetry and art. Tina Beads' interview with Rauna Kuokkanen explores Beads' thinking about Aboriginal feminism and violence against Aboriginal women, beginning with her politicization in childhood by the conditions in her life. Colleen Glenn's interview with Joyce Green focuses on Glenn's feminist solidarity and action with the Canadian organization Indian Rights for Indian Women. Sharon McIvor's interview with Rauna Kuokkanen focuses on McIvor's involvement as a feminist in politics and as vice-president of the Native Women's Association of Canada in the late 1980s and early 1990s. All this writing is wrapped up in the breathtaking art on the book cover by Métis feminist artist Christi Belcourt.

## NOTES

1. In Canada, "Indian" is a subset of the category of Aboriginal peoples, constitutionally recognized in Canada as "Indian, Inuit and Métis."
2. In this chapter and elsewhere I use the term "Aboriginal" to refer to Indigenous people in Canada. I also use the term "Indigenous," particularly when referring to Indigenous peoples from places other than Canada.

Chapter One

# TAKING ACCOUNT OF ABORIGINAL FEMINISM

## *Joyce Green*

Aboriginal (or Indigenous[1]) feminism is a subject that is hotly debated. Some critics say there is no such thing, while others say that feminism is un-traditional, inauthentic, non-libratory for Aboriginal women and illegitimate as an ideological position, political analysis and organizational process. However, I know some Aboriginal feminists. They exist; they choose the label, the ideological position, the analysis and the process. Aboriginal feminists raise issues of colonialism, racism and sexism, and the unpleasant synergy between these three violations of human rights. Aboriginal feminists illuminate topics that, but for their voices, would not be raised at all. Therefore, despite the very small numbers of Aboriginal women who identify their work as feminist, and the small body of literature and theory that can be identified as Aboriginal feminist, these contributions are important.

Feminism is an ideology based on a political analysis that takes women's experiences seriously, and it is played out politically by women's groups that generally have characteristic processes of organization and of action. There are several different kinds of feminism, and it is beyond the scope of this chapter to explore them.[2] Yet, in all of the work on feminism, the women's movement and feminists, there is very little published on or by Indigenous women.[3] Judy Rebick is one of the few published feminists who has paid attention to Aboriginal women (see her chapter, "Indian Rights for Indian Women," in Rebick 2005). Kim Anderson and Bonita Lawrence's collection *Strong Women Stories* (2003) is not about feminism or the women's movement, but it is about Aboriginal women, some of whom are activist in ways that are consistent with feminism and who can be implicitly characterized as feminist. There is virtually no explicit writing on Aboriginal feminism, with the exception of Rosanna Deerchild's discussion of artist Lita Fontaine's notion of tribal feminism as "approaching feminism through a culture lens" (Deerfield 2003: 100) and Andrea Smith, Chapter 5 in this volume, revised and reprinted from Spring 2005 *Feminist Studies*. This gap in the literature points to the invisibility of Indigenous women in the women's movement and, beyond that, to the unthinking racism of a movement that has often failed to see Indigenous women in their full historical and contemporary contexts: as simultaneously Aboriginal and female, and as contemporary persons living in the context of colonial oppression by the occupying state and populations of, for example, Canada, the U.S., Aotearoa/New Zealand and Australia, with their racist mythologies, institutions and practices.

I argue that the emerging Aboriginal feminist literature and politic, while the terrain of a minority of activists and scholars, must be taken seriously as a critique of colonialism, decolonization and gendered and raced power relations in both settler and Indigenous communities. I also argue that the intolerance for feminist analysis in Indigenous communities is problematic, particularly when it takes the form of political intimidation of a marginal segment (critical women) of those communities. This chapter, relying on activists' accounts and the articulation of Aboriginal feminists at the 2002 Aboriginal Feminism Symposium,[4] documents the existence and parameters of Aboriginal feminism in Canada. It concludes that Aboriginal feminism is a valid and theoretically and politically powerful critique of the social, economic and political conditions of Aboriginal women's lives.

## LOCATING ABORIGINAL FEMINISM

So what is Aboriginal feminism? The characteristic of feminism — be it socialist, maternal, radical, liberal, Aboriginal, ecofeminist — is that it takes gender seriously as a social organizing process and, within the context of patriarchal societies, seeks to identify the ways in which women are subordinated to men and how women can be emancipated from this subordination. Feminism is theory that seeks to "describe and explain women's situations and experiences and support recommendations about how to improve them" and is based on "respect for women's own perspectives and authority" (Frye 2000: 195). Feminism is also a social movement fuelled by theory dedicated to action, to transformation — to praxis. Feminism is usually viewed as multiple: *feminisms* analyze the diversity of women's cultural, political and in other ways specific experiences. Marilyn Frye argues that across feminisms, the commonality comes from the analytical approach to social concepts about power relations (196).

Feminist analysis only arises in conditions of patriarchy, as a response to oppression and as a prescription for change. Thus, it is not surprising that women who do not experience patriarchy as oppressive, such as members of the reactionary group REAL (Realistic, Equal, Active for Life) Women, reject and malign feminism. Nor is it surprising that women who consider their communities and cultures to be free of patriarchal oppression and/or to have cultural practices available that recognize the power, dignity and agency of women, also view feminism as irrelevant. Some First Nations historically placed a high value on women's roles in society; indeed, women in most Aboriginal cultures historically enjoyed far more respect, power and autonomy than did their European settler counterparts.

Yet, contemporary Aboriginal women are subjected to patriarchal and colonial oppression within settler society and, in some contexts, in Aboriginal communities. Some Aboriginal cultures and communities are patriarchal, either in cultural origin or because of incorporation of colonizer patriarchy. For example, Gail Stacey-Moore, a Mohawk woman, writes: "The *Indian Act* abolished the traditional matriarchal society for a patriarchal one. Our men turned to the *Indian Act* to get back into a position of strength, and they still use it today" (quoted in Rebick 2005: 112). Fay Blaney (2003: 162) writes: "Present-day systemic and institutionalized patriarchy ensures that the privileged male status in mainstream Canadian society is mirrored in Aboriginal communities." Most Aboriginal women also live with the endemic sexism and racism in the dominant society.

Feminists in all patriarchal societies are denigrated, for they question the common understanding of what it means to be a good woman (and a good man), and they challenge the social, political, economic and cultural practices that validate, perpetuate and enforce these roles. As the British writer Rebecca West said in 1913, "people call me a feminist whenever I express sentiments that differentiate me from a doormat" (Feminismquotes). Challenging the dominant consensus is always difficult. Feminists are viewed with deep suspicion at best, with hostility at worst, by most others in their communities. Thus, the American religious fundamentalist and prominent Republican Pat Robertson claimed, in a caricature that too many believe to be true of this misunderstood ideology, that feminism is a "socialist, anti-family political movement that encourages women to leave their husbands, kill their children, practice witchcraft, destroy capitalism and become lesbians" (Freeman 2005: A3).

Aboriginal anti-colonial political struggle confronts the dominant myths and political, social and economic practices that dignify, deny or perpetuate colonialism — the enforced appropriation of Aboriginal nations' land and resources and the denial of the conditions for self-determination. These colonial processes are primarily initiated by settler state governments, corporations and institutions — to the detriment of Aboriginal peoples, in all their diversity of history and contemporary social experience. As with feminism, anti- and post-colonial analysis and activism attracts hostility, denial and minimization. It too contests the myths and justifications of the economic and political *status quo* of settler states and demands restitution, self-determination and participation in political and economic activity. Fundamentally, this struggle challenges the legitimacy of settler states' claims to sovereignty.

Colonialism is closely tied to racism and sexism. These twin phenomena exist in the context of colonial society, directed at Indigenous people, but they have also been internalized by some Indigenous political cultures in ways that are oppressive to Indigenous women. Liberation is framed by some as a decolonization discourse, which draws on traditional cultural and political mechanisms. It is conceptualized as thoroughly Indigenous in character, while also honouring women in their gendered and acculturated contexts. But Indigenous liberation theory, like so many other liberation movements and theories, has not been attentive to the gendered way in which colonial oppression and racism function for men and women, or to the inherent and adopted sexisms that some communities manifest.

Aboriginal feminism brings together the two critiques, feminism and anti-colonialism, to show how Aboriginal peoples, and in particular Aboriginal women, are affected by colonialism and by patriarchy. It takes account of how both racism and sexism fuse when brought to bear on Aboriginal women. While colonial oppression is identified, so too is oppression of women by Indigenous men and Indigenous governance practices. Aboriginal feminists are the clearest in linking sex and race oppression. They are identified as political adversaries not only by colonial society but also by male Indigenous elites whose power they challenge. And they are also criticized by some Aboriginal women, who deny their analysis and question their motives and authenticity.

## DEPLOYING ABORIGINAL FEMINISM

Some critics allege that Aboriginal feminists use a "white" or "colonial" theoretical approach. Aboriginal feminists counter that they use feminist analysis as a tool for challenging racism and colonialism. Their work looks both at the genesis of colonialism and its consequences, and at the internalization and perpetuation of colonial practices within Aboriginal communities, especially male dominance over women and children. Aboriginal feminist analysis goes further than other Aboriginal libratory critiques in suggesting that not all pre-colonial Aboriginal social practices were innocent of oppression, including sex oppression. This questions the veneration of tradition and also leads to prescriptions for contemporary political formulas for Aboriginal liberation (Green 2001; Dick 2006).

Feminism is also about building bridges to other movements working for social justice. As Aboriginal Women's Action Network (AWAN) activist Fay Blaney (2002) said in her summation of the first roundtable at the Aboriginal Feminism Symposium, "Aboriginal feminists work with non-Aboriginal women, with labour, anti-poverty and environmental groups as well as within Aboriginal communities and focus on issues of social justice; and this attracts political backlash." In another example, Colleen Glenn, a Métis woman who devoted years to the struggle to end sex discrimination in the *Indian Act*, did so because of feminist solidarity and principled commitment to equality, even though the issue did not affect her personally (see the interview with Glenn, Chapter 15).

Aboriginal women activists worked in solidarity with white and other women's organizations and feminists, especially in regard to women's status provisions in the *Indian Act*. For example, the National Action Committee on the Status of Women (NAC)[5] organized a day of mourning to protest the 1971 Supreme Court of Canada decision against Jeannette Lavell and Yvonne Bedard: Gail Stacey-Moore, of the Quebec Native Women's Association, called NAC "incredibly supportive" on the issue of women's status (Rebick 2005: 107, 110).

The groundbreaking *Report of the Royal Commission on the Status of Women in Canada*, filed in 1970, made a number of recommendations concerning the well-being of Aboriginal women, including a recommendation (#106) to end sex discrimination in the *Indian Act*. During the period immediately prior to the Canadian referendum on the constitutional amendments proposed in the Charlottetown Accord,[6] NAC and NWAC (Native Women's Association of Canada) worked closely, with NWAC taking the lead on negotiating positions. Thus, Aboriginal feminism educates movements unfamiliar with issues of colonialism, racism and sexism, and builds critical political consciousness and solidarity, thus contributing to citizenship and democratic development.

## DISCIPLINING ABORIGINAL FEMINISTS

Aboriginal women stigmatized as feminist have endured political and social ostracization and threats of violence and of other punitive tactics, like being denied access to programs, funding and so on (see, for example, Caroline Ennis's account of the inequality of women's access to services and benefits in her community and the threats made against activists [Rebick 2005: 112–15]; see also LaRocque 1997; Silman 1987). This pressure has tainted feminism for many women and has made the label something to be avoided. Addressing the hostility and misconceptions of what feminism is, one symposium participant stated "in our nation there's very little known about feminists.... I don't want to be feared" (Anonymous).

Women who have complained about band politics, or distribution of resources, or violence against women and children, sometimes find they are slapped with the label *feminist*. Jeannette Lavell and Yvonne Bedard, whose challenge to sex discrimination in the pre-1985 *Indian Act* went to the Supreme Court of Canada in 1973, were "attacked by Indian leaders and labelled 'white-washed women's libbers' who were undermining their Indian heritage" (Silman 1987: 13; see also Rebick 2005: 108).

Much of this is similar to what non-Aboriginal feminist women experience. But in addition, Aboriginal women's authenticity is challenged when they are defined as feminist (see Sharon McIvor's experience in Chapter 16).

It is as though some authority has decided that Aboriginal women cannot be culturally authentic, or traditional, or acceptable, if they are feminist. Indeed, some women find themselves criticized for being tools of colonial ideology or for being traitors to their communities. All of this stifles critique — and also political debate.

The typical anti-feminist pressures are amplified for Aboriginal feminists because of their collective position as members of communities occupied and subordinated by settler populations and governments through processes of colonization. In such a relationship, there are very powerful impulses structuring internal allegiance and sustaining traditional social practices of authenticity, resistance and solidarity in the face of colonial assimilative forces. Thus, traditional or putatively traditional social relations are well insulated from critique. Even where contemporary social relations are understood to be shaped by colonial and patriarchal practices, Aboriginal women are reluctant to use a gendered analysis to criticize Aboriginal men. Indeed, feminist analysis is widely considered to be divisive, corrosive of family and community, culturally inappropriate and even colonialist. A number of prominent Aboriginal intellectuals have dismissed feminism's relevance for Aboriginal women while others have celebrated Aboriginal women's traditional and maternalist roles to the exclusion of any analysis of gendered power relations (see LaRocque, Chapter 3). Such analyses celebrate an historic, cultural and/or romantic mythic gender construct, while implicitly or explicitly dismissing a feminist critique of the construct or of its contemporary application.

## THE POWER OF ABORIGINAL FEMINISM

Aboriginal feminism seeks an Aboriginal liberation that includes women, and not just the conforming woman, but also the marginal and excluded, and especially the woman who has been excluded from her community by virtue of colonial legislation and socio-historical forces. Thus, Aboriginal feminism is a theoretical engagement with history and politics, as well as a practical engagement with contemporary social, economic, cultural and political issues. It is an ideological framework not only of intellectuals but also of activists. It is an authentic expression of political analysis and political will by those who express it, who are self-consciously aware of their identities as *Aboriginal women* — with emphasis on the unity of both words. Aboriginal feminism interrogates power structures and practices between and among Aboriginal and dominant institutions. It leads to praxis — theoretically informed, politically self-conscious activism.

While Aboriginal feminists have focused largely on the impositions of imperialism, colonialism, racism and sexism from the dominant societies, the same body of thought has also illuminated impositions of power and practices within Indigenous communities, organizations and families. In other words, it is principled, self-reflective and critical, in the best tradition of transformative thinkers as advocated by Edward Said (1996), and not simply doctrinaire. Aboriginal feminism provides a philosophical and political way of conceptualizing, and of resisting, the oppressions that many Aboriginal people experience. It provides analysis of Aboriginal women's particular experiences of oppression, and it offers some prescriptions for a post-colonial future for Aboriginal peoples. It is anti-oppressive in its intellectual and political foundations. It is not the only way of understanding the world, but it is a valuable, valid conceptual tool, whose practitioners should not be dismissed.

Self-identified Aboriginal feminists see great potential for positive change through feminist praxis in an anti-colonial context. Following are some of the claims made by participants in the 2002 Aboriginal Feminism Symposium:

- "Aboriginal feminism is the tool that will bring about decolonization" (Blaney);
- "Feminism is very important to me and produced a lot of healing for sisters around the world" (Bear);
- "The larger picture of feminism is the genuine caring for humanity and the opposition to any kind of oppression" (McIvor);
- The way to "defend claiming the Aboriginal feminist identity begins by saying patriarchy and sexism is a problem in our community — not just a problem of generic colonialism" (St. Denis).

And now to what Aboriginal feminism is not: it is not a man-hating ideology, nor a unilateral rejection of cultures, traditions or personal and political relationships with men. It is not a subordinate form of other feminisms, nor is it a political stalking horse by colonial ideologies.

## WHAT ABOUT TRADITIONS?

A common claim invoked to reject Aboriginal feminism is that it is un- or anti-traditional. Exploring this criticism means first considering what "traditional" means — and to whom. Tradition consists of valued inter-generational social practices. All societies have them; all venerate them. Not all of the members of a society are similarly faithful to them, nor are all societies monolithic in their identification and replication of them.

For Aboriginal peoples, subjected to colonial forces that have included public policy attacks on Aboriginal cultures and social practices, tradition has come represent a pre-colonial time when Indigenous peoples exercised self-determination. For the most part, this is assumed, and rightly so, to have been a good and appropriate path. But tradition is neither a monolith, nor is it axiomatically good, and the notions of what practices were and are essential, how they should be practised, who may be involved and who is an authority are all open to interpretation. Women around the world have found themselves oppressed through a variety of social, religious, political and cultural practices. Feminism is foundationally about the importance of considering women's experiences, especially through social and cultural practices. Feminism has provided tools to critique oppressive traditions — and to claim and practise meaningful non-oppressive traditions.

Fay Blaney (2003: 167) writes: "The best defense against assimilation is to sustain culture and tradition, but what are we to do when reinstated tradition is steeped in misogyny?" Others have noted that certain Aboriginal elites invoke traditions to sustain *prima facie* violations of women's human rights (Dick 2006; Green 1985, 1993, 2001; LaRocque 1997). Unless we can have conversations about what traditions are, how they affect men and women in their gendered roles and what the implications of this are, we are moving a powerful socio-political critique off the table. Any impulse that represses critical conversation is problematic.

Today, there are a number of versions of tradition in Aboriginal communities. There are many who claim to be authoritative on this subject. They don't always agree, nor should they need to. But neither should they be permitted to deny others a voice. Too many Aboriginal women have been silenced or had their social and political roles minimized by invocations of appropriate tradition relative to women's voices and choices. Sharon McIvor, a symposium participant who had been vice-president of the Native Women's Association of Canada, a national Aboriginal women's organization whose most prominent political objectives had been equal band membership rights and Canadian constitutional protection for Indian women, spoke of her experience: "The first line of offence when you are talking to the [Aboriginal male] political leadership is 'you're destroying our traditions and you're not really traditional. You're not really an Indian and you're not really Aboriginal if you can do this.'"

Rejecting the rhetoric and institutions of the colonizer by embracing the symbols of one's culture and traditions is a strategy for reclaiming the primacy of one's own context in the world, against the imposition of colonialism. But, in the absence of an analysis of the power relations embedded in tradition, it is not necessarily a libratory strategy. Each choice must be interrogated on its own merits, relative to the objective of a contemporary emancipatory formulation that will benefit Aboriginal men, women and children. Feminist critique is an essential part of this process.

At issue, then, is who decides what tradition is — and for whom. Many of us have multiple cultural heritages and historical experiences, and so there can never be a single cultural version of tradition. Secondarily, we need to have conversations about the fact that not all Aboriginal people will choose traditional formulas. Aboriginal feminist voices have much to contribute to these important conversations and to shaping an inclusive future.

## FEMINISTS AND ACTIVISTS

For many years, the few Aboriginal and Indian women who advanced women's issues in the political arena were often criticized for their activities. Always, they sought to locate their claims as thoroughly Indigenous and culturally authentic, while providing a gendered analysis of public policy, political practices and life experiences. In this, they were radical. Here, I document a few of the Canadian organizations and activists whose influence resonates with feminist analysis and action.

Jeanette Corbiere Lavell and Yvonne Bedard mounted a challenge to the infamous section 12(1)(b) of the pre-1985 *Indian Act*, which stripped Indian women who married anyone other than a status Indian man of their Indian status, right to reserve residency and ability to pass status on to their children.[7] The Supreme Court of Canada ruled against Lavell and Bedard in 1973. The case was the catalyst for the formation of a number of Native women's organizations. However, a group of treaty women from Alberta actively opposed the case and any change to the sexist membership provisions of the *Indian Act*. There is no single political position of Indian women. Similar to the situation sketched out by Sharon McIvor in Chapter 16 concerning government funding of organizations to participate in constitutional change, the Department of Indian Affairs was funding the mainstream (malestream) Indian organizations, but Indian women couldn't access federal money to work for *Indian Act* revision and had to raise money through bake sales to lobby the federal government for human rights and justice (Lavell 2005). Thus, the federal government practised discrimination against Indian women in its legislation and again in its selective consultation practices, recognition and support of Indian organizations.

Recounting the aggression, hostility and near-violence by some Indian politicians against women activists, Lavell said the women continued because, "If you believe in principles and values of our people, [it's] worth standing up for.... Our responsibility as women [is] to make things better for our children" (Lavell 2005). And children are still being affected, differentially, by *Indian Act* discrimination (see Green, Chapter 8).

The Tobique-based[8] women known as the Tobique women's group (TWG) emerged as a political force in the mid-1970s to "improve local living conditions for women and children" (Silman 1987: 9). Shirley Bear (see Chapter 14) was part of that group. In 1979 the women organized the 100-Mile Native Women's Walk from Oka, Quebec, to Ottawa, the seat of the Canadian government, mobilizing Indian women across Canada and raising public consciousness about the plight of many Indian women, particularly on the consequences of the sex discrimination of the *Indian Act* membership provisions and on the punitive tactics of some band politicians (Silman 1987: 149–72). Some of the Tobique women participated in the organization, Indian Rights for Indian Women (IRIW), which also focused on the discriminatory membership provisions of the *Indian Act* (Silman 1987: 173–75). Colleen Glenn (Chapter 15), a Métis woman, was part of IRIW.

The Tobique women's group also took the case of Sandra Lovelace (now Lovelace Nicholas and a senator in the Canadian Parliament) to the United Nations Human Rights Commission, and in 1981 succeeded in having Canada declared in violation of section 27 of the Convention on Civil and Political Rights, which guarantees the right to enjoy one's culture in one's community. In the process, Aboriginal women educated the mainstream feminist National Action Committee on the Status of Women about the discrimination facing Indian women, and that in turn generated more education of and support by non-Aboriginal feminists for Aboriginal women (Silman 1987: 177–78).

The Native Women's Association of Canada (NWAC) worked to place Aboriginal women's human rights on the Canadian political agenda and in the Canadian constitution by fighting against sex discrimination in several sections of the pre-1985 *Indian Act*, by arguing for protection of Aboriginal women's rights in the Constitution and Charter of Rights and Freedoms and then again in the constitutional amendments proposed in the failed Charlottetown Accord of 1990. Some former NWAC activists are now involved in the Feminist Alliance for International Action (FAFIA),[9] which works on behalf of women's rights generally and Aboriginal women's rights specifically.

Feminist organizing has served as a political expression of commitment to community and has provided political education and experience for Aboriginal women. The Aboriginal Women's Action Network (AWAN), based in Vancouver's impoverished downtown Eastside, found that organizing created a learning process that was as important as the research and issues on which the organizing was focused. AWAN has struggled to maintain a collective model with consensus-based decision-making, though this has not always been easy or successful. Through AWAN activities, many Aboriginal women have been able to develop their leadership and political skills, as well as their knowledge of the "political opportunity structure." This kind of learning improves individuals' self-confidence as political actors, thus increasing their political efficacy and ability to engage in other political arenas. Tina Beads demonstrates how Aboriginal feminist activism can play out in a mainstream feminist organization, in her case the Vancouver Rape Crisis Collective (Chapter 14).

And yet, in most cases, instead of supporting these political initiatives, the Aboriginal political elites seemed more inclined to challenge their legitimacy, their motives, their analyses and their objectives. Troublingly, Aboriginal women have found themselves under attack for seeking to defend Aboriginal and treaty rights and fundamental human rights for Aboriginal women (see McIvor, Chapter 16). Colleen Glenn recalls hostility from leaders of the National Indian Brotherhood and the Indian Association of Alberta (Chapter 15). Silman recounts numerous incidents of harassment of the Tobique women.

Aboriginal women have also engaged in feminist-like action in the international arena. For example, Indigenous women from around the world participated in the Beijing United Nations Conference on Women in 1995, producing an Indigenous women's declaration that shows much shared terrain with other feminists, while asserting the primacy of the colonial experience common to Indigenous peoples.[10] This declaration also makes it clear that for Indigenous women, liberation is in the context of viable decolonized societies with their own cultural particularities, on their own lands and sustained by their own formulas for economies and for healthy societies.

## CONCLUSION

Aboriginal feminism provides a philosophical and political way of conceptualizing, and of resisting, the oppressions that many Aboriginal people experience. It is not the only way, but it is unique and anti-oppressive in its intellectual and political foundations. Above all, it is critical, in the best tradition of transformative thinkers. While the majority of the brain power has been directed at the imposition of imperialism, colonialism, racism and sexism from the dominating societies, Aboriginal feminism has also illuminated power abuses within Aboriginal communities, organizations and families.

The power of feminist analysis, solidarity and organizing allow women to both consider political and social conditions differently than malestream politicians do and to articulate different kinds of solutions. It enhances the ability of individuals to be political actors — to engage in the activities of citizenship that too few people pursue. And it is done in the service of women, but also of children, men and communities. Contrary to the anti-feminist stereotype, feminism was never articulated as a formula for female dominance and oppression over males. As a body of intellectual work, Aboriginal feminism is demonstrably a libratory critical theoretical approach, fitting comfortably with feminist and post-colonial thought and critical race theory. As a set of political analyses and practices, Aboriginal feminism is a part of the broad and deep stream of feminist activism, wherein theory fuses with strategic action and solidarities.

# NOTES

1. In this chapter I use the term "Aboriginal" as it is the customary and constitutional term in Canada for reference to Indigenous peoples. I use the two terms interchangeably.

2. The interested reader is advised to consult resources such as Jill Vickers's *Reinventing Political Science: A Feminist Approach*, for its accessible language and clear definitions; Janine Brodie's *Politics on the Margins: Restructuring and the Canadian Women's Movement*, for its analysis of the women's movement in the context of contemporary neoliberalism; Penny Kome's *The Taking of Twenty-Eight*, for its documentation of the opposition to the inclusion of women's equality rights in the Canadian Constitution; Judy Rebick's *Ten Thousand Roses: The Making of a Feminist Revolution*, for its documentation of the contemporary Canadian women's movement; and Marilyn Waring's iconic *If Women Counted: A New Feminist Economics*, which shows the sexism inherent in the United Nations system of national accounts, which renders women's work and power invisible. This is not a complete or a systematic list; it simply offers an introduction into primarily Canadian feminist struggles. Rebick (2005: 21) writes that Canadian feminism mirrors two dominant orientations: "those trying to reform the system to improve the state of women and those who believe(d) that a more radical transformation of society was necessary to achieve women's equality." Feminism is associated with the social movement that has components around the globe: the women's movement. It is "one of the most significant and successful social movements in Canada" (Adamson, Briskin and McPhail 1988: 3).

3. This may be changing; a number of scholars from Canada, the U.S., Australia and New Zealand made presentations to the conference "Indigenous Women and Feminism: Culture, Activism, Politics," August 25–28, 2005, at the University of Alberta. Some of this work should find its way to publication.

4. For more discussion of the Symposium, see the Introduction to this book.

5. NAC in its heyday represented over 600 women's organizations across Canada, and regularly met with members of the Canadian government and civil service to lobby for legislation and policy change to improve the status of women. The organization was seriously weakened by systematic underfunding by hostile governments from the late 1980s through to the present, who subsequently also refused NAC regular access (and the consequent legitimacy in the eyes of the public) to policy-makers.

6. The Charlottetown Accord was a package of proposed constitutional amendments, presented to and rejected by Canadians in 1992. It included a section on Aboriginal government. The interested reader is referred to Joyce Green 1993.

7. For a discussion of this, see Jamieson 1978; Silman 1987; Green 2001, 1993; for a 2006 snapshot of the situation, see Dick 2006.

8. Tobique is the name of a reserve, a portion of the traditional territories of the Maliseet First Nation, located in contemporary New Brunswick, on the east coast of Canada.

9. See <http://www.fafia-afai.org>.

10. See <http://www.ipcb.org/resolutions/beijingdec.html> (accessed September 19, 2002).

# REFERENCES

Adamson, Nancy, Linda Briskin and Margaret McPhail. 1988. *Feminist Organizing for Change: The Contemporary Women's Movement in Canada.* Toronto: Oxford University Press.

Anderson, Kim, and Bonita Lawrence (eds.). 2003. *Strong Women Stories: Native Vision and Community Survival.* Toronto: Sumach Press.

Blaney, Fay. 2003. "Aboriginal Women's Action Network." In Kim Anderson and Bonita Lawrence (eds.), *Strong Women Stories: Native Vision and Community Survival.* Toronto: Sumach Press.

Brodie, Janine. 1995. *Politics on the Margins: Restructuring and the Canadian Women's Movement.* Halifax: Fernwood Publishing.

Canada. 1970. *Report of the Royal Commission on the Status of Women.* Ottawa: Supply and Services Canada.

Deerchild, R. 2003. "Tribal Feminism Is a Drum Song." In Anderson and Lawrence.

Dick, Caroline. 2006. "The Politics of Intragroup Difference: First Nations' Women and the *Sawridge* Dispute." *Canadian Journal of Political Science* 39, 1.

Feminismquotes. <http://www.rci.rutgers.edu/~elk/feminismquotes.html> (accessed June 16, 2006).

Freeman, Alan. 2005. "Why hesitate? Assassinate, evangelist suggests." *Globe and Mail*, August 24.

Frye, Marilyn. 2000. "Feminism." In Lorraine Code (ed.), *Encyclopedia of Feminist Theories.* New York: Routledge.

Green, Joyce. 1985. "Sexual Equality and Indian Government: An Analysis of Bill C-31." *Native Studies Review* 1, 2.

_____. 1993. "Constitutionalising the Patriarchy: Aboriginal Women and Aboriginal Government." *Constitutional Forum* 4, 4 (Summer).

_____. 2001 "Canaries in the Mines of Citizenship: Indian Women in Canada." *Canadian Journal of Political Science* XXXIV, 4.

Jamieson, Kathleen. 1978. *Indian Women and the Law: Citizens Minus.* Ottawa: Queen's Printer.

Kome, Penny. 1983. *The Taking of Twenty-Eight: Women Challenge the Constitution.* Toronto: Women's Press.

LaRocque, Emma. 1997. "Re-examining Culturally Appropriate Models in Criminal Justice Applications." In Michael Asch (ed.), *Aboriginal and Treaty Rights in Canada: Essays on Law, Equality, and Respect for Difference.* Vancouver: UBC Press.

Lavell, Jeannette. 2005. Presentation at the Moving Toward Equality Conference, held by Le reseau DIALOG and Quebec Native Women, February 22–24, Montreal.

Rebick, Judy. 2005. *Ten Thousand Roses: The Making of a Feminist Revolution.* Toronto: Penguin Canada.

Said, Edward. 1996. *Representations of the Intellectual.* New York: Beacon Press.

Silman, Janet. 1987. *Enough is Enough: Aboriginal Women Speak Out.* Toronto: Women's Press.

Vickers, Jill. 1977. *Reinventing Political Science: A Feminist Approach.* Halifax: Fernwood.

Waring, Marilyn. 1988. *If Women Counted: A New Feminist Economics.* New York: Harper Collins Publishers.

Chapter Two

# FEMINISM IS FOR EVERYBODY
## Aboriginal Women, Feminism and Diversity

### Verna St. Denis

This chapter tells the story about how and why, as an Aboriginal woman and scholar, I have come to re-evaluate my earlier rejection and dismissal of feminism. There was a time when I believed, as others have stated, that organizing women of the world against gender inequality under a banner of universal sisterhood both minimized and erased social, economic and political differences between vastly differently positioned women, particularly Aboriginal women. I could not and would not prioritize gender inequality over the political and economic marginalization of Aboriginal peoples. It has been through the engagement and critique by feminists of colour, as well as the responses of white feminist scholars to those critiques of feminism, that I have come to appreciate the value of feminist theorizing and analyses for both men and women. My own analyses and understandings of inequality have been greatly enriched by both white women's and women of colour's feminist scholarship, and I believe those of us involved in Native studies and Aboriginal education can no longer deny the relevance of this important body of scholarship, analyses and activism.

Ironically, in the mid- to late 1980s, when I was working on my masters degree, while maintaining that feminist theory and analysis were not relevant to Aboriginal women, I relied on the very important scholarship of feminist women in the academy, especially those who critiqued western male scientific approaches to knowledge and research methodologies (Bowles and Klein 1983; Reinharz 1979). My masters thesis (St. Denis 1989, 1992) is an examination of community-based research methodologies, including an exploration of qualitative methodologies, which were becoming increasingly available in the mid-1980s, thanks largely to feminist scholars. Later, as I researched and wrote a paper exploring racialized minority women's critique of feminism (Davis 1981; hooks 1988; Lorde 1984; Moraga and Anzaldua 1983), I came to reconsider my indiscriminate rejection of feminism.

In that exploration I came across Susan Faludi's *Backlash* (1991), and it is because of that book, in combination with reading the writings of women of colour, who, despite their critique of feminism, nonetheless claimed a feminist identity and politics, that I came to rethink my own position. Rather than rejecting feminism altogether, many feminists of colour have focused on contributing to feminist analyses by calling white feminist colleagues to consider multiple forms of discrimination and inequality, such as racism, classism and heterosexism. I came to realize that, just as Faludi claims, the media has had a big influence in shaping public opinion and encouraging misinformation and hostility towards the inequities that feminists were trying to bring attention to. I was especially affected by Faludi's discussion of the politics of making changes to the Diagnostic Statistical Manual (DSM), which establishes the standard categories for diagnosing psychiatric illnesses. I both laughed and cried my way through her story of the efforts made by women to change the DSM and to challenge the ways in which psychology and psychiatry often positioned women to blame themselves for the many dire effects of the inequitable conditions of their lives. It was in the midst of working on that paper and trying to understand the critiques of feminism made by women of colour that I came to realize how little I knew about feminism in general, how much misinformation had passed as knowledge and finally, that I may have some things in common with feminist struggles, especially against the injustices resulting from patriarchal, misogynist and sexist ideologies and practices that have for so long been a foundation in Euro-western societies.

My initial dismissal of feminism was bolstered by what has been a conventional position taken by many Aboriginal and Indigenous women who reject feminism as not only irrelevant but also racist and colonial. Although we, Aboriginal women, may utilize western forms of knowledge, theory and analysis, and even seek legitimization through educational credentials obtained in western institutions, it is still common for Aboriginal women to disapprove of feminism and sometimes, ironically, citing white men to do so (Giroux cited in Grande 2003: 329; McLaren cited in Grande 2003: 331). But I think feminist theory is no more or no less relevant than a wide variety of western social and political theories and analyses, and I now think there is much to be gained by Aboriginal women's and Aboriginal men's exploration of feminist scholarship. In fact, I could not teach the anti-oppressive education university courses I now do without the very important contributions of feminist scholars and educators.

## HISTORICIZING AND DEFINING FEMINISM

There was neither a Women and Gender Studies department nor a Native Studies department at the University of Saskatchewan when I began attending in 1978. I, like others, missed out on an education in these areas that others now take for granted. Although in recent years I have utilized feminist scholarship both in my research and teaching, I have had to go back and develop an historical understanding of the varied trajectories of feminism.

In developing my knowledge of a history of feminism[1] it became clear that defining feminism is an on-going process involving responding to changing political and social contexts and issues. Unless those Aboriginal women who claim that feminism is not relevant acknowledge this dynamic history and practice of feminism, their engagement, like some, becomes mired in a stereotypic response where feminism is portrayed as merely an expression of a liberal political agenda and is not acknowledged as a complex body of scholarship and activism.

I found it interesting to learn that feminism has always been controversial and never widely popular (Freedman 2002). Sarah Gamble (2000: viii) explains that although feminism may be "generally categorized as the struggle to increase women's access to equality in a male dominated culture, there has never been a universally agreed agenda for feminism"; as such feminism has always been a dynamic and multifaceted movement. But as Freedman maintains, "the political goals of feminism have survived—despite continuing discomfort with the term, a hostile political climate, and heated internal criticism—largely because feminism *has continually redefined itself*" (Freedman 2002: 6, emphasis added).

These "continual redefinitions" of feminism have taken many forms. The reasoning and justification used to assert rights and equality for women have varied over time and place. For example, early western feminists argued for their rights to receive an education, own property and attain citizenship. During first wave feminism, Freedman explains that the pursuit of educational and property rights for women was linked to their authority and rights as mothers. Middle-class women "waged public campaigns to bring the allegedly superior moral values of the home to bear on the world" (Freedman 2002: 65). Motherhood was believed to endow women with social power, and early feminists sought to valorize rather than, as later many feminists would, reject the idealization of motherhood.

This strategy of challenging gender inequality in Judeo-Christian western cultures by valorizing motherhood is described as maternalism. Freedman suggests that although maternalism may be an imperfect term, this concept refers to one way in which women have advocated for political authority. "Maternalism covers a wide range of women's public activism, either as mothers or for the sake of children and families…articulating a powerful defense of female difference as a source of political authority" (Freedman 2002: 65). After 1910, a younger generation of feminists rejected the maternal argument in favour of women's common human identity with men as a basis for equal rights (Freedman 2002: 4). In other words, early feminists challenged social and political inequities between men and women by valorizing their role and responsibilities as women, whereas later feminists would shift from celebrating difference to emphasizing similarities.

A related yet different feminist strategy from maternalism included valorizing femininity and women's culture and difference. Both Charlotte Perkins Gilman and Virginia Woolf wrote about the ways in which gender difference provided women with a uniquely critical perspective (Freedman 2002: 68). Gilman strongly criticized the man-made world for its aggression, competition and destruction of female values of peace, cooperation and life giving (Freedman 2002: 69). The strategy of celebrating the differently positioned place of women in western Judeo-Christian cultures shares some similarities to the strategy that racialized minorities and colonized subjects have employed to resist and disrupt racial inferiorization brought about through colonization.

The "black is beautiful" movement and the development of Afro-centricity in education, which have sought to teach about African heritage and cultural expressions as a way to counter the negative effects of racial inequality is one example. This strategy is also evident in the establishment of Black Studies departments. The movement among Aboriginal and First Nations people towards cultural and language revitalization is another example of a strategy to counter the detrimental effects of colonization and racialization. Feminists, people of colour and Aboriginal people have similarly challenged their marginalization and constructed inferiorization by western institutions through a strategy of valorization of their cultural differences.

In making the effort to learn about feminism, I discovered that feminism is far more complex than is often portrayed or understood. Gamble, in the introduction to the *Critical Dictionary to Feminism and Postfeminism*, explains, "Exactly what 'equality' for women entails, the means by which it is to be achieved, even the exact nature of the obstacles it faces, are all disputed issues. To read feminism's history, therefore, is to uncover a record of debates, schisms and differing viewpoints" (Gamble 2000: viii). I think this is the case, especially in the past four decades, and the debates, schisms and differing viewpoints among western feminisms are often not acknowledged by those Aboriginal women scholars who, in viewing feminism as a static form of analysis and focusing on a liberal agenda,[2] argue that feminism is not relevant to Aboriginal women and their communities.

## ABORIGINAL WOMEN'S CRITIQUE OF FEMINISM

Drawing primarily on the work of Aboriginal scholars and activists (Turpel 1993; Monture-Angus 1995; Monture in Boulton 2003; Tobe 2000; Jaimes with Halsey 1997), I provide here an inventory of some of the reasons why many Aboriginal women reject feminism as not being relevant to their lives and communities. The following list is neither prioritized nor inclusive and many of the reasons overlap. What follows is not a "critique by Aboriginal women" but elements of critique voiced by selected representatives of Aboriginal women. For now I do not specify what form of feminism these critiques are directed towards, nor do I evaluate the positions taken by these scholars, but I develop that analysis later.

First, some Aboriginal women contest the feminist claim that male domination is universal (Jaimes with Halsey 1997; Monture-Angus 1995; Turpel 1993). Insisting that patriarchy is not universal, Turpel explains: "Our communities do not have a history of disentitlement of women from political or productive life" (1993: 180). Monture-Angus also suggests that, "Current thought must recognize that Aboriginal women do not fully share the history of legally sanctioned violence against women with Canadian women" (1995: 175). Both Turpel and Monture-Angus challenge the assumption of universal male domination by referencing historical Aboriginal cultural beliefs and practices that gave high status to women in their societies.

This claim further asserts that there are fundamental differences between Aboriginal and Euro-western cultures in regards to gender relations. Some Aboriginal women claim that Aboriginal cultures do not have a history of unequal gender relations; in fact, it is argued, Aboriginal women occupy or occupied positions of authority, autonomy and high status in their communities. Tobe explains, "We didn't need to fight for our place in our societies because it surrounded us constantly" (2000: 110). Jaimes with Halsey claim, "women have always formed the backbone of Indigenous nations on the North American continent" (1997: 298). They argue that "family structures centered upon the identities of wives rather than husbands — men joined women's families... the position of women was furthered strengthened economically by virtue of their owning all or most property" (Jaimes with Halsey 1997: 304).

Tobe maintains that women in Dine/Navajo culture are valued differently than women in western culture: "Like my mother and other Indian women who grew up in a matrilineal culture, when we cross into the western world, we see how that world values women differently" (Tobe 2000: 107). Tobe explains that the Dine/Navajo culture takes its identity from the female, not the male, through clan membership. As young girls grow into women, their roles in society are determined by age, sex and kinship, which include being groomed for motherhood, which Tobe maintains carries a much different connotation in Dine/Navajo culture than in western culture. Monture-Angus also maintains that

> Aboriginal society is not ordered around the same values, such as sexuality, equality and especially freedom of speech, as Canadian society. Expecting Aboriginal society to be ordered around the same principles as Canadian society ignores the possibility that difference can exist. It also ignores the fact that Aboriginal societies have sur-

37

vived colonization (and that Canadian society colonized). This is a
fundamental difference between the two communities. (1995: 176)

Not only is it asserted by these Aboriginal women that there are substantive
differences in regards to gender relations between Aboriginal and Euro-
western cultures, but also it is claimed that these historical and traditional
gender relations have survived colonization.

Second, some Aboriginal women claim that one important difference
between Aboriginal and Euro-western cultures is the distinct valorizing of
maternalism and motherhood in Aboriginal cultures. For example, Turpel
invokes maternalism and motherhood as central to Aboriginal women's
authority and status within Aboriginal societies:

> It is commonly known that the future of our nations depends upon
> the strength of our women… we must be the hearts of our people….
> We do not want to become part of a movement, which seeks equal-
> ity with men…. Women are at the center. We are the keepers of
> the culture, the educators, the ones who must instruct the children
> to respect the Earth, and the ones who ensure that our leaders are
> remembering and "walking" with their responsibilities demonstrably
> in mind. (1993: 180–81)

In this belief, Aboriginal women are valorized both as mothers and as
caretakers of the nation. In her analysis of Aboriginal women's efforts to
change the *Indian Act*, Krosenbrink-Gelissen reports that the Native Women's
Association of Canada strategically employed the concept of traditional
motherhood in their political struggle for equal rights with Aboriginal men
(Krosenbrink-Gelissen 1994). In other words, Native women argued on
the basis of a cultural connection between motherhood and nationhood
to convince Aboriginal and non-Aboriginal governments that it was not in
the interests of Aboriginal peoples to disenfranchise Aboriginal women and
their children.

Third, some Aboriginal scholars, citing historical and cultural traditions, claim that the concept of equality is neither relevant nor necessary for
Aboriginal women in Aboriginal societies; rather these are concepts imposed
by the colonizers, including feminists. Monture-Angus explains that if she were
to locate herself within the women's movement, that would mean that she
would have to be "willing to accept less than the position accorded to women
of my nation historically. Equality is not a high standard in my way of thinking" (Monture-Angus 1995: 179). Monture (cited in Boulton 2003) argues that,
given the Mohawk culture and tradition of valuing women and the fact that
a gender hierarchy in the traditions of her people is absent, "the idea that a
feminist wants equality with men is a strange idea for Mohawk women."

Turpel states, "equality is not an important political or social concept" (1993: 179) in Aboriginal gender relations. As argued by Buffalohead, "We stem from egalitarian cultural traditions. These traditions are concerned less with equality of the sexes and more with the dignity of the individual and their inherent right — whether they are women, men or children — to make their own choices and decisions" (quoted in Jaimes with Halsey 1997: 306).

Fourth, and related to the rejection of gender equality, some Aboriginal women interpret equality as meaning reproducing the Euro-centric patriarchal system. They reject a form of feminism they understand argues for adopting and imitating white male practices, traditions and processes. If the intention of feminism is to achieve equality on the terms set by men, then equality is regarded as a low priority. Aboriginal women do not want equity in a system they do not support. For example, Turpel argues,

> I do not see it as worthwhile and worthy to aspire to, or desire, equal opportunity with white men, or with the system that they have created. The aspirations of white men in the dominant society are simply not our aspirations. We do not want to inherit their objectives and positions or to adopt their worldview. To be perfectly frank, I cannot figure out why non-Aboriginal women would want to do this either. (1993: 184)

Monture-Angus also rejects the idea that "women's oppression will be eradicated when women assume male-defined positions of status and power" (Monture-Angus 1995: 179).

Aboriginal scholars often interpret the feminist call for equality to mean that women are asking for the right for women to be men. For example, Osennontion, a Mohawk woman cited in Turpel, explains that when she hears feminists

> talk about equality, they mean sameness. They appear to want to be the *same* as man. They wanted to be treated the same as man, make the same money as a man... and, they consider all women, regardless of origin, to be the same, to share the same concerns. I, for one, maintain that Aboriginal women are *different*.... I certainly do not want to be a "man." (1993: 180, emphasis in the original)

Fifth, some Aboriginal women regard it as unnecessary to appeal for the attainment of the same rights as men; rather they appeal for the restoration and reclaiming of cultural traditions and self-government that would allow Aboriginal women to be restored to their once and continuing revered position. They insist that the solution to current problems of gender inequality and violence against Aboriginal women is to assert and reclaim cultural traditions. Part of what this call to tradition accomplishes is the erasure of the larger socio-political context in which Aboriginal women live, including being murdered with impunity.[3] Laura Wittstock, a Seneca leader maintains, "tribalism, not feminism, is the correct route" for Native women to follow (quoted in Jaimes with Halsey 1997: 319). Clara Sue Kidwell, an Anishinabe-Choctaw scholar, also suggests that "recovery of traditional forms is more than ever called for" (quoted in Jaimes with Halsey 1997: 319). "What we need to be is *more* not less Indian" (Lorelei Means, in Jaime with Halsey 1997: 317, emphasis in original). Monture-Angus calls for restoring traditional gender relations: "The relationships among Aboriginal women and Aboriginal men must also be restored and this may require more than just the healing of individuals" (Monture-Angus 1995: 224). She elaborates,

> Striving at all times to re-claim the traditions of my people, the respect and power women once held is the single most important reason why I cannot accept a feminist construction of reality. My ability to re-claim my position in the world as Haudenosaunee woman is preconditioned on the ability of our men to remember the traditions that we have lost. (1995: 179)

Sixth, some Aboriginal women state that gender inequality is neither the only nor the most important form of oppression they face. For example, Janet McCloud disagrees with "many Anglo women [who] try to tell us that our most pressing problem is male supremacy" (quoted in Jaimes with Halsey 1997: 318). Monture-Angus argues that Aboriginal women face multiple forms of discrimination and violence: "Organizing against a single form of violence — men's — is not a luxury I have experienced. The general definition of violence against women is too narrow to capture all of the violence that Aboriginal women face" (Monture-Angus 1995: 171).

Aboriginal women argue that colonization, racism and economic disparity are more pressing concerns than achieving gender equality. As stated by Lorelei Means, "We are *American Indian* women, in that order. We are oppressed, first and foremost as American Indians, as peoples colonized by the United States of America, *not as women*" (quoted in Jaimes with Halsey 1997: 300, emphasis in original). Another American Indian woman, Janet McCloud, a Tulalip activist from Washington State, is quoted as stating,

> *You* join us in liberating *our* land and lives. Lose the privilege *you* acquire at *our* expense by occupying *our* land. Make *that* your first priority for as long as it takes to make it happen. *Then* we'll join you in fixing up whatever's left of the class and gender problems in your society, and our own, if need be. *But*, if you're not willing to do *that*,

then don't presume to tell *us* how we should go about our liberation, what priorities and values we should have. (in Jaimes with Halsey 1997: 301, emphasis in original)

Pam Colorado echoes those same sentiments, claiming, "nothing I've encountered in feminist theory addresses the fact of our colonization or the wrongness of white women's stake in it" (quoted in Jaime with Halsey 1997: 318). Tobe also explains, "When Indian women joined the feminist dialogue in the 1970's, we found that equality for women was generally directed toward white women's issues. The issues that were relevant to our tribal communities were not part of the feminist dialogue. Most Indian families were just struggling to survive…. On an economic hierarchy, Indian women were on the bottom rung and going nowhere" (2000: 109). Turpel states that, "Before imposing upon us the logic of gender equality (with white men), what about ensuring for our cultures and political systems equal legitimacy with the Anglo-Canadian cultural perspective, which dominates the Canadian state?" (1993: 183).

The above reasons form the basis on which some Aboriginal women have rejected feminism as irrelevant. I think it is important to understand and examine these interpretations of feminism as a way to explore and make arguments for the relevance of feminism to Aboriginal women and men.

## REFLECTIONS

At the very moment when the Native intellectual is anxiously trying to create a cultural work he fails to realize that he is utilizing techniques and language which are borrowed from the stranger in his country. (Fanon 1968/1963: 223)

I begin my reflections with this quote from Franz Fanon as one way to acknowledge the extent of the impact and consequences of colonization on Indigenous and Aboriginal people. Some would argue that colonization affected Aboriginal people in varying degrees and scope, and therefore in some places some Aboriginal cultural traditions and practices have remained more or less intact. I argue that the overwhelming majority of Aboriginal people have gone through some degree of socialization into Christianity as well as incorporation into the patriarchal capitalist political economy and education system, and are therefore subject to western ideologies of gender identities and relations. Schools and churches have been described as ideological state apparatuses (Althusser 1971). It is argued that these institutions play a significant role in producing and reproducing ideologies about what it means to be a man or a woman or a family, not through force but through common-sense ideas that are enacted in everyday practices like going to school, courting, getting married and giving birth. Most of us are familiar with how this is done within the boundaries of western traditions and practices, and I argue that we do not stand outside those social and cultural practices. Fanon is also making this point when he comments on the use of the colonizer's language by Indigenous or Aboriginal scholars and activists to make political, poetic and artistic statements (Fanon 1968/1963). This is but one effect of colonization on Aboriginal people. I offer the following reflections about feminism and its relationship to Aboriginal women, while acknowledging that I am both a part of western thinking and practices, as well as separate from them.

## WHOSE THEORY AND WHOSE INSTITUTIONS?

Engaging in social analysis is a political enterprise. It is difficult to find one's way through the myriad forms of analysis and theorizing to find what is useful. Given that the current production of Aboriginal identities and subjectivities has not occurred outside the socio-intellectual traditions and practices of western institutions, I have come to appreciate the importance of being informed about the history, knowledge and institutions of the West. The need to study feminist scholarship and theorizing, before determining its relevance — or lack thereof — to Aboriginal women and their communities is but one example of this need to be informed. As Maori scholar Linda Smith argues, history is about power, and the notion of "subjugated knowledges" must be joined with a critical reading of European knowledge and history (Smith 1999).

Elizabeth Grosz, an American feminist, makes a similar argument in her review of the implications that structural and post-structural theorists, such as Althusser, Lacan, Foucault and Derrida, have on how we think about the human subject. She argues that feminists can "ignore the history and current conceptions of theories of human subjectivity only at their own peril" (1990: 60). She suggests that feminists must use whatever remains worthwhile after considering the limitations of patriarchal discourses "to create new theories, new methods, and values" (61).

After resisting for some time, I have come to appreciate how important it is that we as Indigenous scholars study western canonical knowledge, especially the knowledge of "dead white men." I have found it useful in my research on Aboriginal education to trace the development of, first, the discourse of race and the historical discursive practices of racialization and, second, the discourse of culture and its use as a discursive practice that marks and produces "difference" (St. Denis 2002). In doing so, I have developed a greater appreciation for just how much European history, knowledge and institutions have been, and continue to be, productive of Indigenous and Aboriginal peoples' lives.

I have come to value the merits of drawing on strands of theorizing that intertwine and intersect to produce the analysis required to understand the multiple and sometimes contradictory positioning of Aboriginal peoples. There is much value in trying to follow in the scholarly tradition described by Wright, a feminist scholar, who describes her intellectual engagement as an "experiment in cartography, mapping conceptual and political intersections in order to extend a vital and critical engagement" (1992: xix). I believe that a critical reading entails understanding how inequality and unequal social, political and economic relations have been justified, rationalized and practised within European institutions, and part of this critical reading entails understanding feminist critiques and analyses of western patriarchy.

## FEMINIST THEORY AND PRACTICE: NEITHER STATIC NOR HOMOGENOUS

Just as Aboriginal and Indigenous people are not an homogenous static monolith, neither are feminists and feminist analyses. Kate Shanley, an American Indian who identifies as a feminist, notes that although even she may have in her writing referred to the "women's movement as though it were a single well-defined organization. It is not" (1988: 215). Although feminist scholarship has sometimes been portrayed as an unchanging body of scholarship engaged in male bashing (Jaimes with Halsey 1997), I have found it useful to develop an understanding of the nuanced and complex arguments and analyses that feminists have advanced to challenge gender inequality. Feminist analyses and strategies for overcoming gender oppression have always varied and been debated. An example of the monolithic stereotype is the assumption that feminism is mostly liberal feminism.

I agree with Aboriginal women's claim that equality is not appropriate or relevant in the context of continuing colonization, in which the sovereignty and rights of self-determination of Aboriginal peoples is denied; in other words, equality is not enough and does little to address colonial relations. However, I find it problematic that feminism is interpreted as a desire by women to be treated like men, and equality is interpreted as advocating "sameness" in treatment. Although there may be a strand of feminism that has advocated same treatment as one way to get access to education, employment and political rights, it is a position that has been contested within and by feminists historically and in the present. For example, radical and cultural feminists have not only rejected male power structures, they have also idealized women's culture. As Freedman explains, radical and cultural feminists have "questioned the liberal feminist goal of integrating women into male power structures" (2002: 87). Radical feminists have also resisted "demeaning images in the media" (99) by seeking to celebrate a positive "women's culture" (88).

In another example, Freedman explains that, although Virginia Woolf may have criticized the way in which a patriarchal system relegated women to the home and advocated for access to higher education for women as a path that could lead women to self-sufficiency and political rights, she also, "*did not want* educated women to join the 'procession of the sons of educated men' in perpetuating a society that promulgated social inequalities and waged war" (Freedman 2002: 70, emphasis added). In other words, some feminists may have used equality arguments to gain access to education and other rights, but it did not necessarily mean feminists were advocating for the right to be like men. To some degree, as Shanley suggests, "the women's movement and the Indian movement for sovereignty suffer trivialization" (1988: 215).

First Nations, Métis and Inuit women who participated in an Aboriginal Women's Roundtable on Gender Equality sponsored by Status of Women Canada agreed that sexual discrimination could not "be separated from the twin legacies of colonialism and racism," and on the matter of equality, they agreed with the principle of "equal pay for work of equal value... [and] equality with men in such areas as hiring, training, economic development, decision making and policy development" (Status of Women Canada 2003). In this case, Aboriginal women were discerning interpreters of equality, realizing that in some instances equality must be a requirement in their self-determination as Aboriginal women.

## WESTERN PATRIARCHY: A PROBLEM FOR US ALL

I think feminist analyses of western forms of patriarchy are relevant to both Aboriginal women and men, because western patriarchy has impacted all of us. Monture-Angus has argued that Aboriginal societies are not ordered around the same principles and values as Canadian society, that differences do exist and that "Aboriginal societies have survived colonization" (Monture-Angus 1995: 176). On the other hand, Monture-Angus does call for an analysis of patriarchy in the context of colonization: "Understanding how patriarchy operates in Canada without understanding colonization is a meaningless endeavour from the perspective of Aboriginal people" (Monture-Angus 1995: 175). I argue that most if not all Aboriginal people, both men and women, who are living in western societies are inundated from birth until death with western patriarchy and western forms of misogyny. In this view, I am joined by an increasing number of other Aboriginal women who are also claiming that we have not escaped these social and political structures and ideologies at all.

In *Strong Women Stories: Native Vision and Community Survival,* editors Kim Anderson and Bonita Lawrence bring together a refreshing and fuller alternative to discussions about gender relations, feminism and tradition in Aboriginal communities (see St. Denis 2004 for reviews of this book). In this collection, Aboriginal women explore how patriarchy, Christianity and colonialism have affected their lives and how many women must "wrestle with the patriarchal framework of colonialism and ask what it has done to our traditions, including our social and political systems" (Anderson and Lawrence 2003: 5). In one chapter, Fay Blaney, an Aboriginal woman, describes the work of the Aboriginal Women's Action Network, which seeks to educate Aboriginal women about the impact of patriarchy and misogyny in Aboriginal families. She states that the Native Women's Association of Canada acknowledges that "patriarchy is so ingrained in our communities that it is now seen as a 'traditional trait'" (Blaney 2003: 158). Deerchild explains, "those who question tradition are seen as outsiders to our cultures, or they are seen as people who are misguided about what the teachings mean" (2003: 104).

Anderson and Lawrence challenge doctrinaire notions of traditions as unchanging phenomena. The Aboriginal women authors in the book describe ways in which western and Christian ideologies of gender and gender relations are often incorrectly invoked as Aboriginal tradition and aversely affect women in several ways. For example, in her chapter, Dawn Martin-Hill questions the emergence of the concept of a traditional Indigenous woman whom she identifies as She No Speaks, "a construction born from the tapestry of our colonial landscape," a woman who is encouraged to remain "silent and obedient to male authority" (2003: 108). In a concluding chapter, by Carl Fernandez, a young man reports that in his research one woman observed that, "the teachings about womanhood too often focus on what women *can't* do" (2003: 251, emphasis in the original). Deerchild also points out that the belief and practice of matriarchy in Aboriginal cultures is often "reduced to an obligatory nod" (2003: 101).

Despite the claims that some Aboriginal women have made about the elevated status Aboriginal women occupy in Aboriginal cultures, Aboriginal women do suffer marginalization and oppression within their own communities now and have done in the past. Emma LaRocque, a Métis scholar, disputes assumptions that Aboriginal women have always occupied high-status positions in Aboriginal cultures. She argues, "We cannot assume that all Aboriginal traditions universally respected and honoured women.... It should not be assumed, even in those original societies that were structured along matriarchal lines, that matriarchies necessarily prevented men from oppressing women. There are indications of male violence and sexism in some Aboriginal societies prior to European contact and certainly after contact" (LaRocque 1996: 14). But even if Aboriginal women were once held in high regard and exercised social, economic and political influence, the effects of colonization and Christianity have certainly brought about change.

Colonization has involved the appropriation of sovereignty, lands, resources and agency, and has included the imposition of western and

Christian patriarchy on Aboriginal peoples. Patriarchy is not the only form of oppression experienced by Aboriginal people, but it is certainly a part of that oppression. I agree with Turpel that "We cannot abandon our men; they too have been abused and oppressed by the Canadian state" (1993: 181), but I think understanding how western patriarchy distorts the lives of both men and women is a valuable and significant process in decolonization. We have and can turn to some of the analyses offered by both western and minority feminists, including men who are also concerned with inequitable and unjust gender relations. Certainly the need for education is evident. As Carl Fernandez found, "Most Aboriginal men, particularly the older generation, do not really recognize the ways in which gender inequality affects their community" (2003: 253).

In my anti-racist teaching, I draw on the work of feminists who provide critiques and analyses of how western patriarchy shapes the lives of both men and women, and I think it is something that Aboriginal people can also learn from. For example, I often assign readings from Alan Johnson's book *The Gender Knot: Unraveling Our Patriarchal Legacy*, in which he makes the case that "patriarchy isn't simply about relationships between women and men. It encompasses an entire world organized around principles of control, domination and competition" (1997: 51). Johnson claims,

> Patriarchy encourages men to seek security, status, and other rewards through control; to fear other men's ability to control and harm them; and to identify being in control as both their best defense against loss and humiliation and the surest route to what they need and desire. In this sense, although we usually think of patriarchy in terms of what happens between men and women, it is more about what goes on *among men*." (1997, 26, emphasis in the original)

He argues that our journey out of western patriarchy "begins with seeing how it works and what it does to us, how we participate in it and how we might choose differently" (52). For example, in explaining the high levels of violence against women, Johnson argues that in a patriarchal system, "women's place is to help contain men's resentment over being controlled by *other men*... men are allowed to dominate women as a kind of compensation for their being subordinated to other men because of social class, race, or other forms of inequality" (37).

There is some merit to this analysis, and I think it offers a partial explanation for the high levels of physical and sexual violence committed by both Aboriginal and non-Aboriginal men against Aboriginal women. "Women's powerful economic, political, social, and religious positions within most tribes are not honoured as they once were, violence against Indigenous women has escalated" (Mihesuah 2003: xiv). LaRocque also points out that there is no question that "Aboriginal men have internalized white male devaluation of women" (1994: 74–76).

Furthermore, LaRocque asks important questions about the impact of a sexist and misogynist popular mainstream culture on Aboriginal people: "What happens to Aboriginal males who are exposed not only to pornography but also to the racist/sexist view of the 'Indian' male as a violent 'savage' and the Aboriginal female as a debased sexually loose 'squaw'?" (76). We must be able to draw on the important work that feminists have done in exploring the impact of pornography on gender relations and gendered violence. Aboriginal people are not immune to popular culture, and we must therefore, as LaRocque suggests, explore how "pornography in popular culture is affecting sexual attitudes and behaviour within Aboriginal communities" (76). I remember how disturbing the National Film Board film *This is Not a Love Story* was for me when I was required to watch it as part of an undergraduate sociology course on crime and deviance. This documentary film produced in the late 1970s provides a feminist critique of the pornography industry.

Aboriginal people live for the most part in a western capitalistic and patriarchal context; it is that social, economic and political context that irrevocably shapes our lives, and denying this or minimizing these conditions will not change it. Tobe acknowledges this when she states: "When we leave our traditional world and step into the western world, feminism becomes an issue, and we must confront and deal with the same issues that affect all women (2000: 109). As Shanley argues, "Indian feminists are united with mainstream feminists in outrage against woman and child battering, sexist employment and educational practices, and in many other social concerns" (1988: 215). In regards to these social issues, there is place in feminist theory and action for dialogue and alliances among diverse women.

## INTERSECTION OF RACE, CLASS, NATIONHOOD IN FEMINISM

Feminist analysis and activism have evolved over time and have generated new understandings of the effects of the multiple positions women occupy — for example, how social and economic class and racial positioning, sexual identity and disability intersect. There is much in the literature that takes up the contentious relationship between Aboriginal and minority women and feminism. Some of these issues have already been discussed in this chapter. Aboriginal and minority women have also had to contend with pressure from within Aboriginal and minority communities to reject and deny the relevance of feminist theory and activism. Additionally, Aboriginal and minority women have not always been welcomed within the feminist community. Freedman acknowledges this history.

The denial, inability or resistance on the part of some feminists to address racism is a real issue that affects Aboriginal and minority women within the feminist movement and in the larger society. This issue has been discussed and written about extensively over the past two or three decades. As Freedman and many others have stated, many women of colour have felt excluded from a theory that elevated gender at the expense of race or class identity. In particular, the example of African American women has long provided a critical perspective for white women, alerting them to the integral connections between race and gender (Freedman 2002: 83).

In early twentieth century efforts to create an international women's movement, concern was expressed with how those efforts often reproduced colonial relations (Freedman 2002: 105). In a more recent example, Freedman explains that when U.S. feminists arrived in Mexico City in 1975 for the first international conference on women, which launched the United Nations declaration of the Decade for Women, they encountered criticism from delegates who did not want to discuss gender outside the context of movements for national self-determination (2002: 109). This is similar to the claims that many Aboriginal women have made. It was the non-governmental organizations that both worked with women internationally and also attended the international conferences on women beginning in the mid-1970s to the mid-1980s that convinced many western women that world poverty and national liberation were feminist issues because they affected women's lives around the globe (Freedman 2002: 110). Feminism has responded to the multiple and sometimes contradictory positioning of women locally and internationally. As Freedman explains "Most western feminists have learned that global economic and political justice are prerequisites to securing women's rights" (2002: 3).

Racialized women who claim a feminist politics have provided me with an opening to feminist scholarship. Even though some Aboriginal women maintain that the processes of racialization do not solely define their identity, there are similarities in Aboriginal women's criticisms of feminism and the criticisms made by other racialized and minority women. My own race and gender analysis was greatly enhanced by researching the scholarship of these feminists of colour. The concerns raised by Lata Mani, a South Asian feminist scholar, are ones that are shared by other racialized and minority women, including Aboriginal women. Her concern is with "how to argue for women's rights in ways that are not complicit in any way with patriarchal, racist or ethnocentrist formulations of the issues" (1989: 8).

One issue that I have found particularly relevant to Aboriginal and Indigenous women is the claim that one's first loyalty is to one's nation, race or culture, above gender, and that to challenge oppression by one's own community is to betray it. This is a discussion engaged in by racialized and Third World women as well. Algerian feminist Marie-Aimee Helie-Lucas explains that women hesitated for years to speak out against unjust laws because they felt "silenced by fears of accusations of betrayal and by the nationalist myth" (Freedman 2002: 104).

Native American women risk being dismissed as "assimilated" if they identify with feminist politics. For example, Jaimes with Halsey argue that those Native women activists who have most openly identified themselves as feminists

> have tended to be among the more assimilated of Indian women activists… these women are devoted to "civil rights" rather than liberation per se. Native American women who are more genuinely sovereigntist in their outlook have proved far more dubious about the potentials offered by feminist politics and alliances. (1997: 317)

One of the effects of this has been to discourage Aboriginal and Native women from not only writing about feminism, but even from learning about how feminism tries to intervene in sexism and misogyny. Mihesuah challenges the belief that Aboriginal and Indigenous women who identify with feminism are being divisive. She writes,

> My position as a Native female who has observed and encountered these relationships is that we are not being divisive; we are being realistic. Misogyny, colorism, ethnocentricism, and physical abuse are sad realities among Native people and unless Natives do something about these problems, no one else will. (2003: xiii–viv)

Although earlier scholarship by some Aboriginal women argued that feminism was not compatible with Aboriginal culture and nationhood, more recent Aboriginal women's work disputes those claims. Not unlike other racialized women who argue that feminism is not incompatible with nationalism or religion, "some international feminists have argued for higher education, professional jobs, and an insistence that feminism is compatible with Islam and nationalism" (Freedman 2002: 102). There is a wide-range of analysis to be found in feminist scholarship that is potentially relevant and compatible with the needs of Aboriginal women and men and their communities.

## CONCLUSION

> Although Indigenous scholars *do not always agree* with each other, it is critical that we present our opinions and concerns not only to Natives but also to non-Natives. (Mihesuah 2003: xiii, emphasis added)

I want to conclude with the message offered in the above quote, because Aboriginal people are all too familiar with the way in which disagreement within our communities can not only discourage critical debate among ourselves but can be used as a justification by dominant institutions to ignore Aboriginal claims for social justice. Aboriginal people, researchers and scholars must have the freedom to debate and discuss the contradictions and paradoxes that arise in our strategies as we move towards decolonization, including the merits of feminism for Aboriginal people. The diversity of perspectives among Aboriginal peoples in our analyses and strategies for change cannot be used as justification for maintaining the status quo of inequality and marginalization.

I too once maintained that feminism was not relevant to Aboriginal people, and I once thought that to be feminist meant that one had to choose between gender and culture or nation. I no longer hold this view. Increasingly more Aboriginal women are beginning to identify as feminists, or at least with some of the goals of feminism, such as ending violence against women and children. As I have found out in my own use of feminist scholarship, feminism can no longer be dismissed as merely advancing a liberal agenda. Feminist scholarship is very important to my anti-racist teaching, in which I draw upon on a wide range of feminist writing on issues including race, nationhood, class, disability and sexual identity. I have begun encouraging Aboriginal students, both women and men, to take courses in women and gender studies if they have that option in their university programs. We miss an important body of scholarship when we in the Aboriginal community dismiss feminism as irrelevant. This dismissal has the effect of discouraging Aboriginal students from reading feminist scholarship, which is no less relevant than other components of the large body of scholarship we study in any university. As bell hooks (2000) declares, "Feminism Is for Everybody."

## NOTES

1.   In this section I draw heavily on Estelle Freedman's *Not Turning Back: The History of Feminism and the Future of Women* (2002), where she provides, as the title suggests, a history of feminist theory and activism in western societies, including a discussion of the effects of the engagement by racialized and Third World feminists with white and western feminisms. Freedman provides a broad overview of the development of feminism and a history of the debates that have occurred within both scholarly and activist feminist communities. I also draw upon the *Encyclopedia of Feminist Theories*, edited by Lorraine Code (2000), and *The Routledge Critical Dictionary of Feminism and Postfeminism*, edited by Sarah Gamble (2000), which also provide general overviews of the history of feminism.

2.   Liberal feminists work "towards an egalitarian society, which would uphold the right of each individual to fulfil their potential" (Gamble 2000: 264). In the case of women, liberal feminism was a call to "give women the same status and opportunities as men" (Gamble 2000: 264), it advocates "equal rights for women" (Code 2000: 303). I once assumed that to be a feminist meant liberal feminism. Liberal feminism has been widely critiqued as an inadequate response to the needs of vastly differently positioned raced and classed women. The assump-

tion of liberal feminism that equality could be attained through formal and legal declaration did not take into account the needs of women marginalized by racism and classism.

3. Crawford murders and Pickton murders and many others.

## REFERENCES

Althusser, L. 1971. *Lenin and Philosophy, and Other Essays*. Translated from the French by Ben Brewster. London: New Left Books.

Anderson, K., and B. Lawrence (eds.). 2003. *Strong Women Stories: Native Vision and Community Survival*. Toronto: Sumach Press.

Blaney, F. 2003. "Aboriginal Women's Action Network." In Anderson and Lawrence.

Boulton, M. 2003. "Monture Takes Advocacy for Aboriginal Women to National Stage on Person's Day." *On Campus News* 11, 6 (October 31). Available at <http://www.usask.ca/communications/ocn/03-oct-31/news12.shtml> (accessed March 2007).

Bowles, G., and R.D. Klein. 1983. *Theories of Women's Studies*. Boston: Routledge and Kegan Paul.

Code, L. 2000. *Encyclopedia of Feminist Theories*. New York: Routledge.

Davis, A. 1981. *Women, Race, and Class*. New York: Random House.

Deerchild, R. 2003. "Tribal Feminism Is a Drum Song." In Anderson and Lawrence.

Faludi, S. 1991. *Blacklash: The Undeclared War Against American Women*. New York: Crown Publishers.

Fanon, F. 1968/1963. *Wretched of the Earth*. New York: Grove Press.

Fernandez, C. 2003. "Coming Full Circle: A Young Man's Perspective on Building Gender Equity in Aboriginal Communities." In Anderson and Lawrence.

Freedman, E. 2002. *No Turning Back: The History of Feminism and the Future of Women*. New York: Ballantine Books.

Gamble, S. (ed.). 2000. *The Routledge Critical Dictionary of Feminism and Postfeminism*. New York: Routledge.

Grande, S. 2003. "Whitestream Feminism and the Colonialist Project: A Review of Contemporary Feminist Pedagogy and Praxis." *Educational Theory* 53, 3 (Summer) ProQuest Education Journals.

Grosz, E. 1990. "Contemporary Theories of Power and Subjectivity." In S. Gunew (ed.), *Feminist Knowledge: Critique and Construct*. London: Routledge.

hooks, b. 1988. *Talking Back: Thinking Feminist, Thinking Black*. Toronto: Between the Lines.

_____. 2000. *Feminism Is for Everybody: Passionate Politics*. Cambridge, MA: South End Press.

Jaimes, A.M., with T. Halsey. 1997. "American Indian Women: At the Center of Indigenous Resistance in Contemporary North American." In A. McClintock, A. Mufti and E. Shohat (eds.), *Dangerous Liaisons: Gender, Nation and Postcolonial Perspectives*. Minneapolis: University of Minnesota Press.

Johnson, A. 1997. *The Gender Knot: Unravelling our Patriarchal Legacy*. Philadelphia: Temple University Press.

LaRocque, E. 1994. *Violence in Aboriginal Communities*. Ottawa: National Clearinghouse on Family Violence, Family Violence Prevention Division, Health Programs and Services Branch, Health Canada.

_____. 1996. "The Colonization of a Native Woman Scholar." In C. Miller and P. Chuchryk (eds.), *Women of the First Nations: Power, Wisdom and Strength*. Winnipeg: University of Manitoba Press.

Lorde, A. 1984. *Sister Outsider: Essays and Speeches*. Trumansburg, NY: Crossing Press.

Krosenbrink-Gelissen, L.E. 1994. "Caring Is Indian Women's Business, But Who Takes Care of Them? Canada's Indian Women, the Renewed Indian Act, and Its Implications for Women's Family Responsibilities, Roles and Rights." *Law and Anthropology: International Yearbook for Legal Anthropology* 8.

Mani, L. 1989. "Multiple Mediations: Feminist Scholarship in the Age of Multinational Reception." *Inscriptions* 5.

Martin-Hill, D. 2003. "She No Speaks and Other Colonial Constructs of 'The Traditional Woman.'" In Anderson and Lawrence.

Mihesuah, D.A. 2003. *Indigenous American Women: Decolonization, Empowerment, Activism*. Lincoln: University of Nebraska Press.

Monture-Angus, P. 1995. *Thunder in My Soul: A Mohawk Woman Speaks*. Halifax: Fernwood Publishing.

Moraga, C., and G. Anzaldua (eds.). 1983. *This Bridge Called My Back: Writings by Radical Women of Color*. Latham, NY: Kitchen Table, Women of Color Press.

Reinharz, S. 1979. *On Becoming a Social Scientist*. New Brunswick, NJ: Transaction Books.

Shanley, K. 1988. "Thoughts on Indian Feminism." In B. Brant (ed.), *A Gathering of Spirit: A Collection by North American Indian Women*. Ithaca: Firebrand Books.

Smith. L.T. 1999. *Decolonizing Methodologies: Research and Indigenous Peoples*. London: Zed Books Ltd.

St. Denis, V. 1989. "A Process of Community-based Participatory Research: A Case Study." Unpublished masters thesis. University of Alaska/Fairbanks, Fairbanks, Alaska.

_____. 1992. "Community-Based Participatory Research: Aspects of the Concept Relevance for Practice." *Native Studies Review* 8, 2.

_____. 2002. "An Exploration of the Socio-cultural Production of Aboriginal Identities: Implications for Education." Unpublished doctoral dissertation. Stanford University, Stanford California.

_____. 2004. "Book Review: Strong Women Stories: Native Vision and Community Survival." *Resources for Feminist Research* 31, 1/2.

Status of Women Canada. 2003. Aboriginal Women's Roundtable on Gender Equality. Available at <http://www.swc-cfc.gc.ca/pubs/abwomenroundtable/section3_e.html> (accessed March 2007).

Tobe, L. 2000. "There Is No Word for Feminism in My Language." *Wicazo sa Review: A Journal of Native American Studies* Fall.

Turpel, M.E. 1993. "Patriarchy and Paternalism: The Legacy of the Canadian State for First Nations Women." *Canadian Journal of Women and the Law* 6.

Wright, E. 1992. *Feminism and Psychoanalysis: A Critical Dictionary*. Cambridge, MA: Blackwell Publishers.

# Chapter Three

# MÉTIS AND FEMINIST
## Ethical Reflections on Feminism, Human Rights and Decolonization

### Emma LaRocque

To speak or write on matters of human rights for Aboriginal peoples, especially for Aboriginal women, is to be confronted with extraordinary challenges, in part because there are so many issues to address. I have struggled with what issues to foreground with respect to Aboriginal women and feminism, reviewing a menu of socio-political items such as poverty, racism/sexism, violence and the culturalization of violence, the criminal justice system, self-government, exclusions of Aboriginal women in constitutional processes and so forth. Yet, one feels compelled to offer a more positive portrait of the ways in which Aboriginal women live: as victims of colonization and patriarchy, yet as activists and agents in their lives; as oppressed, yet as fighters and survivors; and as among the most stereotyped, dehumanized and objectified of women, yet as the strong, gracious and determined women that they are. I also wondered whether I should just concentrate on Métis Nation women as their histories and contemporary concerns are frequently submerged, if not erased, under the umbrella terms and treatment of Aboriginal women (which almost always means dealing exclusively with status Indian issues).

Perhaps a way to bring together some of these wide-ranging concerns is to offer reflections on my engagement with feminism as a scholar and educator, a writer and social critic, a human rights advocate and most pertinently, as a Métis woman who grew up with all the contradictions and burdens of a community wracked with the colonial situation, and in a society inured to this situation.

I am aware that many, perhaps even the majority of, status Indian and Métis women do not identify with or readily use the label "feminist." Joyce Green has observed that

> Feminist identification and feminist analysis [are] weak within Aboriginal communities and organizations, and [are] not widespread among individual women. Aboriginal women have been urged to identify as Aboriginal, in the context of the domination and exploitation by the newcomer community, to the exclusion of

identification as women with women across cultures, and with the experience of exploitation and domination by men within Aboriginal communities. (1993: 111)

Reasons for this are complex and include political, historical, cultural and socio-economic factors as well as some misunderstanding about feminism. For some Aboriginal women, such misunderstanding reflects their disadvantaged socio-economic position and marginalization, which, among other things, deprives them of attaining adequate education. But there are also Native women intellectuals who charge white feminism with having little or no understanding of colonial history, Aboriginal peoples or race oppression (Stevenson 1993; Monture-Angus 1995; Ouellette 2002).

Given that feminism is neither well-understood nor readily received by many Aboriginal women, it is useful to offer some basic assumptions, definitions and understandings about feminism. Josephine Donovan writes that "historical and anthropological studies reveal" four "determinant structures under which women, unlike men, have nearly universally existed" (1990: 172). I find her concise overview of these structures helpful:

> First and foremost, women have experienced political oppression.... Second, nearly everywhere and in nearly every period, women have been assigned to the domestic sphere.... Third, women's historical economic function has been production for use, not production for exchange.... Fourth, women experience significant physical events that are different from men's. (1990: 172–73)

Is this also true for Aboriginal women? Without going into all the possible nuances and exceptions to the rule, and taking somewhat of a different direction from Donovan, I have no hesitation in accepting that such determinant structures are most definitely present in the lives of the majority of Aboriginal women. While there are some notable exceptions in history, such as some semi-matriarchal societies among Indigenous peoples, and while we can pinpoint colonization as the major factor in our present conditions, it remains true that we currently live under structures that proscribe or marginalize our lives. Aboriginal women experience political oppression in a number of ways. Our alienation from constitutional processes and from positions of leadership in white and Native male-dominated institutions are evidence of this. Aboriginal women have not enjoyed automatic inclusion or leadership roles in the public sphere of either Canadian society or in the upper echelons of national Aboriginal political organizations. Nor have they enjoyed equal treatment in Canadian legislation or in Aboriginal governance. They continue to face discrimination in a wide spectrum of social and economic settings. Even in areas of religion or spirituality, Aboriginal women's roles are circumscribed by church doctrines or by some renderings of Aboriginal traditions. Women are politically oppressed when their roles and standing in the political and cultural life of their societies are restricted when compared to men.

While much has been made of "balance" between genders in Aboriginal traditions, there is overwhelming evidence that, by and large, Aboriginal women's roles have been confined to the domestic sphere. As Donovan explains, women have "been consigned to the domestic sphere and to domestic duties — including child-rearing or mothering — throughout recorded history" (1990: 172). We also need to ask what is meant by balance. Does the rhetoric of "balance" necessarily or automatically mean gender equality? It could merely mean that male and female roles are to be interdependent or complementary but from within gender-specified stations. The problem is in the definition of the roles. For instance, I have heard a male elder baldly declare that "man is the law, and woman is to serve the man and to nurture the family." Here, the elder is equating balance not with gender equality but with maintaining the status quo, that men maintain their over-arching dominance in the family, the stuff of patriarchy. "Balance" then becomes a new buzzword for keeping women to domestic and nurturing roles. I am sure not all people who promote balance between genders mean to say that women's roles should be restricted to home life. However, it does remain that for many, idealization of nurturing/motherhood has been reified and has gained political currency within nationalist and cultural difference discourses. I come back to this later.

Concerning women's economic function, I would be careful — as is Donovan — not to apply western-based economic ideas onto pre-industrial societies, and in our case, original Indigenous societies. Concepts such as "production for use" versus "production for exchange" may not be applicable to land-based, non-capitalist cultures. Living off the land does tend to encourage greater flexibility in gender/labour roles. However, we can see that Aboriginal women's gender roles, including economic roles, became more restricted with the arrival of European missionaries, "explorers" and fur traders. Separation between home (domestic) life and work (productive) life (the public/private dichotomy identified by feminist analysis) certainly increased. The fur traders, for example, encouraged male labour and travel, which of course meant that women were left to attend to child-rearing and other family and home demands. Missionaries twisted such gender role and economic changes into moral mandates. Within a few years of Confederation in 1867, the Canadian government legislated Indian status/non-status identity, rights and gender roles along patriarchal lines.

Donovan invokes "significant physical events that are different from men's," citing menstruation, childbirth and breastfeeding as examples, and uses these differences as a springboard towards formulating a particularly female epistemology and ethic (1990:173). Donovan does not name sexuality or sexual violence here. However, Aboriginal women need to consider violence as a significant physical event (or series of events) as Aboriginal females of all ages continue to suffer from child abuse, wife battering, sexual assault and murder in epidemic proportions. As Patricia Monture-Angus explains: "It is likely Aboriginal women experience violence in their lives with greater frequency than any other collective of women in Canadian society"; further, that "violence is not a mere incident in the lives of Aboriginal women" (1995: 170).

Deploying Donovan's approach, then, we can see that Aboriginal women's experiences and socio-political positions in both Native and white communities fall within these structural determinants. Thus, we cannot remove Aboriginal women's concerns from other women's concerns for we too live under over-arching male-dominated conditions both as Canadian citizens and Aboriginal people. And although we must be sensitive to racial, cultural or economic differences, we can address Aboriginal women's multiple layers of oppressions from a feminist perspective.

## FEMINISM

What then is "Feminism"? I understand feminism as a struggle to end sexism and gender-based inequality in society. "Feminism… is comprised of the well-founded belief that girls and women are legally, politically and socially disadvantaged on the grounds of their sex; the ethical stance that this oppression is morally wrong; and the pragmatic commitment to ending injustice to all female human beings" (Overall 1998: 15).

bell hooks has a more comprehensive definition:

> Feminism is the struggle to end sexist oppression. Its aim is not to benefit any specific group of women, any particular race or class of women. It does not privilege women over men. It has the power to transform in a meaningful way all our lives. Most importantly, feminism is neither a lifestyle nor a ready-made identity or role one can step in to. (1994: 24)

Feminism, then, does not belong to any particular group, and those who understand and practise this social idea of ending gender inequality and injustice are feminist. In this sense, men and women of all backgrounds can be feminists, and feminists should be among our best allies, and many are. Aboriginal writers, artists, scholars and community activists resisting our dehumanization and our dispossession are doing work very similar to feminist principles and objectives. Feminist and Aboriginal resistance entails both deconstruction and reconstruction. Aboriginal, non-Aboriginal, male and female feminists will especially examine theories, portrayals, political positions or social treatments of Aboriginal women. Feminism provides us with theoretical tools with which we can analyze historical realities such as patriarchy. Feminism is not so much about complaining about one particular man, event or even piece of legislation (i.e., the *Indian Act*); rather, feminism is an analysis of how social systems work to privilege men and disadvantage women. Feminism has an ethical component in that feminist analysis interrogates, confronts and seeks to transform those realities that compromise women's well-being and human rights.

## BEING MÉTIS

Given the seemingly innocuous and even grand principles and objectives for human rights embedded in feminism, I have often been surprised, at times even startled, at the negative reactions to this concept. Because the labels "feminist" or "feminism" carry such a negative or unclear meaning for many women, perhaps it is best not to fixate on terminology or on oppositional politics but rather to begin by trying to find what is important to us as Aboriginal women. Here I outline what is important to me with the inference that what is important to me may or ought also to be important to other women.

I do not come from any racially or economically equal, much less privileged, background.[1] The Métis in my community have been written up from an urban-centric bias as "bush people" living in "isolated" or "remote Indian" communities along a railroad line in northeastern Alberta (Garvin 1992). Although we spoke Plains Cree (with Michif) and lived off the land, legally we were/are not status Indians and so never lived on reserves. We were/are Métis but never lived in the Alberta Métis Settlements, or "Colonies" as they were once called. We knew ourselves as Apeetowgusanuk (or "half-sons" in Cree) who were descended from both the Red River Métis and locally originated Métis[2] communities with deep kinship connections to both status and non-status Indian peoples. And although Métis do originate from the early fur trade era of First Nations and European peoples, both my maternal and paternal family histories are grounded in Métis Nation lineage with no remembrance of or relational ties with non-Aboriginal people. My parents, aunts and uncles all spoke of "scrip"[3] and how Apeetowgusanuk lost and were continuing to lose beloved domains of lands either through scrip or simply through urban, industrial and farming encroachments. Legally, we did not own any land but in those years we could still definitely live on, from and with the land, for morally, it was our land.[4] My grandparents occupied, used and loved this land long before Confederation, and my father was born before Alberta became a province.

My parents' generation made a living from the many resources of the land, including hunting and trapping, as well as from wage labour, wherever such could be found. And although most Apeetowgusanuk were hard-working, proudly independent, or Ootayemsuak peoples, they/we were suffering from unimaginable poverty and racism, complete with layers and waves of both legal and social dispossession.

Among the multiple sites of dispossession, public schooling contributed significantly to my generation's sense of cultural dislocation and intellectual alienation. Not only did schooling aim to extract us from our mother language and our motherland with its particular western ethos, it failed to teach us basic classroom reading and writing skills, thereby failing to prepare us for the new brave world of industrialization/urbanization, even as this world was fast overtaking us, especially after World War II. Undergirding this pedagogy was the colonialist version of history and the "National Dream," all equated with "progress." Not surprisingly, the vast majority of Métis students left school as fast as they could do so legally. In 1971, the average grade level for Métis people in Alberta was four. This and more have left many people of my generation and their children in a socio-cultural vacuum. This is the direct and continuing legacy of colonization, and it is the sociological after-effects of this colonial earthquake that has dislocated and disoriented many of our youth.

Two things have always followed me from my early years: on one hand, our richly woven cultural life based on our blended land and railroad line ways, textured with our Métized (my coin) Cree oral literature, language and worldview; and on the other hand, our extreme poverty and alienation from the financial and material privileges of mainstream Canada. I do not speak of poverty in any abstract sense. Depending on seasons (trapping or non-trapping), wage-labour employment or non-employment, we could also go without much food for months, for years. My parents typically struggled to outfit us with adequate or socially acceptable clothing, lunches and other school supplies during school terms. Poverty in my family and community translated into social warfare on our bodies. As virtually penniless people of the land who spoke only Cree and often lived miles away from town, we had minimal access to doctors or hospitals throughout the 1900s, but most relevant for my generation, in the 1940s–70s. Consequently, many people died, often from tuberculosis or other diseases. Many of my relatives were sent away to sanitoriums due to TB, among them, my older sister and brother. Some came back in coffins. We were lucky: my older brother and sister survived and came home. Some children were never returned from hospitals, and those who were orphaned (but were taken care of within extended kinship systems) were often confiscated by state welfare agencies. The now infamous "sixties scoop," social welfare systems taking children away from Native families, was also practised on northern Métis communities. Those who survived were left with bewilderment and broken hearts along with a wide array of medical or social problems. Some individuals and some families increasingly displayed fragmentation, depression, alcohol abuse, anger and violence.

Yet, remarkably, numerous Métis individuals and families kept body and soul together, and I hasten to add, many men including my father did not take to violence under any circumstances. In my home there was no physical violence (except for the rare disciplinary willow lashings from my mother); as a rule, I grew up safe and secure inside our home. But my mother (1918–1981) did not grow up so safe. Somewhere, during the Depression, my maternal grandfather had been dispossessed of his scrip, his store, his land and dairy farm, uprooting his large family. Apparently, he took to drinking and family violence. Overnight my mother's young life had become one of abject poverty, and she and her sisters suffered the most immediate consequences. As part of making ends meet, my grandfather pushed his many daughters out of the home as soon as they became "of age." In a patriarchal world, they were left to find men who could take care of them.

I cannot say whether my grandfather's treatment of his daughters was typical of Métis attitudes of those times but I can say that patriarchy did not end with my grandfather. The Métis community of my generation was by no means free from patriarchal notions and practices. Take the name we had for ourselves: Apeetowgusanuk, or "half-son." Why not "half-daughters"? In my own family, all the men got two given names, and all the women had one name. This practice goes back to my grandparents and great grandparents. There was also the typical double standard about male and female sexual behaviour. To put it in the vernacular, men could "run around," women could not. If women exercised sexual freedom they could expect censorship. In the Roman Catholic Church, boys could assist priests in the service, girls could not. In our home, however, my mother, who integrated Cree traditions with Roman Catholic rituals, assumed spiritual leadership. She also led the way in many of our family decisions and activities. Although my own parents allowed the girls as much freedom of expression as the boys, I do recall one incident that indicated they had been much influenced by male-favoured thinking. When I was quite young I was told by my mother not to walk over my father's and brothers' trapping/hunting supplies and preparations. I immediately asked why not? She explained that it would bring bad luck to their trapping/hunting. I do not remember her answer, if any, to my next "why?" but I called on natural justice — if my brothers could walk over them, so could I. I was left to my youthful logic but the message was disturbing: girls are contaminated, girls bring bad luck and girls can't do all the things boys can, simply because they are girls. I am aware that today people attach spiritual power to menstrual taboos, but I was premenstrual, indicating that this taboo reflected wider and deeper gender biases and could be generalized at will.

To me all this problematizes human customs that are biology-linked. World-wide, women and girls suffer horrific mutilations as well as extreme confinements, which the international post-colonial community has largely tolerated in deference to nationalisms, cross-culturalism or tradition. Given our scientific knowledge today,[5] it seems to me we should ask whether any biology-based restrictions, even if spiritualized, are benign. Of course, I am raising normative questions, unlike my parents who tended to let things be for they were raised in an ethic of non-interference.[6] I am of a different generation — I marvel at the power tradition has over human beings. Yet, my mom was by no means sanguine about traditions that impacted her more directly.

Even though my mom was a remarkably resourceful woman who took exceptional care of us, she was by no means a happy homemaker. She most definitely did not romanticize motherhood; if anything, she resented the fact that responsibility fell on her to do the major portion of child-rearing and other home-related duties. This is all the more interesting because my amiable father assisted with many of the household chores, such as cooking, making our lunches for school and so forth, whenever he was home. Conversely, my mother enjoyed working outside alongside my dad. My mom was as free to trap and do many other so-called masculine-assigned tasks as my father was free to work in the home. Yet the key difference for my mom lay in the fact my father had a choice concerning childcare and kitchen work whereas my mother did not. And she really had no other choice. Although highly gifted and creative, my mom, along with the vast majority of other Métis women of her generation (and even my older sisters' generation), never had any opportunity to go to school or to develop her many gifts, much less to have a career or even get a job. So my mom lived with the frustration of remaining financially dependent on my father — something she viewed as an affront to her dignity.

Poverty also sets up social conditions that facilitate violence against women. In my mother's generation, white males, including police and priests, attacked Native women because they knew the women were in no position to bring them to justice. Similarly, predators in our communities targeted the most defenceless because they too knew they could get away with it. Generally, many women in our area were bullied, battered or assaulted. Aboriginal women's relocations to urban centres is in part a result of such poverty and violence.

Previously, I have addressed the topic of violence against women within Native communities (1993, 1997). I have tried to place this troubling issue in the context of colonialism, yet at the same time, have emphasized that for many reasons, male violence cannot be fully explained by social or political conditions. In other words, neither colonization nor poverty explains everything about why or how Native men (and societies) may assume sexist attitudes or behaviours. This point has to be emphasized because male violence continues to be much tolerated, explained or virtually absolved by many women of colour, including Aboriginal women, usually in defence of cultural difference, community loyalties or nationalist agendas, or out of reaction to white feminist critiques. I am concerned too that sexual violence, in particular, is often treated as only one of many colonial-generated problems that we face. But as numerous studies show, this is no ordinary social problem. Sexual violence devastates human dignity and freedom and rips apart the lives of victims, their families, kinships and other crucial community seams (Shkilnyk 1977). As far back as humans have existed this crime against humanity has existed and remains global in scope and obviously requires much greater analysis and confrontation than it has received.

Clearly, poverty is a social evil that steals from poor people a quality of life each Canadian citizen should have the right to expect. Poverty severely compromises the physical, cultural and psychological well-being of children, women and men, but it is the case that the most defenceless, usually women, children and the elderly, often bear the greatest burdens. These are issues that centrally concern women who most certainly have a great stake in working towards a society in which every citizen has access to fundamental resources for a safe and decent quality of life. Indeed, this should be a fundamental human right in our world. At the very least, this must mean ending poverty and violence.

## CRITICISM AND FEMINISM

On a philosophical level, freedom to choose is fundamental to our humanity. It is theorized (Freire 1970; Puxley 1977) that what makes us human is our capacity to make choices, which in turn, gives us moral agency. This is why colonization or any other form of coercion is a form of dehumanization. The human need and the human right to be able to have and to make choices, then, is an act of humanization. The freedom, the means or the capacity to make choices is really what self-determination is all about. Although the international community recognizes self-determination as a basic human right, all too often the concept of self-determination is applied only to cultural, ethnic or political forms and movements. But self-determination cannot be limited to constitutions, cultures or collectivities; it must be extended to individuals. Self-determination must mean that all individuals have a basic right to a certain quality of life, free from the violence of colonialism, racism/sexism and poverty, as well as from the violence of other humans, even if these other humans are one's people, or even one's relations, or are themselves suffering from colonial conditions. For multiple reasons, Aboriginal women have the greatest stake in self-determination, both as part of a people struggling to decolonize and as individuals struggling to enjoy basic human rights.

Self-determination must also mean intellectual freedom. I turn to this issue from the context of my work in Native studies for three decades now. Many of us in Native studies have made a living deconstructing the Euro-Canadian master narrative with its canons and ideologies; but we must also have the right to exercise our analytical skills and training in the service of advancing Aboriginal scholarship and humanity. We must maintain our freedoms to practise our scholarship. I emphasize intellectual and academic freedom because as feminist scholars or professors, we face political problems in pedagogical settings. I used to teach what I thought was a fairly benign seminar on Native women. I noticed that students responded well to history or information on the social conditions confronting Aboriginal women. However, when I presented them with literature or thinking that was remotely "feminist," I was greeted with silence. Interestingly, my student numbers from this course started dwindling. I do not know whether or not this was the result of an organized effort, but I certainly received the message about any critical reflection on the place of Aboriginal women in Aboriginal communities. I was, on one hand, chided by a Native male student for "airing our dirty laundry in public," and on the other, I was labelled and psychologized by white students unhappy with their marks. These are two tactics used to discredit Aboriginal and feminist analyses.

I am painfully aware that social and political realities place Native academics in unusual circumstances. In the first place, we are still a very small community, making it difficult to treat each other's works critically. I feel this pressure with this chapter! Moreover, there seems to be an unstated expectation that women not criticize women, or that Native scholars not criticize Native scholars. This is unfortunate because it detracts from the important theoretical work that needs to be done, and it hampers intellectual vibrancy. Aboriginal scholars walk a tightrope between keeping a wary eye on western-defined canons and negotiating cultural and/or community interests. Of course, cultural issues are urgently important to contemporary Native peoples. Issues of cultural, social or political urgency can, however, present conflicting interests for scholars as critical thinkers and as decolonizing educators.

For example, stereotypes about traditional knowledge and how this is expected to function in gender roles, usually with inferences that Native women be all-embracing mothers and healers, poses particular problems to those who disagree or practise roles outside of these expectations. Many popular creeds portray Aboriginal women as centrally maternal, nurturing and feminine. Typically authenticated by biology, culture or tradition, such characterizations are widely articulated by academics, writers and policy-makers as well as many community platforms. I am partial to a female epistemology and appreciate what is nurturing and feminine but I find certain idealizations of this role quite problematic.

For purposes of discussion I will take up some representations from Kim Anderson's *A Recognition of Being: Reconstructing Native Womanhood* (2000). This is an important and substantial book, one of a handful of books that focuses on Aboriginal women's experiences and issues. It is compassionate, thoughtful and well written, and the author made an effort to respectfully include a wide variety of views, including mine. This book has gained wide readership and is a useful springboard for debate on Aboriginal feminist theory.

Anderson's objective is to facilitate as many Native women's voices as possible. However, although Anderson allows for different voices, no debate is generated, for she foregrounds those views of motherhood as central to Aboriginal women's epistemology. She writes: "Motherhood was an affirmation of a woman's power and defined her central role in traditional Aboriginal societies" (2000: 83). To be sure, Anderson takes great pains to extend the "Aboriginal ideology of motherhood" (2000: 171) to those women without children and employs the concept of "aunties" in a very positive way. She also points to special women who have done great international work of healing, women with no biological children but "their role is the same as that of any mother: to teach, nurture and heal all people" (2000: 171). This is indeed a sterling vocation and ethic, echoing some feminist directions which have argued for a maternal-based "moral vision" (Donovan 1990: 173). Nonetheless, such maternalization is totalizing and exclusionary. Many women today choose not to be mothers, and they neither have desire nor appreciate being forced into what is essentially an heterosexist framework, even if a feminine one. Ultimately, motherhood does imply biology, and, as deployed in Anderson, defines "womanhood."

Even more disconcerting is the notion that a skirt is a way of accessing connectedness to the earth (2000: 167). Anderson explains that the skirt is "another symbol related to woman's ability to produce and nurture life" (2000: 166). This is then extrapolated into a rather startling view of what constitutes womanhood, or femininity. Anderson quotes a young woman who remarks: "The skirt itself represents the hoop of life. So, as a woman, you need to walk like a woman, you need to sit like a woman, you need to conduct yourself like a woman, and part of that is being recognized, not only on this earth, but also in the spirit world, as a woman" (2000: 168).

Such an assertion reflects a statement of faith, and while we must respect people's faiths, what do we do when faith turns to dogma that requires submission or contradicts other rights? I do not wear skirts, and I most certainly do not feel any less connected to the earth. Indeed, I take umbrage to any suggestion that my spirituality is wanting simply because of clothing or ceremony! But my take here is much more than personal: as a scholar and as a feminist, I too question such a remark. In the first instance, this view is strikingly similar to patriarchal Christian and other fundamentalist constructions of "woman," and one wonders to what extent the influence of residential schools and other patriarchal agencies and attitudes, both old and new, is at work here.

It is simply not true that there was any universalized Aboriginal under-standing about "womanhood," especially one that made much of masculin-ity or femininity in the western sense. In fact, archival records reveal that European men reacted to the fact that, in several Aboriginal nations, there was little difference between men and women in roles, appearance, clothing or even physical strength.[7] Furthermore, there were widely divergent tradi-tions around gender roles.

Equally problematic is the naturalizing of human gestures to biological determinism, which has every potential to discriminate against those who do not fit certain expectations. Gender stereotypes such as walking "like a woman" or "like a man" carry heterosexist preferences and prejudices that perpetuate the oppression of gay people, among others. And I might add, as one who grew up in the bush with no modern amenities, we did not think in terms of gender-proscribed ways of walking when we picked berries, chopped wood, carried water or walked for miles to towns or to our traplines, and so forth. There is much scholarly evidence to suggest that gender, and with it notions of femininity, or masculinity, are constructed (Roscoe 1998). It remains debatable whether one walks, talks or gestures "like a woman" or "like a man" naturally, or is taught to do so. The other and perhaps more important point is that traditionally, Indigenous nations demonstrated much tolerance for difference and individuality (LaRocque 1997). Even in cultures that practised fairly rigid sex roles there were allowances, even honour, for those who assumed cross-gender roles, although it appears there was more honour given to women who took on male roles than men who took on female ones (Hungry Wolf 1980: 60–64, 67). This implies a cultural bias in favour of male-defined roles.

With respect to assigning gender quality to certain clothing, a study of Native women's roles in the fur trade shows that European men, reflecting their westernized notions about femininity, modesty and chastity (sexual mo-res), pressured their Native wives and their halfbreed daughters to conduct themselves with "lady-like" manners and to adopt the wearing of western clothing such as skirts and other "feminine," usually English, accoutrements (Van Kirk 1980). Further, many Aboriginal cultures did not produce skirts or dresses as we know them today, and both men and women wore either robes, pants or pant-like leggings. It was European husbands and fathers assuming authority over their Native families who pressured Native peoples to associate clothing with gender roles or even with spirituality. We see here that colonization is almost completely about over-arching male dominance, which clearly had a domino effect on Aboriginal cultures and practices.

While intending to affirm Aboriginal women and cultures, both much beleaguered in white North American archival records, histories and popular culture, many writers readily criticize Euro-Canadian colonial forces (not a bad thing in and of itself), but they tend to both gloss over Aboriginal practices that discriminate(d) against women, and they generalize and romanticize traditions. There is an over-riding assumption that Aboriginal traditions were universally historically non-sexist and therefore, are universally liberating today. Besides the fact that not all traditions were non-sexist, we must be careful that, in an effort to celebrate ourselves, we not go to the other extreme of biological essentialism of our roles as women by confining them to the domestic and maternal spheres, or romanticizing our traditions by closing our eyes to certain practices and attitudes that privilege men over women.

There is no doubt that many pre-Columbian cultures developed political systems and spiritual practices in which women held significant power and influence. Nor was this power relegated to the domestic sphere. And there is no question that colonial forces have seriously disrupted Aboriginal thought and institutions. There is no question that we need to rebuild and restore ourselves and our cultures. However, this cannot mean that we refrain from confronting patriarchal and sexist attitudes or oppressive behaviours. The fact remains that there is an awful lot of gender inequality within Native families, communities, organizations and governments. In the final analysis, it does not much matter what the ultimate cause of sexism or misogyny may be. What matters is that, on a fairly universal level, it permeates the lives of women throughout the world today, and it certainly permeates our lives, and that is what feminism attends to.

Women cannot saddle ourselves with the staggering responsibility of teaching or nurturing the whole world; nor should we assume sole responsibility for "healing" or "nurturing" Aboriginal men. To assume such roles is tantamount to accepting patriarchal definitions about the nature and role of women, and it results in assuming responsibility for our oppression and our inequality. And to do this is to deny our historical and sociological experience as women. This is not in any way to dismiss men's experiences or to suggest we should be aloof or callous towards those men who also suffer from racism and colonialism (and in some instances, even from female violence). I know too well how hard my beloved Bapa worked to take care of us because he had no other opportunities than to be a labourer; I know too well how much my two brothers continue to struggle to make ends meet even today because school failed them. However, men and women experience colonialism differently. This is not about "blaming our men" but of assessing women's situation in an historical and social context. The point is, colonialism and patriarchy are systemic problems, and we cannot address these adequately by assuming personal or collective female responsibility for how the world hurts or how men may behave.

I believe that some of the maternalist claims about roles and positions are taken without adequate historical or anthropological research, and without awareness about their implications. But they are also taken in an effort to outline our difference from western definitions. "Difference" serves rhetorically as part of an anti-colonial arsenal in the process of culture re-building. However, in decolonization movements traditions about women are often framed as largely domestic and supportive in nature. The disturbing pattern in nationalist movements is that while women are celebrated abstractly as carriers of culture and guardians of tradition, their fundamental human rights are often denied (Young 2003). "Historically... women do not reap equal benefits from decolonisation for reasons of gender inequality [because] the decolonised nation is hardly interested in female liberation [as men become] chief beneficiaries of political and economic power gained through the nationalist struggle" (McLeod 2000: 115). My hope is that First Nations and Métis peoples can avoid these pitfalls. But it is worrisome that a discernable pattern is already there: Native women are "honoured" as "keepers" of tradition, defined as nurturing/healing, while Native men control political power. What concerns me even more is that in the interest of being markers of difference, many non-western women are apparently willing to accept certain proscriptions, even fundamental inequalities. Why is it women who are always the ones to do this? In Canada, much of the rhetoric of Indigenous nationalism is filtered through the language of "cultural difference" requiring "culturally appropriate" responses and models.

The question is, to what extent is difference discourse serving us as women? How different are we, and from whom, exactly, are we to be different? Who is defining the difference? Feminism invites us to think seriously about difference, but to also remain focused on women's human rights.

This is not to say that we are exactly the same as white Canadians or that we want to be. Of course we are different! But our difference today, as it was in pre-Columbian times, is much more dynamic, diverse, complex and nuanced than what the popularized and stereotyped "cultural differences" discourse suggests. That these "differences" are often neatly typologyzed into a handful of traits[8] may be convenient for many, and they are certainly more political than cultural, but I believe they serve to entrench the colonizer's model (to borrow J.M. Blaut's [1995] phrase) of "the Indian," rendering women marginalized and vulnerable to unequal treatment.

The irony is that, generally, there is a tendency to lump Native scholars and/or writers, perhaps especially Native women, under certain universalized and prescribed notions of experience or of expression. For all the talk on difference we continue to be stereotyped as some mother-earthly mass of battered bodies. Both Aboriginal and non-Aboriginal writers tend to do this. While many of us may have much in common, the generalized treatment to our selves or to our work is an act of erasure, to each of us.

Further, it is unacceptable that many feminist writers, perhaps especially white and African American writers, seem unaware of our existence, both as politically situated women and/or as intellectuals and scholars. There is in mainstream Canadian and American feminist writings a decided lack of inclusion of our experience, analysis or perspectives. Recently, I perused about fifteen textbooks on feminist theory, most of them published in the 1990s. With the exception of about three authors,[9] not one of them wrote a single word on Aboriginal people (American or Canadian), including women, much less referred to any of our deconstructions, Indigenous-based anti-colonial theories; to the contemporizing of Aboriginal epistemologies in our classrooms; or to our matrifocal societies and traditions, even though most of them had several chapters on "women of colour." However, there are some more recent works, especially by women of colour, that have treated Aboriginal women seriously and respectfully.[10]

Clearly, there remain problems with white-constructed feminism, and just as clearly, Aboriginal women must deal with multiple sites of being othered. But, to use an old aphorism, let's not throw out the baby with the bath water! As we address white feminist exclusions we must be careful that we not sabotage our human rights or our critical capacities. I do not think it is fruitful for us to weaken our resources or our analysis by fixing upon what is now a very common argument, namely, that feminism is irrelevant because white women have conceptualized it (and presumably know nothing about racism or colonial history), or because race/racism is more urgent and fundamental to Native women than sex/sexism. Racism/sexism is a package experience and it is virtually impossible to untangle one from the other (LaRocque 1990a). But the integrity of my sexuality and my body will not be sacrificed for race, for religion, for "difference," for "culture" or for "nation."

Much work is needed to decolonize the feminist/academic community concerning the treatment and reading of Aboriginal women's material and intellectual locations. That we are diverse, complex and divided is all the more reason for greater efforts to be made by all intellectuals. New theoretical directions are urgently needed to help think through the issues confronting Aboriginal women today.

Nonetheless, despite these problems, and despite the substantive socio-economic disparities between Native and non-Native women (Frideres 2003), and even despite the colonial chasms that do exist, I do believe that feminism is viable as a basis for analysis and as an ideal for equitable gender relations. This feminism though cannot be read as solely belonging to white women; Aboriginal women have fought for their rights long before and long after European arrival or influence even if they have not used white feminist language. Further, being feminist cannot and does not mean abandoning our commitments to the Aboriginal community.

The relationship between Native and white women cannot be unidirectional. The Canadian or international women's movements cannot define all the terms nor expect Native women to assume dominant cultures as their own, even if we share common interests around gender. Native women's cultures challenge state and cultural systems. White women must do some consciousness-raising about the quality of life and the nature of political and intellectual colonialism in our country.

Aboriginal values and worldviews offer genuine alternatives to our over-industrialized, over-bureaucratized, corporate-controlled society. Many Aboriginal beliefs and practices, *the real* traditionally based practices — and those reinvented — also offer models and concepts on gender equality that can enhance woman-centred notions of equality and valuation. Naturally, we need to transform those traditions that obstruct gender equality; we need to confront thinking and institutions that violate our rights and we need to ensure that our contemporary First Nations and Métis liberation efforts move away from that either-or pattern of sacrificing women's equality in the interests of the ever amorphous "collective." We must be both decolonizers and feminists.

Finally, I am painfully aware that I have raised questions and issues that are politically charged and may cause discomfort. I am highly conscious of the fact that there are ideological divisions among us as we seek to find common ground in the theorizing of our lives, both as women and as diverse Aboriginal peoples. I am equally aware that we are oppressed peoples and that we are making valiant efforts to restore ourselves to rebuild our stolen and fragmented cultures and traditions. I appreciate that it is difficult for us to bear any further criticism. Yet, history teaches us that it is in moments of nationalisms that we are most vulnerable not only to essentialisms/fundamentalisms (Green 2003), but to the disempowerment of women. It is in moments of nationalisms that we must exercise our critical capacities towards the enhancement of our human freedoms.

Freedom from imperial, systemic and personal dominations must remain the basis of our emancipatory efforts. This must mean that, paramount among our principles, is an abhorrence of violations against other human beings. Specifically, in this discussion, no injustice against any persons, whether constitutional, cultural or physical/sexual, should ever be tolerated in the name of advancing any collective or political interests, even when idealized as some kind of a decolonizing reconstructive process. We must understand that it is not in the interest of any collective or culture to dismiss or abuse individual rights, particularly matters as crucial as citizenship, identity or personal safety and integrity. It is not deliverance if some people's rights within any decolonizing or liberation movements are sacrificed.

In the final analysis, what matters to me is that, as we rebuild, we have an opportunity to create contemporary cultures based on human rights that extend to all members of our communities. Such rights will respect cultures and traditions but, at the same time we must be vigilant that cultures and traditions uphold the human rights of all peoples, certainly children and women.

## NOTES

1.  As part of my resistance scholarship theory, I have refused to stand aloof from some of my research and published works, and accordingly locate some family or community contexts. For more biographical information see my essay "Tides, Towns and Trains," in J. Turner (ed), 1990.
2.  Some capitalize "Métis" to indicate those who originate from the Red River in order to make distinctions from other métis who do not have Red River lineage. See Peterson and Brown (1985).
3.  Between 1870 and 1900, the federal government issued a series of tickets with monetary or land value (scrip) to "Halfbreed Heads of Families" as a form of recognizing Métis rights to land. However, in large part, the Métis were divested of the scrips by speculators, fraud, government legislation and cultural processes alien to them (see RCAP 1996).
4.  I am grateful to my younger brother, who has remained on our original land area but like my father before him, can only lease the land as we have never had resources to purchase this land. But if there was any justice for Métis people the governments should simply transfer ownership to those Métis families who have loved and tended specific lands — and continue to do so — long before Confederation.
5.  It is theorized that most biology-linked customs that tend to injure or constrict females in "traditional" societies were created in pre-scientific eras when people did not understand bodily functions and so tended to mystify them. It is interesting, however, that so many such customs were invented to circumscribe women more than men.
6.  There is much beauty to this ethic as it facilitates tolerance for difference, among other things. But ethically it does have its limitations for many social evils such as slavery, which existed because it was tolerated by society. Similarly, sexism flourishes because it is tolerated. What should we tolerate and to what extent?
7.  In a scathing critique of Alexander Mackenzie's journals, Parker Duchemin notes that MacKenzie interpreted Sekani women's height and "lusty make"

(that Mackenzie imagined) as "inverting normal distinctions of gender" (1990: 60–61).

8. See my analysis of this (LaRocque 1997).

9. The authors (in my collection at the time) that included some treatment of Aboriginal women are Emberly (1993), Hunter (1996), and Stalker and Prentice (1998). While Emberly and Hunter take a respectful and considered approach, Stalker and Prentice include one puzzling chapter on "Native Students and Quebec Colleges," which is written by a non-Aboriginal woman.

10. I am thinking especially of Sherene Razack's works, *Looking White People in the Eye* (1998) and *Race, Space and the Law* (2002). See also Bannerji (1993).

## REFERENCES

Anderson, Kim. 2000. *A Recognition of Being: Reconstructing Native Womanhood.* Toronto: Second Story Press.

Bannerji, Himani (ed.). 1993. *Returning the Gaze: Essays on Racism, Feminism and Politics.* Toronto: Sister Vision Press.

Blaut, J.M. 1993. *The Colonizer's Model of the World: Geographical Diffusionism and Eurocentric History.* New York/London: Guilford Press.

Donovan, Josephine. 1990. *Feminist Theory: The Intellectual Traditions of American Feminism.* New York: Continuum Publishing.

Duchemin, Parker. 1990. "'A Parcel of Whelps': Alexander Mackenzie Among the Indians." In W.H. New (ed.), *Native Writers Canadian Writing.* Vancouver: University of British Columbia Press.

Emberly, Julia. 1993. *Thresholds of Difference: Feminist Critique, Native Women's Writings, Postcolonial Theory.* Toronto: University of Toronto Press.

Freire, Paulo. 1970. *Pedagogy of the Oppressed.* New York: Herder and Herder.

Frideres, James S. 2003. *Aboriginal Peoples in Canada: Contemporary Conflicts.* Scarborough: Prentice Hall Allyn and Bacon.

Garvin, Terry. 1992. *Bush Land People.* Calgary: Arctic Institute of North America of the University of Calgary.

Green, Joyce. 1993. "Constitutionalising the Patriarchy: Aboriginal Women and Aboriginal Government." *Constitutional Forum* 4, 4.

_____. 2003. "A Cultural and Ethnic Fundamentalism: The Mixed Potential for Identity, Liberation, and Oppression." *The Scholar Series.* University of Regina: Saskatchewan Institute of Public Policy. (This also appears as a chapter in Carol Schick, JoAnn Jaffe and Alisa Watkinson [eds.], 2004, *Contesting Fundamentalisms*, Halifax, Fernwood Publishing.)

hooks, bell. 1984. *Feminist Theory: From Margin to Center.* Boston: South End Press.

Hungry Wolf, Beverly. 1980. *The Ways of My Grandmothers.* New York: William Morrow and Company.

Hunter, Lynette. 1996. *Outsider Notes: Feminist Approaches to Nation/State Ideology, Writers/ Reads and Publishing.* Vancouver: Talon Books.

LaRocque, Emma. 1990a. "Racism/Sexism and Its Effects on Native Women." *Public Concerns on Human Rights: A Summary of Briefs.* Ottawa: Canadian Human Rights Commission.

_____. 1990b. "Tides, Towns and Trains." In J. Turner (ed.), *Living the Changes.*

Winnipeg: University of Manitoba Press.

_____. 1993. "Violence in Aboriginal Communities." *The Path to Healing: Report of the National Round Table on Aboriginal Health and Social Issues.* Ottawa: Royal Commission on Aboriginal Peoples.

_____. 1997. "Re-examining Culturally Appropriate Models in Criminal Justice Applications." In M. Asch (ed.), *Aboriginal and Treaty Rights: Essays on Law, Equality and Respect for Difference.* Vancouver: University of British Columbia Press.

McLeod, John. 2000. *Beginning Postcolonialism.* Manchester: Manchester University Press.

Monture-Angus, Patricia. 1995. *Thunder in my Soul: A Mohawk Woman Speaks.* Halifax: Fernwood Publishing.

Ouellette, Grace J.M.W. 2002. *The Fourth World: An Indigenous Perspective on Feminism and Aboriginal Women's Activism.* Halifax: Fernwood Publishing.

Overall, Christine. 1998. *A Feminist I: Reflections from Academia.* Peterborough: Broadview Press.

Peterson, Jacqueline, and J. Brown (eds.). 1985. *The New Peoples: Being and Becoming Métis in North America.* Winnipeg: University of Manitoba Press.

Puxley, Peter. 1977. "The Colonial Experience." In M. Watkins (ed.), *Dene Nation: A Colony Within.* Toronto: University of Toronto Press.

Razack, Sherene. 1998. *Looking White People in the Eye: Gender, Race and Culture in Courtrooms and Classrooms.* Toronto: University of Toronto Press.

_____ (ed.). 2002. *Race, Space and the Law: Unmapping a White Settler Society.* Toronto: Between the Lines.

Roscoe, William. 1998. *Changing Ones: Third and Fourth Genders in Native North America.* New York: St. Martin's Press.

Royal Commission on Aboriginal People (RCAP). 1996. *Perspectives and Realities.* Volume 4. Ottawa: Supply and Services.

Shkilnyk, Anastasia. 1985. *A Poison Stronger than Love: The Destruction of an Ojibwa Community.* New Haven: Yale University Press.

Stalker, Jacqueline, and Susan Prentice (eds.). 1998. *The Illusion of Inclusion: Women in Post-Secondary Education.* Halifax: Fernwood Publishing.

Stevenson, Winona, et al. 1993. "Peekiskwetan." *Commentaries/Commentaires Canadian Journal of Women and the Law/Revue Femmes et Droit* 6.

Van Kirk, Sylvia. 1980. *"Many Tender Ties": Women in Fur Trade Society, 1670–1870.* Winnipeg: Watson and Dwyer Publishing.

Young, Robert J.C. 2003. *Postcolonialism: A Very Short Introduction.* Oxford: Oxford University Press.

# Chapter Four

# MYTHS AND REALITIES OF SAMI WOMEN
## A Post-colonial Feminist Analysis for the Decolonization and Transformation of Sami Society

### Rauna Kuokkanen

In Sami society, there is a common and persistent image of strong Sami women (see, for example, Aikio 1998; Lukkari 1998). While this may be true in some cases both traditionally and presently, I argue in this chapter that there is a pressing need to revisit this myth as it may hinder the necessary processes of decolonization and healing of contemporary Sami women and Sami society at large.

The Sami are the Indigenous people of Northern Europe who, in the course of colonial history, have been divided by the nation-states of Norway, Sweden, Finland and Russia.[1] Faced with similar colonial practices of assimilation, usurpation of territories and eradication of languages and cultures as other Indigenous peoples worldwide, the Sami have, since the late 1960s, been engaged in a process of reclaiming their self-determination and rights to land, language and cultural heritage.

Compared to many other Indigenous peoples, such as the Maori in Aotearoa and First Nations/Native Americans on Turtle Island, the Sami fall behind in critically examining the effects of colonial and assimilation policies on us and in embarking on the path to decolonizing and reshaping the various spheres of Sami society. Quite obviously, this analysis would necessarily include an in-depth assessment of women's conditions and realities beyond "the traditional roles of Sami women." As other Indigenous women scholars have pointed out, it is necessary to critically assess the numerous ways in which colonial and patriarchal policies and practices have affected and still affect Indigenous societies (Green and Voyageur 1999; Irwin 1988; LaRocque 1996; Mihesuah 2003; L.T. Smith 1999; Green 2001). Moreover, it is crucial to recognize that it is not only Indigenous women but the entire society that is negatively affected, for example, through psychological stress, mental disorders, identity crises, self-hatred, violence, increased alcoholism and other social problems. As a result, Indigenous communities experience breakup of families, communication gaps between generations and loss of connection with traditional livelihoods and the land, forcing many people to move away from their communities to cities (Mihesuah 2003).

When critically employed, particularly post-colonial feminist analyses of patriarchal hegemony can be useful in the process of decolonizing contemporary Sami society. "Post-colonial" here refers to the critical analysis and deconstruction of colonial discourses, practices and relations of power, and it does not suggest that colonialism belongs to the past. As patriarchy is an inseparable part of colonization, trying to dismantle one without the other may prove both ineffective and inadequate. I suggest that the confluence of Indigenous and feminist discourses (which are by no means singular or homogeneous) may help to move beyond stereotypical misunderstandings of feminism prevalent in Sami society and offer a more attentive understanding and critical perspective of the ways in which colonial practices always overlap with patriarchy and gender imbalances. In this chapter, I discuss three themes affecting Sami women and their participation in Sami society: challenges Sami women face in participating in political processes; discriminatory reindeer herding policies and practices; and sexual violence against women and girls. First, however, I consider the myth of strong Sami women more closely to establish a context for my discussion.

## THE MYTH OF STRONG SAMI WOMEN

While there are Sami women who feel it is artificial to separate women from the rest of their communities, there are others who are forging a strong feminist agenda and contesting the myths of "strong Sami matriarchs," which are often employed to ignore demands by Sami women's organizations and groups. According to Sami feminist scholar Jorunn Eikjok, notions of powerful Sami women and traditional Sami society as matriarchal are myths created by the Sami ethnopolitical movement in the 1970s, which needed to distinguish the Sami people from the surrounding Nordic peoples and cultures.[2] Until the late 1980s, it was common in the Sami movement to stress that Sami women were not as oppressed as Nordic women and that in Sami society, women were equal with men.[3] Besides as a marker of distinctiveness, the notion of strong Sami women also had to do with a desired ideal of Sami society rather than the everyday reality of Sami women. Today, this myth is often used against Sami women who advocate women's issues, particularly by Sami men who have either internalized the myth or who benefit from the patriarchal system that is the reality of contemporary Sami society (Eikjok 2000). A common way to disregard Sami women's concerns is to refer to the fact that Sami women are already "better off" than Sami men because they are stronger and because the loss of traditional livelihoods has not impacted them as radically as men.[4]

In daily life, Sami women are often torn between two sets of demands. On the one hand, they are required to uphold cultural values and customs connected with the traditional subsistence economy and on the other, they are required to fulfill the expectations placed upon contemporary women. Eikjok suggests that this is due to the internalization of patriarchal social relations in Sami society while at the same time, there is very little social or societal support for Sami women's efforts. The adoption of the mainstream gender roles and devaluation of the private sphere has had the effect of diminishing the status of Sami women also in the public sphere (Eikjok 1988; 1990; see also Paltto 1989).

To critique the stereotype of strong Sami women does not imply that it has not existed in traditional Sami society. Like many other Indigenous and/or traditional societies in the world, women in Sami society historically had a form of equality with men, characterized by a symmetrical complementarity of domains, roles and tasks. Sami scholar of religion and history Louise Bäckman notes: "In a society in which hunting is a prerequisite for survival itself, it is obvious that everyone, regardless of sex, shared the burden of work, and that the division of labour is made upon a practical basis" (1982: 148).

The symmetrical complementarity of domains, roles and tasks resulted in a situation where Sami women were independent and possessed power and control over certain domains. Often these spheres were domestic and private but in some cases also economic. Erik Solem (1970), a Norwegian sexton in the Sami community of Tana in the early twentieth century, observed the respected and independent status of Sami women both within the family and in society at large. Traditionally, particularly reindeer herding women were often in charge of their family economies (Solem 1970; Valkeapää 1998; Bäckman 1982; Sámi Instituhtta 1979).

Moreover, it was customary for women and men to have separate properties. Skolt Sami women, for example, traditionally owned everything that they prepared and made, including clothing for their husbands. Women and men also used to manage their own loans (Paulaharju 1921). According to Sami customary law, women and men inherited on equal footing. It was also common for a Sami widow to move back to her own family and community, taking her property with her (Balto 1997). Further, Solem (1970) proposes that Sami naming customs and terminology indicate a relatively strong matrilinearity and matrilocality. This does not mean, however, that patrilinearity did or does not exist in Sami society, nor can Solem's findings be considered a proof of the equal status of Sami women in contemporary society.

Sami educator Asta Balto's (1997) study on Sami gender roles and control partially supports the ethnographic information above. There have been and there are Sami women who have a higher status and more power than others. The status of a Sami woman might be dependent on her family and wealth. Today, matrilocality is no longer more common than patrilocality, and traditions have been replaced by practical factors such as employment. Balto contends that both matrilinearity and patrilinearity are common and important in Sami society. She points out, however, that modernization of Sami society especially since the mid-1950s changed many of these practices and customs, an indication of the influence of patriarchal ideologies that followed the societal changes (Balto 1997).

It is these subtle and sometimes not so subtle influences that many Sami, including women, are reluctant to address or analyze, preferring to fall back on the argument of strength and power of Sami women. Personally, I have witnessed many occasions where Sami representatives (at conferences, symposia, meetings, etc.) are asked about the role and status of Sami women. It is interesting how Sami male representatives always very politely let their female counterparts reply, as if they have no knowledge or authority over these issues. When the question is asked directly of a Sami man, a standard response is to invoke the notion of strong Sami women, usually accompanied with a story either about the "matriarch" mother in the man's family or a personal encounter with a "strong Sami woman." I have never witnessed a Sami man telling about the less glamorous realities of Sami women, either past or present, such as institutional discrimination within traditional or contemporary livelihoods, or the negative influence of Christianity on general attitudes and perceptions of women in Sami society, not to mention domestic and sexual violence against Sami women — an issue that very much remains a taboo among the Sami.

In *No Beginning, No End: The Sami Speak Up* (Helander and Kailo 1998a), an anthology of front-line Sami artists and cultural workers discussing and analyzing current issues affecting the Sami people and culture, several contributors address the influence of Christianity on women. Sami writers Kirsti Paltto (1998) and Rauni Magga Lukkari (1998) and Sami musician Inga Juuso (1998) suggest that Christian ideology has introduced a hierarchical understanding between genders, prioritizing men and resulting in low self-esteem of many Sami women.[5] Since the mid-1800s, Laestadianism, an evangelical, revivalist movement inside the Lutheran Church influential in the Northern parts of Scandinavia,[6] has had a particularly strong effect in Sami society. It has introduced certain concepts of female piety and humility in addition to common Christian dualistic notions of women as either good or evil.[7]

In other words, Christianity and Laestadianism in particular have affected Sami society for several generations. Contemporary perceptions of and attitudes toward women in Sami society are, therefore, an entangled combination of influences of various origins and from different periods of time, making it rather difficult trace back the traditional status and roles of Sami women (whatever is implied by the always problematic notion of "traditional"). While the Sami as a people have been colonized by surrounding nation-states, many Sami women have also been oppressed and susceptible to sexism and male violence within their own communities. Though not a new phenomenon, anecdotes and also official reports about such incidents are only now beginning to surface in Sami society.

## SAMI WOMEN AND POLITICAL PARTICIPATION

Inspired by several other civil and human rights movements around the world, the Sami women's movement culminated in the establishment of the Sami women's organization Sáráhkká in 1978.[8] Many of the women involved in the organization had been (and in many cases, remain) active in the Sami ethnopolitical movement and other forms of cultural revitalization that emerged in the early 1970s (Eidheim 1997). The history of the struggle for Sami rights, however, goes back to the late nineteenth and early twentieth centuries. In this struggle, Sami women have always had a central and significant role.

The first national Sami conference, in 1917, was organized particularly due to the efforts and vision of Elsa Laula Renberg (1877–1930), the chair of the first Sami women's organization. She also established the first (though short-lived) national Sami organization in 1904 and several local associations in both the Swedish and Norwegian sides of Samiland. A well-known figure of the time, Renberg actively promoted Sami land rights and livelihoods and advocated the education of women. Despite her deep commitment to her people — she even wrote a pamphlet entitled "Life or Death," in which she encouraged Sami to claim their rights to land — Renberg's role in the early Sami rights movement has usually been minimized or left out in historical accounts (including those written by Sami men), which focus on her male contemporaries and their activities (Lundmark 1978; Stien 1976; Hirvonen 2000).

Sami women also played a central role in the Alta River conflict in the late 1970s and early 1980s, although their actions have generally received much less attention than those of the male activists. The Alta River conflict, considered a watershed in Sami-Nordic relations, involved a plan by the Norwegian government to build a hydroelectric dam in Northern Norway (see, for example, Brantenberg 1985; Paine 1982; Parmann 1980; Sanders 1980). In its original form, the dam would have submerged the Sami village of Máze (Masi) and a considerable portion of important reindeer grazing and calving areas in the heart of the reindeer herding region. The government plans were met with unexpected resistance by the Sami as well as by environmentalists and fishers who wanted to protect the salmon river. The conflict culminated in a massive demonstration at the construction site by the river and a hunger strike in the front of the Norwegian Parliament building in Oslo in 1979. The office of the Norwegian prime minister Gro Harlem Brundtland was occupied by fourteen Sami women in 1981. The prime minister met with the Sami women but did not consider their concerns worthy of her time and left the meeting after half an hour.[9] The women refused to leave the office and the next morning were forcibly removed by the police. In spite of my close connection to the conflict — my parents attended the demonstration by the river — I only recently learned from a Sami newspaper about these fourteen women and their action. Ignored in most accounts of the Sami political movement of the 1970s and 1980s, the fourteen women and their actions were finally recognized in 2005 by the Norwegian Sami Association in a special ceremony (Min Áigi 2005).

The forms of Sami women's activism have had and continue to have several objectives and concerns not limited to issues stereotypically associated with women's organizations. They include revitalizing and maintaining the Sami language and cultural heritage, promoting the participation of Sami women in leadership (see Nystad 1995; Stordahl 1990) and increasing Sami women's economic opportunities as well as fighting for the recognition of previously held economic rights within traditional livelihoods, particularly reindeer herding (Joks 2001; Sárá 2002).

Although there are several Sami women in prominent political positions, a large number of contemporary Sami women do not consider running for office at local or regional levels such as in municipal or Sami Parliament elections. The three Sami parliaments in Norway, Sweden and Finland — elected bodies representing the Sami especially at the national level to their respective state governments — have been male-dominated, and in the case of Sweden and Finland, continue to be so (the percentage of women is 35 and 21 respectively). The Norwegian Sami Parliament has had special campaigns to recruit more women as candidates and to encourage women to vote in its elections. At its last election in the fall 2005, women formed, for the first time, the majority (51 percent) of the Norwegian Sami Parliament's thirty-nine elected representatives. (Before the 2005 elections, the percentage of women representatives was as low as 12). Also, for the first time in the history of all three Sami parliaments, the newly elected president of the Sami Parliament in Norway is a woman.[10]

There is, however, a need to look beyond numbers and percentages. Although significant, the female majority in the Norwegian Sami Parliament does not automatically guarantee political practices or procedures that revoke or even challenge the patriarchal structures, priorities and political processes. Moreover, there are other powerful Sami organizations, such as the Norwegian Sami Reindeer Herders' Association, that continue to be strongly male-dominated. With an executive board consisting of only 22 percent women, the organization also breaks the Norwegian law that requires minimum 40 percent of women representatives on organizations' boards (J.I. Utsi 2005c). In a similar fashion, women play a minor role in the municipal politics in Ohcejohka/Utsjoki, the northernmost and only municipality in Finland where the Sami are in majority. In the most recent municipal elections, in 2004, only one woman (Finnish) was elected as a councillor despite the fact that all the parties had female candidates.[11] A female candidate on the Sami List notes that the results suggest that the voters in Ohcejohka/Utsjoki do not seem to trust women as politicians (Johnskareng 2004).

In spite of the prominent roles some Sami women play in local politics, practices of trivialization of and discrimination against women continue in contemporary Sami and other local organizations and political processes. Generally, these practices are subtle and difficult to expose as discrimination (such as jokes and insinuations), but as feminist scholars have pointed out, they function as powerful mechanisms of control (e.g., Enloe 2004: 5; Plumwood 1993). Sami female politicians' perspectives and attempts to participate in political debate are particularly trivialized when the topic is considered traditionally belonging to the "male sphere," such as all-terrain vehicle permits — a hot topic in the Norwegian side of Samiland before the 2005 Sami Parliament elections. Aili Keskitalo, the new president, challenged the practice of trivializing women's perspectives on the issue. As an example, she mentions a male candidate who had called the female vice-president of the Sami Parliament a "coffee maker" when she expressed her views on the all-terrain vehicle debate (J.I. Utsi 2005d).

Like other Indigenous societies worldwide, contemporary Sami society is shaped by processes of colonial and patriarchal history. Sami political and representative bodies, such as the Sami parliaments and the Sami Council, are, in many ways, copies of their Nordic counterparts, thus often reflecting similar ideologies and biases as institutions in mainstream societies. Although the Sami political bodies have limited decision-making power even with regard to issues affecting the Sami, they exert power internally by dealing only with issues considered important within the patriarchal political system.[12] Issues such as health, social services, education and other concerns internal to Sami society are often neglected. While topics such as the European Union, globalization, government-relations and funding feature in seminars by the Sami parliaments, the Sami Council and other main Sami organizations year after year, rarely are concerns pertaining to the well-being of Sami society topics of long-term policy-making. Initiatives on issues pertaining to Sami women are often ignored or limited to the realm of Sami women's organizations.

## SAMI WOMEN AND TRADITIONAL LIVELIHOODS

Policies and laws imposed by the nation-states regulating and controlling reindeer herding and the way of life associated with it are an excellent example of the interconnectedness of colonial and patriarchal discrimination and domination. These government policies have made women invisible in the livelihood in which they have always played a central role. In many cases, they have erased the traditionally held right of ownership of woman's own reindeer and in official records placed reindeer-owning Sami women under their husbands — an act that has had ramifications ranging from allocation of subsidies and grants to the status and recognition of women within the livelihood, often considered one of the central markers of Saminess and Sami identity (Sárá 1990–91; Sámi Instituhtta 1979; Sárá 2003).

These sexist policies make it very difficult for reindeer-herding Sami women to continue their traditional livelihoods if, for example, there is a divorce or the husband dies. In 2005 in Kárásjohka, Norwegian Samiland, a young Sami woman who separated from her husband lost her share of the reindeer-herding subsidies. She and her husband had a joint reindeer household but she had always had her own reindeer and reindeer mark. Since the divorce, however, the full amount of subsidies have been paid to her ex-husband, although she has the custody of their three small children. The *Reindeer Herding Act* in Norway does not indicate how the subsidies ought to be distributed in cases of divorce, and the director of the Reindeer Herding Administration does not want to get involved, stating that it is the responsibility of the household to find a way to share the subsidies (J.I. Utsi 2005b).

Some Sami female politicians, however, are concerned about the situation and note that issues such as divorce have never been taken account of within the *Reindeer Herding Act*. The Act, which came into force in 1978, did not protect both the husband's and wife's rights, only the rights of the owner of the reindeer household, who were and still are mostly men.[13] The Act was amended in 1996 and the rights were extended to the spouse of the owner, but nothing was said about the rights upon divorce, still a taboo topic in reindeer herding, where, traditionally, separation has been rare. Usually it is the women who lose their economic and livelihood rights, although there is at least one case where, upon a divorce, a woman kept the reindeer household while the man kept the reindeer but lost his rights to the pasture and the household (J.I. Utsi 2005a).

Another recent case involves an older Sami woman who lost the right to the family summer pasture after the death of her husband. Their summer pasture area — where the reindeer herders are mandated to migrate annually, according to the *Reindeer Herding Act* — was seized by other reindeer herders of the area, making it impossible for the widow and her son to conduct the annual summer migration. As a result, the Reindeer Herding Administration threatened the family with a forced slaughter of their herd (Utsi 2006).

Jorunn Eikjok suggests that, presently, reindeer herding is commonly regarded both inside and outside Sami society as synonymous with men's activity, while in reality, women continue to "stand for much of the production and ... for a versatile management of the resources" (Eikjok 1992: 7). Many women are also more prone to keep up the traditional Sami *verdde* system, the practice of establishing and sustaining economic relations and social bonds with individuals and families of different livelihoods (Eikjok 1992). What is more, Sami scholar Solveig Joks (2001) contends that if reindeer herding is viewed only as a meat industry, an emphasis of state policies and regulations since the 1950s, rather than as a traditional way of life, women's input and role are made invisible. This focus on meat production has also been adopted by Sami reindeer herding associations and their politics, which generally do not recognize the special tasks of Sami women as part of the livelihood (Eikjok 1988; Joks 2001). This has resulted in an increased number of women giving up reindeer herding as a viable source of living and moving to other livelihoods and occupations (Landbruksdepartementet 1991–92).

There is, however, an increasing number of reindeer herding Sami women who are critically assessing reindeer-herding practices and traditions such as traditional child-rearing and the practice of marking more reindeer to male children in the family (Somby Sara 2005). For example, the chair of the Guovdageaidnu Reindeer Herding Women's Network demands the establishment of a educational centre for reindeer herding and for other Sami livelihoods and activities to promote equality among genders, among other things (E.M. Utsi 2005b).

## SEXUAL VIOLENCE

Besides the image of strong women, another prevalent myth about the Sami is that of a peaceful people who never fought any wars. This myth was created in the 1960s particularly by well-meaning anthropologists who wanted to portray the Sami as the victims of outside settlement and development projects and as a people who "deserved" to be protected (see especially Nickul 1970). While the idea of the Sami as a peaceful people who never fought any wars is not quite true, those who created the myth and those who continue to uphold it have been also blind to incidences of violence *within* Sami society.

What has gone mostly unnoticed, both in the past and the present, is sexual violence such as incest, rape, sexual abuse and child molestation and other forms of sexual and physical violence. Mainly due to Laestadianism, women's sexuality especially has been a major taboo in Sami society. Moreover, because of the shame surrounding sexual violence and the tendency to blame the victim (usually women), incidences of rape and sexual harassment have remained largely unreported until very recently.

There has been a particularly sharp escalation in sexual abuse cases within a short period of time in Guovdageaidnu, one of the Sami communities where the language and traditional livelihoods, especially reindeer herding, remain very strong.[14] Some of the recent reports of rape involve victims who were fourteen-year-old girls (Pulk 2005d). The Sami head of the local police is quoted as saying that the recent cases indicate that the situation in Sami society is not as good as people have previously thought (Pulk 2005c).

Thus far, sexual violence in Sami communities has not been addressed in any serious or systematic manner. However, there are signs that some individuals and groups have started to take the issue of sexual violence seriously. A few months after recurrent reports of rape in Guovdageaidnu a group of local Sami men initiated and organized a public meeting against rape and sexual harassment (Pulk 2005b).[15] One topic discussed at the meeting was the commonplace sexual harassment of girls at the local secondary school. A teacher reported how he had seen boys grabbing girls' genitals while walking by in the hall. When he stopped and questioned the boys, they did not understand what was wrong with their behaviour. Others also reported an increase in disconcerting attitudes among boys toward girls (Pulk 2005e).

In the view of Sami psychiatrist Marit Triumf, one explanation can be found in the traditional upbringing of girls in Guovdageaidnu. Girls and women were expected to be chaste and say "no" even if they agreed to a man's advances. It was the girls' and women's responsibility if the man did not control himself and proceeded to have intercourse (Pulk 2005a). This kind of double standard in behaviour, blaming the victim (woman) is, of course, very common in all societies. However, in Sami society, Laestadianism has played a central role in forming views and methods of upbringing with a strong focus on the dualistic patriarchal paradigm of female chastity on the one hand and the fallen woman who is to be blamed, on the other.

Christianity is part of the colonial legacy that continues to affect Indigenous communities worldwide. Cherokee scholar Andrea Smith argues that sexual violence in Indigenous societies is inseparably connected to colonization (2005b). In other words, the subjugation of Indigenous communities depended on the subjugation of women. Because Indigenous societies were largely egalitarian and characterized by complementary gender roles, colonial administrators facilitated colonization by first establishing and naturalizing hierarchy through the introduction of patriarchy (Allen 1986; A. Smith 2005a: 23). For Smith, the link between state violence and interpersonal violence is most obvious in the legacy of abuse from boarding schools. This has resulted in individualizing the trauma and increased personal shame and self-blame but also continuing the cycle of abuse by inflicting violence on self and others (126–27).

The Sami also have a history of boarding schools but the physical, sexual and psychological abuse that took place in those institutions has been a taboo subject until very recently and is even less debated than in the North American context. As long as we cling to the myths that do a huge disservice to those Sami women who are most vulnerable, rather than give them necessary support, Sami society cannot start healing, essential in the process of restoring a healthy and strong self-determination. As Métis scholar Emma LaRocque (1997) asserts, healing cannot take place without justice. As long as we insist on believing that Sami women do not face any oppression, we remain blind to contemporary realities that are crying for attention and that may, in the worst cases, result in such tragedies as a recent incest case involving a well-known Sami writer who had sexually abused two girls related to him. When the case became public and he was sentenced to prison and a literary award was withheld from him, he committed suicide (Anti 2005). Selective blindness can be particularly damaging especially when we as women continue the legacy of silence, for example, in the name of false and misguided ideas about family reputation. In reality, we are protecting the perpetrators of violence at the cost of the health and sometimes lives of women in our communities.

In struggling for self-governance, I believe that we Sami must ask ourselves some critical questions. What do we do with self-governance if a considerable part of our people is unable to either contribute to and participate in it or receive any benefits? What do we do with self-governance if it is built on myths and illusions rather than on realities of Sami society? Or as Andrea Smith notes, "Before Native peoples fight for the future of their nations, they must ask themselves, who is included in the nation?" (2005b: 121). In short, it is imperative that we re-evaluate our institutions and political structures and aspire to create a self-determination that reflects our own values, principles and models of governance.

As Eikjok notes, "in discussing self-government schemes for Indigenous peoples, we must carefully evaluate *which* of our traditions are worth basing our community upon" (2000: 41). We have to be careful when talking about "traditions" and remain critical of Christian, patriarchal, liberal or New Age reinventions of our traditions (see LaRocque 1997). Remodeling Indigenous traditions along colonial and patriarchal paradigms can be employed against Indigenous women to silence, subordinate and remove them from their previously held positions of authority (see Martin-Hill 2003).

## POST-COLONIAL FEMINIST ANALYSIS AND SAMI WOMEN

As both colonialism and patriarchy employ analogous forms of domination, there are certain similarities in experiences of Indigenous peoples (and other colonized groups) on the one hand and women on the other. With Indigenous women, these two forms of oppression often result in multiple marginalization. Sami scholar Vuokko Hirvonen, for example, proposes that it is possible to compare the situation of Sami women to that of Third World women. If the Sami in general are characterized as the Other, Sami women have been in the multiple margins because most research on Sami society has been conducted in the light of male activities. What has been recorded as Sami culture or tradition is, therefore, mainly tradition produced and sustained by Sami men. In such a context, Hirvonen argues, feminist criticism is valuable in casting light on the biased premises and perspectives on knowledge production. Moreover, employing feminist analyses in Sami research can produce new information about Sami women's lives and the hierarchies between the genders (Hirvonen 1999).

Similarities can also be found in ways in which post-colonial and feminist critiques oppose forms of oppression. Post-colonial and feminist discourses both aim at asserting a denied or alienated subjectivity and agency, whether of women or colonized peoples. In other words, post-colonial feminist analysis seeks to deconstruct and demonstrate the "interrelationship of oppressions of race, class, ethnicity, gender and sexuality in both a national and a transnational frame" (Clough 1994: 118).

As a critique of hegemonic relations implicated in patriarchy, colonialism and imperialism, post-colonial feminist approaches have introduced a more nuanced consideration of the multiple ways in which gender is constructed and employed in colonial and imperial processes. Early post-colonial feminist critics such as Chandra Mohanty (1984), Gayatri Spivak (1985) and Sara Suleri (1992) also demonstrated that, while imposed upon everybody, colonialism affected men and women in different ways. Spivak (1985) in particular examined and criticized the gender bias and blindness of anti-colonial nationalist movements, which often reproduce patriarchal, hierarchical models as the ideals for sovereignty.

It could be argued that there are Sami who have internalized and benefited from the colonial and patriarchal structures that have, in many ways, also permeated Sami society. There are quite a few Sami who deny the impact of colonization on Sami people and culture (even when the signs, such as loss of language, identity and possibilities to practise Sami culture and livelihoods, are anywhere), but there are even more people who refuse to recognize the influence of the mainstream patriarchal structures. As in many other Indigenous communities, one often hears the argument that sexism is only a problem in dominant societies. But as Maori scholar Kathy

Irwin notes,

> Colonisation brought with it capitalism and a new set of patriarchal relations. We cannot deny the impact of colonisation upon our culture.... It would be unrealistic to suggest that the relations between Maori men and women have been able to withstand the impact of colonisation and capitalism, in a way that race and economic relations have not. The truth is that sexism: that is, the economic exploitation and social domination of members of one sex by the other, specifically of women by men, is alive and well in Maori culture *today*. (1988: 35; see also A. Smith 2005b)

The same applies, no doubt, to Sami society. It would be misleading and naive to seriously believe that in some miraculous way, Sami gender relations have remained entirely unaffected through the centuries-long colonizing process that changed every other aspect of the lives and cultural practices of our people. One only has to look around to see that as a result of the colonial process, contemporary Sami life hardly differs from that of mainstream Nordic societies. In such a situation, how could we expect that we would have not internalized the patriarchal, hierarchical power relations and mechanisms of control? In such circumstances, it is peculiar indeed that thus far there has not been a systematic analysis of colonial processes — many of which continue today — including assimilation policies, racism, marginalization and erasure of our epistemic foundations and value system.

Feminist critique may assist us to expose not only the patriarchal, hierarchical structures of our governing bodies and models but also the (perhaps unconscious) internalization of hegemony,[16] which prevents us from achieving a meaningful self-determination. It needs to be emphasized here that the question is not merely how many women there are in Sami politics but more fundamentally, what are the ways and structures, discourses and processes in which Sami politics is practised. As French feminist Luce Irigaray pointed out,

> women merely "equal" to men would be "like them," therefore not women.... So it is essential for women themselves to invent new modes of organization, new forms of struggle, new challenges.... If women allow themselves to be caught in the trap of power, in the game of authority, if they allow themselves to be contaminated by the "paranoid" operations of masculine politics, they have nothing more to say or do *as women*. (1985: 166)

Irigaray's words could be paraphrased to also apply to the Sami (or other Indigenous peoples) in general and Sami women specifically — that if we as the Sami people allow ourselves to be caught in the trap of power, if we allow ourselves to be contaminated by colonial, patriarchal politics, we will have nothing to say as Sami. Moreover, if we as Sami women are caught in the trap of masculine, colonial power, we will have nothing to say as Sami women. Colonial and patriarchal policies and practices have affected Sami men and women differently. Feminist analysis can help us expose these differences and thus reinforce and facilitate our decolonizing strategies. Certain post-colonial feminist criticisms may also effectively illuminate the forms of involvement and roles of Sami women that have been overlooked and excluded from official historiographies, including those written by Sami men.[17]

Even if some Sami women may be able to claim that sexism is not their problem, our society is heavily influenced and permeated by colonial and patriarchal practices affecting all of us (but even more so Sami women). Post-colonial feminist critique can assist us in recognizing and understanding these practices in a way that can help up on the road to decolonization and transformation. I strongly believe that our survival as a people is dependent on embarking on the path of transforming and decolonizing the colonial, patriarchal discourses reflected in every aspect of our society, hindering and distracting us from restoring and re-envisioning our communities and the future of our people. It is a process of challenging the very foundation of the social and cultural order that is prescribed by the colonial and patriarchal systems, that is, addressing interlocking oppressions and mechanisms of power on institutional and structural levels.

Many Sami women are, however, hesitant to engage with feminist analysis. They may consider feminist analysis irrelevant or fear being stigmatized or ridiculed by others, particularly Sami men (see Eikjok 2000), and they may hold misconceptions and stereotypical views about feminism. Like their Indigenous sisters elsewhere, many Sami women argue that as long as the Sami people's right to self-determination has not yet been adequately addressed and recognized, the priority needs to be given to colonization over sexism.

According to Sami scholar Elina Helander, the Sami women's movement scared some women off as the idea of women as victims was alienating for them. Moreover, as the women's movement was labelled as "radical" and a threat to Sami family and other central social structures, it was misunderstood and rejected even by Sami women themselves (Helander and Kailo 1998b). As elsewhere, many Sami women have internalized the common but false impression of feminism as male-bashing or as an attempt to merely reverse the power dynamics and, in turn, have control over and oppress men. Clearly, these views serve certain interests and are thus reinforced and perpetuated through media and other public discourses. Yet, the roots of colonialism can be found in patriarchy (see, for example, Mies 1998; A. Smith 2005a).

Eikjok notes: "Feminism is perceived as very negative in the Indigenous world; it has been reduced to being *anti men*, as opposed to being *pro women*" (2000: 40). It is, however, also crucial to recognize that feminism is not limited to being pro-women, but that it extends to the analysis of the interlocking systems of oppression inherent in patriarchy, sexism, racism and colonialism. As Black feminist scholar bell hooks argues, feminism is "a movement to end sexism, sexist exploitation, and oppression" that eventually benefits the entire society (2000: viii).

If we want to adequately understand and dismantle complex colonial processes — many of which have become internal — it is necessary to recognize that colonial and patriarchal practices usually form interlocking and inseparable discourses and practices of oppression in which each informs and reinforces the other. It is necessary, as Sami and Indigenous women, to have the courage and vision to call attention to the realities and circumstances in which many of us live, even if it is not always our own lives. We must stop interpreting colonial and patriarchal practices as two separate forms of oppression, only one of which affects Indigenous peoples, and start examining the historical roots of colonialism in patriarchy. As Andrea Smith reminds us: "It is precisely through sexism and gender violence that colonialism and white supremacy have been successful" (2005b: 127).

We also have to stop falling prey to superficial, stereotypical misconstructions of feminism and its objectives as "anti-men." Instead of statements about irrelevancy of feminism to Sami or Indigenous women in general, we can reclaim it as one of our strategies for restoring our communities and strengthening our people. Instead of retreating behind the barricades of assumed incommensurable differences, it would be more fruitful to recognize the similarities in the various struggles against colonial and patriarchal subjugation and engage in the "politics of affinity" — i.e., collaboration with other women and marginalized groups (Kailo 1994).

I have no doubt that there are traces of the traditionally strong Sami women left everywhere in Sami society. However, to use the notion as a means to dismiss issues and concerns critical and important to Sami women, to bash or trivialize women and their initiatives, either for one's own reinforced sense of power or in the fear of losing the unified front (which is yet another common myth) in the struggle for self-determination is shortsighted, selfish and deleterious to Sami society. We are losing people through increased physical and sexual violence — suicides, mental illnesses, substance and alcohol abuse — but also through structural violence manifested in the lack of participation, further assimilation and integration into mainstream societies and, ultimately, the loss of what makes us Sami.

Instead of repeating the myth of Sami women as an excuse to remain passive and as a means of accepting current circumstances, we can start employing it for a proactive strategy of healing and transformation of not only women but all of Sami society. We could start advocating and implementing our powerful female legacies found, for example, in the Sami worldview and cosmic order that may well have been centred around the female deity Máttáráhkká ("Ancestral Mother") and her three daughters Sáráhkká, Juksáhkká and Uksáhkká, to advance and rebuild our communities. We could use our strength to call for accountability of our current leadership to enhance the well-being of all our people, not just a handful of individuals. Such a strategy would not only empower us and foster the Sami self-determination process in the present, but it also would constitute an invaluable gift for future Sami generations.

## NOTES

An earlier version of this article was published in Finnish in *Tasa-arvon haasteita globaalin ja lokaalin rajapinnoilla* [Global and Local Challenges of Equality], ed. K. Kailo, V. Sunnari and H. Vuori (Oulu: Women's Studies Program, University of Oulu, 2004). I wish to express thanks to the Finnish Academy for partial funding of this article under the research project "Monoacculturation, Gender and Violence in Educational Institutions," led by Dr. Kaarina Kailo at the University of Oulu, Finland (2000–2003).

1. Previously called Lapps or Laplanders, the Sami have claimed their collective term deriving from their own languages (*sápmelas* in Northern Sami). The terms "Lapp" or "Laplander" are considered derogative. Moreover, some Finns living in Northern Finland (also known as Lapland) have started to refer to themselves as Lapps to further confuse the already complex and conflicting issue of Sami land rights.

2. In a similar fashion, scholar of religion (and the first Sami woman to receive a Ph.D. in 1975) Louise Bäckman (1982) contends that the notion of Sami matriarchy is at best speculative.

3. There are still some Sami women who maintain that view. Sami poet Rauni Magga Lukkari, for instance, comments that, "I do not feel downtrodden like my sisters in the western world" (1998: 109). In her view, Sami women are not oppressed because one of the ways for women to exercise power is through making traditional Sami clothing.

4. As Lillian Ackerman notes, this is not necessarily so although it is a common explanation with regard to Indigenous societies. Discussing the context of the Colville Reservation in Washington State, she points our that there is as little continuity in women's traditional roles as there is in men's. Childbearing and rearing are roles that continue to be female-dominated, but everything else has changed: "Office employment is as different from gathering and preserving wild foods as lumbering is from hunting." Ackerman suggests that women's ability to better adjust "may result from their being accustomed to sustained rather than strenuous intermittent work" (2002: 30; see also Allen 1986).

5. This is the case of many other Indigenous societies as well. Dawn Martin-Hill observes that the adoption of Christian practices into Indigenous traditions is

common in the North American Indigenous communities. According to her, it has resulted in "the exclusion of women from ceremonies and to exalting female servitude as 'traditional'" (2003: 109).

6. The movement was named after its founder, Lars Levi Laestadius (1800–1861), who was of South Sami ancestry and who travelled across Samiland preaching and delivering his healing sermons, which partly drew upon Sami culture and oral traditions. A central characteristic of the Laestadian faith is the confession of sins followed by absolution "in the name and blood of Jesus." Laestadianism requires an abstinence from alcohol and disapproval of contraception.

7. Such perceptions of women are evident, for example, in some of the works of Sami writers, including Eino Guttorm, a male writer who has been criticized for his dualistic, simplistic descriptions of Sami women (see Guttorm 1998). In her collection of short stories *Guovtteoaivat nisu* ("Two-Headed Woman"), Kirsti Paltto (1989) analyzes common images and representations of Sami women in a society strongly influenced by Christianity (see also Poikajärvi 1996).

8. The name of the organization refers to one of the female deities of Sami cosmology. A daughter of Máttáráhkká ("the ancestral mother"), Sáráhkká governs particularly the realm of childbirth.

9. Ironically, only a few years later, Gro Harlem Brundtland chaired the World Commission on Environment and Development convened by the United Nations. The Commission produced the much-cited report, *Our Common Future* (1987), introducing the concept of sustainable development into mainstream parlance. The report is one of the first United Nations documents to recognize the sustainable ways of life of Indigenous and tribal communities and the role of Indigenous and tribal institutions and ideas in envisioning more sustainable futures for everybody in the planet. Significantly, the report also proposes that human activities should "meet the needs of the present without compromising the ability of future generations to meet their own needs" (Brundtland 43). This suggestion echoes the traditional teachings of many Indigenous peoples in North America, according to which we need to consider our actions in the light of well-being of seven future generations.

10. There is an interesting tendency in Sami politics to elect young women with limited experience to some of the most high-ranking positions of Sami organizations and political power. Most of the new female Sami Parliament representatives in Norway are relatively young, including the new president and the minister of fisheries in the government of Norway, while the more experienced and senior female Sami politicians are cast aside. One could ask whether this represents the beginning of a new and different dynamics in Sami politics or whether it is a old boys' network strategy to fend off charges of inequality while maintaining control over the political agenda and decision-making through "training" and "advising" the junior female leadership.

11. Finland also has a law mandating a minimum of 40 percent of women on government representative bodies. In order to comply with the law, two other female candidates were nominated as municipal councillors.

12. The Norwegian Sami Parliament today has the most decision-making power, especially since the *Finnmark Act* came into force in the beginning of 2006. The Act forms a co-management board for the northernmost county and its resources

in Norway. However, as the president of the Sami Parliament Aili Keskitalo notes, the executive committee of the board lacks equality, having only two women representatives. She suggests that the board elect a woman as the chair to amend the situation (Johnskareng 2005b). The male Sami candidate for the chair disputes this and maintains that party politics are more important than equality (Johnskareng 2005a).

13. In Norway, where only Sami can own reindeer, only 17 percent of women are heads of reindeer households, although 45 percent of reindeer owners are women. These women own approximately one third of all the reindeer (E.M. Utsi 2005b).

14. In the municipality of Guovdageaidnu, with a population of 3,000, there were sixteen reported cases of rape in 2005, three times more than the previous year (E.M. Utsi 2005a).

15. These men have recently established an association to improve male attitudes toward women in the community. They intend to publish a book on sexual harassment and abuse based on experiences of local women as well as visit schools to raise awareness (E.M. Utsi 2005a).

16. Hegemony, defined by Antonio Gramsci, is a form of ideological and cultural domination whereby the consciousness of subordinate groups is constructed by the discourse of those in power (Hoare and Smith 1971). It is a concept that appears to explain quite well the processes of Sami society discussed above.

17. See, for example, Lehtola (1998), who discusses the early days of Sami politics in Finland only in light of activities of Sami men.

## REFERENCES

Ackerman, Lillian A. 2002. "Gender Equality in a Contemporary Indian Community." In L. Frink, R.S. Shepard and G.A. Reinhardt (eds.), *Many Faces of Gender: Roles and Relationships through Time in Indigenous Northern Communities*. Boulder/Calgary: University Press of Colorado/University of Calgary Press.

Aikio, Inger-Mari. 1998. "I Write to Get Loads Off My Chest." In E. Helander and K. Kailo (eds.), *No Beginning, No End. The Sami Speak Up*. Edmonton: Canadian Circumpolar Institute/Nordic Sami Institute.

Allen, Paula Gunn. 1986. *The Sacred Hoop: Recovering the Feminine in American Indian Traditions*. Boston, Beacon Press.

Anti, Máret Láilá. 2005. "Gáibida mánáidgirgeruđa ruovttoluotta." *Min Áigi*. Kárásjohka. 5.

Bäckman, Louise. 1982. "Female — Divine and Human: A Study of the Position of the Woman in Religion and Society in Northern Eurasia." In Å. Hultkrantz and Ø. Vorren (eds.), *The Hunters*. Tromsø: Universitetsforlaget.

Balto, Asta. 1997. *Sámi mánáidbajásgeassin nuppástuvvá*. Oslo: Ad Notam Gyldendal.

Brantenberg, Terje. 1985. "The Alta-Kautokeino Conflict: Saami Reindeer Herding and Ethnopolitics." In J. Brosted, J. Dahl, A. Gray et al. (eds.), *Native Power: The Quest for Autonomy and Nationhood of Indigenous Peoples*. Oslo: Universitetsforlaget.

Clough, Patricia Ticineto. 1994. *Feminist Thought. Desire, Power, and Academic Discourse*. Oxford and Cambridge, Blackwell.

Eidheim, Harald. 1997. "Ethno-political Development among the Sami after World

War II: The Invention of Selfhood." In H. Gaski (ed.), *Sami Culture in a New Era: The Norwegian Sami Experience*. Kárásjohka: Davvi Girji.

Eikjok, Jorunn. 1988. "Sámi almmái- ja nissonrolla rievdamin." *Diehtogiisá* 1.

_____. 1990. "Indigenous Women's Situation: Similarities and Differences, Common Struggle for our Future." International Conference and VI General Assembly of the World Council of Indigenous Peoples. Tromsø.

_____. 1992. "The Situation of Men and Women in the Reindeerherding Society." *Diehtogiisá* 1.

_____. 2000. "Indigenous Women in the North: The Struggle for Rights and Feminism." *Indigenous Affairs* 3.

Enloe, Cynthia. 2004. *The Curious Feminist. Searching for Women in a New Age of Empire*. Berkeley: University of California Press.

Green, Joyce. 2001. "Canaries in the Mines of Citizenship: Indian Women in Canada." *Canadian Journal of Political Science* 34, 4.

Green, Joyce, and Cora Voyageur. 1999. "Globalization and Development at the Bottom." In M. Porter and E. Judd (eds.), *Feminists Doing Development: A Practical Critique*. London, Zed Books.

Guttorm, Eino. 1998. "Everybody is Worth a Song." In Helander and Kailo.

Helander, Elina and Kaarina Kailo. 1998a. *No Beginning, No End: The Sami Speak Up*. Edmonton, Canadian Circumpolar Institute/Nordic Sami Institute.

_____. 1998b. "The Nomadic Circle of Life: A Conversation on the Sami Knowledge System and Culture." In Helander and Kailo.

Hirvonen, Vuokko. 1999. *Sámeeatnama jienat. Sápmelaš nissona bálggis girječállin*. Guovdageaidnu: Dat.

_____. 2000. "Elsa Laula — sámiid álbmotbeaivvi eadni. Elsa Laula — saamelaisten kansallispäivän äiti." In K. Vuolab (ed.), *Giibat don leat? Sámi albmotbeaivve seminára 6.2.1998 Oulus. Kukapa se sinäkin olet? Saamen kansallispäivän seminaari 6.2.1998 Oulussa*. Oulu: Oulun yliopisto.

Hoare, Quintin, and Geoffrey Nowell Smith (eds.). 1971. *Selections from the Prison Notebooks of Antonio Gramsci*. London: Lawrence and Wishart.

hooks, bell. 2000. *Feminism is for Everybody: Passionate Politics*. Boston: South End Press.

Irigaray, Luce. 1985. *This Sex Which Is Not One*. Ithaca: Cornell University Press.

Irwin, Kathy. 1988. "Maori, Feminist, Academic." *Sites* 17 (Summer).

Johnskareng, Ámmun. 2004. "Álbmat stivrejit Ohcejogas." *Min Áigi*. Kárášjohka.

_____. 2005a. "Bellodatpolitihkka dehálat go dásseárvu." *Min Áigi*. Kárášjohka.

_____. 2005b. "Dásseárvu váilu FO:s." *Min Áigi*. Kárášjohka.

Joks, Solveig. 2001. *Boazosámi nissonolbmot — guovddážis báike — ja siidadoalus, muhto vajálduvvon almmolaččat*. Guovdageaidnu: Sámi Instituhtta.

Juuso, Inga. 1998. "Yoiking Acts as Medicine for Me." In Helander and Kailo.

Kailo, Kaarina. 1994. "Trance-Cultural Travel: Indigenous Women and Mainstream Feminisms." In M. Peepre (ed.), *Trans-Cultural Travels: Essays in Canadian Literature and Society*. Nordic Association for Canadian Studies.

Landbruksdepartementet. 1991–92. "En bærekraftig reindrift." Oslo.

LaRocque, Emma. 1996. "The Colonization of a Native Woman Scholar." In C. Miller, P. Chuchryk, M.S. Marule, B. Manyfingers and C. Deering (eds.), *Women of the First Nations: Power, Wisdom, and Strength*. Winnipeg: University of

Manitoba Press.

———. 1997. "Re-examining Culturally Appropriate Models in Criminal Justice Applications." In M. Asch (ed.), *Aboriginal and Treaty Rights in Canada: Essays on Law, Equity and Respect for Difference.* Vancouver: UBC Press.

Lukkari, Rauni Magga. 1998. "Where Did the Laughter Go?" In Helander and Kailo.

Lundmark, Bo. 1978. "Hon var en förgrundsgestalt i samernas moderna historia." *Samefolket* 6.

Martin-Hill, Dawn. 2003. "She No Speaks and Other Colonial Constructs of 'the Traditional Woman.'" In K. Anderson and B. Lawrence (eds.), *Strong Women Stories: Native Vision and Community Survival.* Toronto: Sumach Press.

Mies, Maria. 1998. *Patriarchy and Accumulation in the World Scale: Women in the International Division of Labour.* London: Zed Books.

Mihesuah, Devon A. 2003. *Indigenous American Women: Decolonization, Empowerment, Activism.* Lincoln: University of Nebraska Press.

Min Áigi. 2005. "Historjjálas vuollástahttin." *Min Áigi.*

Mohanty, Chandra. 1984. "Under Western Eyes: Feminist Scholarship and Colonial Discourse." *Boundary* 2, 12–13(3–1).

Nickul, Karl. 1970. *Saamelaiset kansana ja kansalaisina.* Helsinki: SKS.

Nystad, Ragnhild. 1995. "Urfolkskvinner mellom etnisitet og kjønn." In T. Brantenberg, J. Hansen and H. Minde (eds.), *Becoming Visible: Indigenous Politics and Self-Government.* Tromsø: University of Tromsø, Sámi dutkamiid guovddás — Centre for Sámi Studies.

Paine, Robert. 1982. *Dam a River, Damn a People?* Copenhagen: International Working Group on Indigenous Affairs.

Paltto, Kirsti. 1989. *Guovtteoaivvat nisu.* Ohcejohka: Gielas.

———. 1998. "One Cannot Leave One's Soul by a Tree Trunk." In Helander and Kailo.

Parmann, Georg. 1980. *Kampen om Alta — en trusel mot vårt demokrati?* Oslo: Dreyer.

Paulaharju, Samuli. 1921. *Kolttain Mailta: Kansatieteellisiä Kuvauksia Kuollan-Lapista.* Helsinki: Kirja.

Plumwood, Val. 1993. *Feminism and the Mastery of Nature.* London: Routledge.

Poikajärvi, Ulla. 1996. "Árbevirolas nissongovva." Review of *Guovtteoaivvat nisu. Gába.* 3/4.

Pulk, Åse. 2005a. "Boasttut bajásgeassán nieiddaid." *Min Áigi.* Kárásjohka.

———. 2005b. "Dolkan veagalváldinsteampilii — lágidit álbmotčoahkkima." *Min Áigi.* Kárásjohka.

———. 2005c. "Fas dutkame veagalváldinássi." *Min Áigi.* Kárášjohka.

———. 2005d. "Olu veagalváldináššit Guovdageainnus." *Min Áigi.* Kárásjohka.

———. 2005e. "Ártegis guottut hirbmáhuhttet." *Min Áigi.* Kárásjohka.

Sámi Instituhtta. 1979. "Boazosámi æmidiid bargodilálásvuodat. Flyttsamekvinnens arbeidssituasjon. Poronhoitossaamelaisnaisten työtilanteesta." *Diedut* 4.

Sanders, Ed. 1980. "Urbefolkningens rettiheterer og Alta-Kautokeino-utbyggningen." In T. Thuen (ed.), *Samene — urbefolkning og minoritet.* Tromsø: Universitetsforlaget.

Sárá, Máret. 1990–1. "Reindeer herding women are oppressed." *Sáráhkká. Newsletter of Sami Women's Association.*

_____, ed. 2002. *Boazodoalloealáhusa nissonpolitihkalas seminára*. Romsa: Boazodoallohálddahus.

_____. 2003. "Mann of kvinne like viktig. FN kvinnekonvensjon inn i Reindriftsloven." *Reinddriftsnytt/Boazodoallo-oddasat* 2.

Smith, Andrea. 2005a. *Conquest: Sexual Violence and American Indian Genocide*. Boston: South End Press.

_____. 2005b. "Native American Feminism, Sovereignty, and Social Change." *Feminist Studies* 31, 1.

Smith, Linda Tuhiwai. 1999. *Decolonizing Methodologies: Research and Indigenous Peoples*. London: Zed Books.

Solem, Erik. 1970. *Lappiske rettstudier*. Oslo: Universitetsforlaget.

Somby Sara, Elle Máret. 2005. Dásseárvu nieidamánáid ja gándamánáid gaskka boazodoalus. *Min Áigi*. Kárášjohka.

Spivak, Chakravorty Gayatri. 1985. "Three Women's Texts and a Critique of Imperialism." *Critical Inquiry* 12.

Stien, Laila. 1976. "Elsa Laula Renberg, en samisk foregangskvinne." *Ottar* 88.

Stordahl, Vigdis. 1990. "Why are they so few in numbers? Women leaders in a sample of Saami institutions." *Indigenous Women on the Move*. Copenhagen: International Working Group of Indigenous Affairs.

Suleri, Sara. 1992. "Woman Skin Deep: Feminism and the Postcolonial Condition." *Critical Inquiry* 18, 4.

Utsi, Elle Merete. 2005a. "Dievddut bargagoahtán." *Min Áigi*. Kárásjohka.

_____. 2005b. "Vuordá oahpahusguovddáža boazoealáhussii." *Min Áigi*. Kárásjohka.

Utsi, Josef Isak. 2005a. "Earráneapmi saddamin váttisvuohtan." *Min Áigi*. Kárásjohka.

_____. 2005b. "Massii rivttiiid go earráneigga." *Min Áigi*. Kárásjohka.

_____. 2005c. "NBR stivrras ii gávdno dásseárvu." *Min Áigi*.

_____. 2005d. "Nissonolbmot dahkkojit bogostahkan." *Min Áigi*.

_____. 2006. "Nihttet bákkus njuovvat ealu." *Min Áigi*. Kárásjohka.

Valkeapää, Nils-Aslak. 1998. "I Have No Beginning, No End." In Helander and Kailo.

# Chapter Five

# NATIVE AMERICAN FEMINISM, SOVEREIGNTY AND SOCIAL CHANGE

## *Andrea Smith*

When I worked as a rape crisis counsellor, every Native client I saw said to me at one point, "I wish I wasn't Indian." My training in the mainstream anti-violence movement did not prepare me to address what I was seeing — that sexual violence in Native communities was inextricably linked to processes of genocide and colonization. Through my involvement in organizations such as Women of All Red Nations (Chicago) and Incite! Women of Color Against Violence, and other projects, I have come to see the importance of developing organizing theories and practices that focus on the intersections of state and colonial violence and gender violence. In my ongoing research projects on Native American critical race feminisms, I focus on documenting and analyzing the theories produced by Native women activists that intervene in both sovereignty and feminist struggles.[1] These analyses serve to complicate the generally simplistic manner in which Native women's activism is often articulated within scholarly and activist circles.

### NATIVE WOMEN AND FEMINISM

One of the most prominent writings on Native American women and feminism is Annette Jaimes (Guerrero) and Teresa Halsey's early 1990s article, "American Indian Women: At the Center of Indigenous Resistance in North America." Here, they argue that Native women activists, except those who are "assimilated," do not consider themselves feminists. Feminism, according to Jaimes, is an imperial project that assumes the "givenness" of U.S. colonial stranglehold on Indigenous nations. Thus, to support sovereignty Native women activists reject feminist politics:

> Those who have most openly identified themselves [as feminists] have tended to be among the more assimilated of Indian women activists, generally accepting of the colonialist ideology that Indigenous nations are now legitimate sub-parts of the U.S. geopolitical corpus rather than separate nations, that Indian people are now a minority within the overall population rather than the citizenry of their own distinct nations. Such Indian women activists are therefore usually

more devoted to "civil rights" than to liberation per se.... Native American women who are more genuinely sovereigntist in their outlook have proven themselves far more dubious about the potentials offered by feminist politics and alliances. (1992: 330–31)

According to Jaimes and Halsey, the message from Native women is the same, as typified by these quotes from one of the founders of Women of All Red Nations (WARN), Lorelei DeCora Means:

> We are *American Indian* women, in that order. We are oppressed, first and foremost, as American Indians, as peoples colonized by the United States of America, *not* as women. As Indians, we can never forget that. Our survival, the survival of every one of us — man, woman and child — *as Indians* depends on it. Decolonization is the agenda, the whole agenda, and until it is accomplished, it is the *only* agenda that counts for American Indians....
>
> You start to get the idea maybe all this feminism business is just another extension of the same old racist, colonialist mentality. (quoted in Jaimes and Halsey 1992: 314, 332, emphasis in original)

The critique and rejection of the label of feminism made by Jaimes and Halsey is important and shared by many Native women activists. However, it fails to tell the whole story. Consider, for instance, this quote from Madonna Thunder Hawk, who co-founded WARN with Lorelei Means:

> Feminism means to me, putting a word on the women's world. It has to be done because of the modern day. Looking at it again, and I can only talk about the reservation society, because that's where I live and that's the only thing I know. I can't talk about the outside. How I relate to that term feminist, I like the word. When I first heard, I liked it. I related to it right away. But I'm not the average Indian woman; I'm not the average Indian activist woman, because I refuse to limit my world. I don't like that.... How could we limit ourselves? "I don't like that term; it's a white term." Pssshhh. Why limit yourself? But that's me.

My point is not to set Thunder Hawk in opposition to Means: both talk of the centrality of land and decolonization in Native women's struggle. While Thunder Hawk supports many of the positions typically regarded as "feminist," such as abortion rights, she contends that Native struggles for land and survival continue to take precedence over these other issues. Rather, my argument is that Native women activists' theories about feminism, about the struggle against sexism both within Native communities and the society at large and about the importance of working in coalition with non-Native women are complex and varied. These theories are not monolithic and cannot simply be reduced to the dichotomy of feminist versus non-feminist. Furthermore, there is not necessarily a relationship between the extent to which Native women call themselves feminists, the extent to which they work in coalition with non-Native feminists or value those coalitions, whether they are urban or reservation-based, and the extent to which they are "genuinely sovereigntist." In addition, the very simplified manner in which Native women's activism is theorized straightjackets Native women from articulating political projects that both address sexism *and* promote Indigenous sovereignty simultaneously.

Central to developing a Native feminist politic around sovereignty is a more critical analysis of Native activist responses to feminism and sexism in Native communities. Many narratives of Native women's organizing mirrors Jaimes and Halsey's analysis — that sexism is not a primary factor in Native women's organizing. However, Janet McCloud recounts how the sexism in the Native rights movement contributed to the founding of the Indigenous Women's Network in 1985:

> I was down in Boulder, Colorado, and Winona LaDuke and Nilak Butler were there and some others. They were telling me about the different kinds of sexism they were meeting up with in the movement with the men, who were really bad, and a lot of these women were really the backbone of everything, doing a lot of the kind of work that the movement needed. I thought they were getting discouraged and getting ready to pull out and I thought, "Wow, we can't lose these women because they have a lot to offer." So, we talked about organizing a women's conference to discuss all the different problems.... Marsha Gomez and others decided to formally organize. I agreed to stay with them as a kind of a buffer because the men were saying the "Indignant Women's Organization" and blah, blah, blah. They felt kind of threatened by the women organizing. (n.d.)

My interviews with Native women activists also indicate that sexism in Native communities is a central concern:

> Guys think they've got the big one, man. Like when [name of Native woman in the community] had to go over there and she went to these Indians because they thought they were a bunch of swinging dicks and stuff, and she just let them have it. She just read them out. What else can you do? That's pretty brave. She was nice, she could have laid one of them out. Like you know [name of Native

man in the community], well of course this was more extreme, because I laid him out! He's way bigger than me. He's probably five foot eleven, I'm five feet tall. When he was younger, and I was younger, I don't even know what he said to me, it was something really awful. I didn't say nothing because he was bigger than me, I just laid him out. Otherwise you could get hurt. So I kicked him right in his little nut, and he fell down on the floor — "I'm going to kill you! You bitch!" But then he said, you're the man! If you be equal on a gut and juice level, on the street, they don't think of you as a woman anymore, and therefore they can be your friend, and they don't hate you. But then they go telling stuff like "You're the man!" And then what I said back to him was "I've got it swinging!" (Interviewee #1)

And while many Native women do not call themselves feminists for many well-thought-out reasons, including but not limited to the reasons Jaimes and Halsey outline, it is important to note that many not only call themselves feminist but argue that it is important for Native women to call themselves feminists. And many activists argue that feminist, far from being a "white" concept, is actually an Indigenous concept white women borrowed from Native women.

I think one of the reasons why women don't call themselves feminists is because they don't want to make enemies of men, and I just say, go forth and offend without inhibition. That's generally why I see women hold back, who don't want to be seen as strident. I don't want to be seen as a man-hater, but I think if we have enough man-haters, we might actually have the men change for once.... I think men, in this particular case, I think men are very, very good at avoiding responsibility and avoiding accountability and avoiding justice. And not calling yourself a feminist, that's one way they do that. Well, feminism, that's for white women. Oh feminists, they're not Indian. They're counterrevolutionary. They're all man-haters. They're all ball-busters. They've gotten out of order. No, first of all that presumes that Native women weren't active in shaping our identity before white women came along. And that abusive male behaviour is somehow traditional, and it's absolutely not. So I reject that. That's a claim against sovereignty. I think that's a claim against Native peoples. I think it's an utter act of racism and white supremacy. And I do think it's important that we say we're feminists without apology. (Interviewee #2)

I think that's giving that concept to someone else, which I think is

> ridiculous. It's something that there has to be more discussion about what that means. I always considered, they took that from us, in a way. That's the way I've seen it. So I can't see it as a bad thing, because I think the origins are from people who had empowered women a long time ago. (Interviewee #3)

This reversal of the typical claim that "feminism" is white then suggests that Native feminist politics is not necessarily similar to the feminist politics of other communities or that Native feminists necessarily see themselves in alliance with white feminists. In addition, the binary between feminist versus non-feminist politics is false as Native activists have multiple and varied perspectives on this concept. For instance, consider one woman's use of "strategic" feminism with another women's affirmation of feminist politics coupled with her rejection of the term "feminist." These women are not neatly categorized as feminists or non-feminists.

> Well, you know I vary that from situation to situation. Because when I'm back home, I'll say I'm a feminist just to rile the guys so they know where I still stand. So there's nothing tricky about who I am and what I'm doing. And when I'm out here in a white women's studies department, I won't call myself, because I don't want to align myself with their politics. (Interviewee #2)

> It's not the term that fits within my culture. I'm an Indian woman, first and foremost. I'm a strong Indian woman, very directed, and I believe in feminism as I understand society, and that I would be a part of that…. The word doesn't equate with any Indian word that I would know. That's what I mean, there isn't a word. (Interviewee #3)

These analyses suggest that sexism is not necessarily a secondary concern to Native women, and Native women's engagement with feminist politics to address sexism is much more complex that generally depicted.

## NATIVE FEMINISM AND SOVEREIGNTY

If we successfully decolonize, the argument generally goes, then we will necessarily eliminate problems of sexism as well. But the reality is, regardless of its origins in Native communities, sexism operates with full force today and requires strategies that directly address it. Before Native peoples fight for the future of their nations, they must ask themselves, who is included in the nation? It is often the case that gender justice is often articulated as being a separate issue from issues of survival for Indigenous peoples. Such an understanding presupposes that we could actually decolonize without addressing sexism, which ignores the fact that it has been precisely through gender violence that we have lost our lands in the first place (Smith 1999: 31–52). In my activist work, I have often heard the sentiment expressed in Indian country: we do not have time to address sexual/domestic violence in our communities because we have to work on "survival" issues first. However, Indian women suffer death rates twice as high as any other women in this country because of domestic violence (Rennison 2001). They are clearly *not* surviving as long as issues of gender violence go unaddressed. Scholarly analyses of the impact of colonization on Native communities often minimize the histories of oppression of Native women. In fact, many scholars argue that men were disproportionately affected by colonization because the economic systems imposed on Native nations deprived men of their economic roles in the communities more so than women (Murphy 1995; Purdue 1995). By narrowing our analysis solely to the economic realm, we fail to account for the multiple ways women have disproportionately suffered under colonization — from sexual violence to forced sterilization. As Paula Gunn Allen argues:

> Many people believe that Indian men have suffered more damage to their traditional status than have Indian women, but I think that belief is more a reflection of colonial attitudes toward the primacy of male experience than of historical fact. While women still play the traditional role of housekeeper, childbearer, and nurturer, they no longer enjoy the unquestioned positions of power, respect, and decision making on local and international levels that were not so long ago their accustomed functions. (1986: 202)

This tendency to separate the health and well-being of women from the health and well-being of our nations is critiqued in Winona LaDuke's 1994 call to not "cheapen sovereignty." She discusses attempts by men in her community to use the rhetoric of "sovereignty" to avoid paying child support payments:

> What is the point of an Indian Child Welfare Act when there is so much disregard for the rights and well-being of the children? Some of these guys from White Earth are saying the state has no jurisdiction to exact child support payments from them. Traditionally, Native men took care of their own. Do they pay their own to these women? I don't think so. I know better. How does that equation better the lives of our children? How is that (real) sovereignty? The U.S. government is so hypocritical about recognizing sovereignty. And we, the Native community, fall into the same hypocrisy. I would argue

the Feds only recognize Indian sovereignty when a First Nation has a casino or a waste dump, not when a tribal government seeks to preserve ground water from pesticide contamination, exercise jurisdiction over air quality, or stop clear-cutting or say no to a nuclear dump. "Sovereignty" has become a politicized term used for some of the most demeaning purposes. (LaDuke 1996)

Beatrice Medicine (1993) similarly critiques the manner in which women's status is often pitted against sovereignty, as exemplified in the 1978 *Santa Clara Pueblo v. Martinez* case. Julia Martinez sued her tribe for sex discrimination under the *Indian Civil Rights Act* because the tribe had dictated that children born from female tribal members who married outside the tribe lost tribal status whereas children born from male tribal members who married outside the tribe did not. The Supreme Court ruled that the federal government could not intervene in this situation because the determination of tribal membership was the sovereign right of the tribe. On the one hand, many white feminists criticized the Supreme Court decision without considering how the Court's affirmation of the right of the federal government to determine tribal membership would have constituted a significant attack against tribal sovereignty (MacKinnon 1987: 63–69). On the other hand, as Medicine notes, many tribes take this decision as a signal to institute gender-discriminatory practices under the name of sovereignty (1993: 121–30). For these difficult issues, it is perhaps helpful to consider how they could be addressed if we put American Indian women at the centre of analysis. Is it possible to simultaneously affirm tribal sovereignty *and* challenge tribes to consider how the impact of colonization and Europeanization may impact the decisions they make and programs they pursue in a manner that may ultimately undermine their sovereignty? Rather than adopt the strategy of fighting for sovereignty first and then improving Native women's status second, as Jaimes and Halsey suggest, we must understand that attacks on Native women's status are themselves attacks on Native sovereignty. Lee Maracle illustrates the relationship between colonization and gender violence in Native communities in her groundbreaking work, *I Am Woman* (1988):

> If the State won't kill us
> We will have to kill ourselves.
> It is no longer good etiquette to head hunt savages.
> We'll just have to do it ourselves.
> It's not polite to violate "squaws"
> We'll have to find an Indian to oblige us.
> It's poor form to starve an Indian
> We'll have to deprive our young ourselves.

Blinded by niceties and polite liberality
We can't see our enemy,
    so, we'll just have to kill each other. (12–13)

It has been through sexual violence and through the imposition of European gender relationships on Native communities that Europeans were able to colonize Native peoples in the first place. If we maintain these patriarchal gender systems, we will be unable to decolonize and fully assert our sovereignty.

## NATIVE FEMINIST SOVEREIGNTY PROJECTS

Despite the political and theoretical straightjacket in which Native women often find themselves, there are several groundbreaking projects today that address both colonialism and sexism through an intersectional framework. One such attempt to tie Indigenous sovereignty with the well-being of Native women is evident in the materials produced by the Sacred Circle, a South Dakota based national American Indian resource centre for domestic and sexual violence. Their brochure, *Sovereign Women Strengthen Sovereign Nations*, reads:

| Tribal Sovereignty | Native Women's Sovereignty |
|---|---|
| All Tribal Nations Have an Inherent Right To | All Native Women Have an Inherent Right To: |
| 1) A land base: possession and control is unquestioned and honored by other nations. To exist without fear, but with freedom. | 1) Their body and path in life: the possession and control is unquestioned and honored by others. To exist without fear, but with freedom. |
| 2) Self-governance: the ability and authority to make decisions regarding all matters concerning the Tribe without the approval or agreement of others. This includes the ways and methods of decision-making, social, political and other areas of life. | 2) Self governance: the ability and authority to make decisions regarding all matters concerning themselves, without others' approval or agreement. This includes the ways and methods of decision-making in social, political and other areas of life. |

| | |
|---|---|
| 3) An economic base and resources: the control, use and development of resources, businesses or industries the Tribe chooses. This includes resources that support the Tribal life way, including the practice of spiritual ways. | 3) An economic base and resources: the control, use and development of resources, businesses or industries that Native women choose. This includes resources that support individual Native women's chosen life ways, including the practice of spiritual ways. |
| 4) A distinct language and historical and cultural identity: Each tribe defines and describes its history, including the impact of colonization and racism, tribal culture, worldview and traditions. | 4) A distinct identity, history and culture: Each Native woman defines and describes her history, including the impact of colonization, racism and sexism, tribal women's culture, worldview and traditions. |
| ****** | ****** |
| Colonization and violence against Native people means that power and control over Native people's life way and land have been stolen. | Violence against women, and victimization in general, means that power and control over an individual's life and body have been stolen. |
| As Native people, we have the right and responsibility to advocate for ourselves and our relatives in supporting our right to power and control over our tribal life way and land — tribal sovereignty. | As relatives of women who have been victimized, it is our right and responsibility to be advocates supporting every woman's right to power and control over her body and life — personal sovereignty. |

Another such project is the Boarding School Healing Project, which seeks to build a movement to demand accountability and reparations for U.S boarding school abuses. This project, founded in 2002, is a coalition of Indigenous groups across the United States, such as the American Indian Law Alliance, Incite! Women of Color Against Violence, Indigenous Women's Network and Native Women of Sovereign Nations of the South Dakota Coalition Against Domestic Violence and Sexual Assault. In Canada, Native peoples have been able to document the abuses of the residential school system and demand accountability from the Canadian government and churches. The same level of documentation has not taken place in the United States. The Boarding School Healing Project is documenting these abuses. However, the strategy of this project is not to seek remedies on the individual level, but to demand a collective remedy by developing links with other reparation struggles that fundamentally challenge the colonial and capitalist status quo.

The project organizes around the boarding school issue as a way to address gender violence in Native communities.

One of the harms suffered by Native peoples through state policy was sexual violence perpetrated by boarding school officials. The continuing effect of this human rights violation has been the internalization of sexual and other forms of gender violence *within* Native American communities. Thus, the question is, how can we form a demand around reparations for these types of continuing effects of human rights violations that are evidenced by violence *within* communities, but are nonetheless colonial legacies. The Boarding School Healing Project organizes against interpersonal gender violence *and* state violence simultaneously by framing gender violence as a continuing effect of human rights violations perpetrated by state policy. Consequently, this project challenges the mainstream anti-domestic/sexual violence movement to conceptualize state-sponsored sexual violence as central to its work. As I have argued elsewhere, the mainstream anti-violence movement has relied upon the apparatus of state violence (in the form of the criminal justice system) to address domestic and sexual violence without considering how the state itself is a primary perpetrator of violence (Smith 1999: 31–52). The issue of boarding schools forces us to see the connections between state violence and interpersonal violence. It is through boarding schools that gender violence in our communities was largely introduced.

Prior to colonization, Native societies were, for the most part, not male dominated. Women served as spiritual, political and military leaders. Many societies were matrilineal and matrilocal. Violence against women and children was infrequent or unheard of in many tribes (Sacred Shawl Women's Society; Division of Indian Work Sexual Assault Project n.d.; Allen 1986). Native peoples did not use corporal punishment against their children. Although there existed a division of labour between women and men, women's and men's labour was accorded similar status (Jaimes and Halsey 1992: 311–44; Allen 1986). In boarding schools, by contrast, sexual/physical/emotional violence proliferated. Particularly brutalizing to Native children was the manner in which school officials involved children in punishing other children. For instance, in some schools, children were forced to hit other children with the threat that if they did not hit hard enough, they themselves would be severely beaten. Sometimes perpetrators of the violence were held accountable, but generally speaking, even when teachers were charged with abuse, boarding schools refused to investigate. In the case of just one teacher, John Boone at the Hopi school, FBI investigations in 1987 found that he had sexually abused over 142 boys, but that the principal of that school had not investigated any allegations of abuse (*American Eagle* 1994: 19). Despite the epidemic of sexual abuse in boarding schools, the Bureau of Indian affairs did not issue a policy on reporting sexual abuse until 1987 and did not issue a policy to strengthen the background checks of potential teachers until 1989. While not all Native peoples see their boarding school experiences as negative, many believe that much if not most of the current dysfunctionality in Native communities can be traced to the boarding school era.

The continuing effects of boarding school abuses continue today because these abuses have not been acknowledged by the larger society. As a result, silence continues within Native communities, preventing Native peoples from seeking support and healing from the inter-generational trauma. Because boarding school policies are not as acknowledged as human rights violations, Native peoples individualize the trauma they have suffered, which increases their sense of shame and self-blame. If both boarding school policies and the continuing effects from these policies were recognized as human rights violations, then it might take away the shame associated with talking about these issues and thus provide an opportunity for communities to begin to heal.

Unfortunately, we perpetuate this colonial violence through domestic/ sexual violence, child abuse and homophobia. No amount of reparations will be successful if we do not address the oppressive behaviours we have internalized. Women of colour have for too long been presented with the choices of prioritizing either racial justice or gender justice. This dualistic analysis fails to recognize that it is precisely through sexism and gender violence that colonialism and white supremacy have been successful. A question to ask ourselves then is: What would reparations really look like for women of colour who suffer state violence and interpersonal gender violence simultaneously? The Boarding School Healing Project provides an opportunity to organize around the connections between interpersonal gender violence and state violence, and this could serve as a model for the broader anti-violence movement.

In addition, this project makes important contributions to the struggle for reparations as a whole. The project asserts that reparations must call into question the capitalist and colonial status quo. No matter how much financial compensation the U.S. may give, such compensation does not ultimately end the colonial relationship between the United States and Indigenous nations. What is at the heart of the struggle for Native sovereignty is control over land and resources rather than financial compensation for past and continuing wrongs. If we think about reparations less in terms of financial compensation for social oppression and more about a movement to transform the neo-colonial economic relationships between the U.S. and people of colour, Indigenous peoples and Third World countries, we see how critical this movement could be to all of us. The articulation of reparations as a movement to cancel Third World debt, for instance, is instructive in thinking of strategies that could fundamentally alter these relations.

## NATIVE FEMINISM AND THE NATION STATE

Native feminist theory and activism make a critical contribution to feminist politics as a whole by questioning of the legitimacy of the United States specifically and the nation-state generally as the appropriate form of governance. Progressive activists and scholars, while prepared to make critiques of the U.S. government, are often not prepared to question its legitimacy. A case in point is the strategy of many racial justice organizations in the U.S. to rally against hate crimes resulting from the attacks of 9/11 under the banner, "We're American too." However, what the analysis of Native women activists suggests is that this implicit allegiance to "America" legitimizes the genocide and colonization of Native peoples, as there could be no "America" without this genocide. Thus by making anti-colonial struggle central to feminist politics, Native women make central to their organizing the question of what is the appropriate form of governance for the world in general. Does self-determination for Indigenous peoples equal aspirations for a nation state, or are there other forms of governance we can create that are not based on domination and control?

Questioning the U.S. in particular and questioning the nation-state as the appropriate form of governance for the world in general allow us to free our political imagination to begin thinking of how we can build a world we would actually want to live in. Such a political project is particularly important for colonized peoples seeking national liberation because it allows us to differentiate "nation" from "nation-state." Helpful in this project of imagination is the work of Native women activists who have begun articulating notions of nation and sovereignty that are separate from nation-states. Whereas nation-states are governed through domination and coercion, Indigenous sovereignty and nationhood is predicated on interrelatedness and responsibility. As Crystal Ecohawk states:

> Sovereignty is an active, living process within this knot of human, material and spiritual relationships bound together by mutual responsibilities and obligations. From that knot of relationships is born our histories, our identity, the traditional ways in which we govern ourselves, our beliefs, our relationship to the land, and how we feed, clothe, house and take care of our families, communities and Nations. (1999: 21–22)

This interconnectedness exists not only among the nation's members but among all creation — human and non human. As Sharon Venne states:

> Our spirituality and our responsibilities define our duties. We understand the concept of sovereignty as woven through a fabric that encompasses our spirituality and responsibility. This is a cyclical view

of sovereignty, incorporating it into our traditional philosophy and view of our responsibilities. There it differs greatly from the concept of western sovereignty which is based upon absolute power. For us absolute power is in the Creator and the natural order of all living things; not only in human beings.... Our sovereignty is related to our connections to the earth and is inherent. The idea of a nation did not simply apply to human beings. We call the buffalo or, the wolves, the fish, the trees, and all are nations. Each is sovereign, an equal part of the creation, interdependent, interwoven, and all related. (1998: 23–25)

These models of sovereignty are not based on a narrow definition of nation that would entail a closely bounded community and ethnic cleansing. One activist distinguishes between a chauvinistic notion of "nationalism" versus a flexible notion of "sovereignty":

Nationalism is saying, our way is the only right way.... I think a real true sovereignty is a real, true acceptance of who and what's around you. And the nationalist doesn't accept all that.... Sovereignty is what you do and what you are to your own people within your own confines, but there is a realization and acceptance that there are others who are around you. And that happened even before the Europeans came, we knew about the Indians. We had alliances with some, and fights with some. Part of that sovereignty was that acceptance that they were there. (Interviewee #5)

It is interesting to me, for instance, how often non-Indians presume that if Native people regained their land bases, that they would necessarily call for the expulsion of non-Indians from those land bases. Yet, it is striking that a much more inclusive vision of sovereignty is articulated by Native women activists. For instance, this activist describes how Indigenous sovereignty is based on freedom for all peoples:

If it doesn't work for one of us, it doesn't work for any of us. The definition of sovereignty [means that]... none of us are free unless all of our free. We can't, we won't turn anyone away. We've been there. I would hear stories about the Japanese internment camps... and I could relate to it because it happened to us. Or with Africans with the violence and rape, we've been there too. So how could we ever leave anyone behind.

This analysis mirrors much of the work currently going on in women of colour organizing in the U.S. and in other countries. Such models rely on this dual strategy of what Sista II Sista (Brooklyn) describes as "taking power" and "making power" (Sista II Sista members). On one hand it is necessary to engage in oppositional politics to corporate and state power (taking power). However, if we only engage in the politics of taking power, we will have a tendency to replicate the hierarchical structures in our movements. Consequently, it is also important to "make power" by creating those structures within our organizations, movements and communities that model the world we are trying to create. Many groups in the U.S. try to create separatist communities based on egalitarian ideals. However, if we "make power" without also trying to "take power," then we ultimately support the political status quo by failing to dismantle those structures of oppression that will undermine all our attempts to make power. The project of creating a world governance system not based on domination, coercion and control does not depend on the unrealistic goal of being able to fully describe such a utopian society for all at this point in time. From our position of growing up in a patriarchal, colonial and white supremacist world, we cannot even fully imagine how a world not based on structures of oppression could operate. Nevertheless, we can be part of a collective, creative process that can bring us closer to such a society. To quote Jean Ziegler from the 2003 World Social Forum, held in Porto Alegre, Brazil: "We know what we don't want, but the new world belongs to the liberated freedom of human beings. 'There is no way; you make the way as you go.' History doesn't fall from heaven; we make history."

## NOTES

This chapter first appeared in *Feminist Studies* 31, 1 (Spring 2005), copyright Andrea Smith; reprinted with permission.

1.  Quotes that are not cited come from interviews from my research. These interviews are derived primarily from women involved in Women of All Red Nations and the American Indian Movement. All are activists today.

## REFERENCES

Allen, Paula Gunn. 1986. *The Sacred Hoop*. Boston: Beacon.

_____. "Violence and the American Indian Woman." *The Speaking Profits Us*. Seattle: Center for the Prevention of Sexual and Domestic Violence.

*American Eagle*. 1994. "Hello New Federalism Goodbye BIA." *American Eagle* 2.

Division of Indian Work Sexual Assault Project. "Sexual Assault is Not an Indian Tradition." Minneapolis.

Ecohawk, Crystal. 1999. "Reflections on Sovereignty." *Indigenous Woman* 3, 1.

Jaimes, M. Annette, and Theresa Halsey. 1992. "American Indian Women: At the Center of Indigenous Resistance in North America." In M. Annette Jaimes (ed.), *State of Native American*. Boston: South End Press.

LaDuke, Winona. 1996. "Don't Cheapen Sovereignty." *American Eagle*. Available at <www.alphacdc.com/eagle/op0596.html> (accessed March 2007).

MacKinnon, Catherine. 1987. *Feminism Unmodified*. Cambridge: Harvard University Press.

Maracle, Lee. 1988. *I Am Woman*. North Vancouver: Write-On Press Publishers.

McCloud, Janet. N.d. "The Backbone of Everything," *Indigenous Woman* 1, 3.

Medicine, Beatrice. 1993. "North American Indigenous Women and Cultural Domination." *American Indian Culture and Research Journal* 17, 3.

Murphy, Lucy Eldersveld. 1995. "Autonomy and the Economic Roles of Indian Women of the Fox-Wisconsin Riverway Region, 1763–1832." In Nancy Shoemaker (ed.), *Negotiators of Change: Historical Perspectives on Native American Women*. New York: Routledge Press.

Purdue, Theda. 1995. "Women, Men and American Indian Policy: The Cherokee Response to 'Civilization.'" In Nancy Shoemaker (ed.), *Negotiators of Change: Historical Perspectives on Native American Women*. New York: Routledge Press.

Rennison, Callie. 2001. "Violent Victimization and Race 1993–1998." Washington, DC: Bureau of Justice Statistics.

Sacred Shawl Women's Society. "A Sharing: Traditional Lakota Thought and Philosophy Regarding Domestic Violence." South Dakota.

Sista II Sista members. Quoted from personal conversations. (See <www.sistaiisista.org>.)

Smith, Andrea. 1999. "Sexual Violence and American Indian Genocide." In Nantawan Lewis and Marie Fortune (eds.), *Remembering Conquest: Feminist/Womanist Perspectives on Religion, Colonization and Sexual Violence*. Binghamton: Haworth Press.

Venne, Sharon. 1998. "Mining and Indigenous Peoples." *Indigenous Woman* 2, 5.

Chapter Six

# GENDER, ESSENTIALISM AND FEMINISM IN SAMILAND

## Jorunn Eikjok (translation by Gunhild Hoogensen)

At a recent meeting for Arctic Indigenous people, the theme of gender was raised. Two different views of reality were presented. A young male politician opened the discussion by stating that the problem of gender and equality was not relevant for us as Indigenous people, but that it is a western phenomenon and problem. He further stated that men and women were equally valued within the Indigenous community and used as an example his own community, where the men hunt and women take care of the meat and skins. The other view was presented by a young Indigenous woman from East Siberia. She stated that her community was in serious crisis since the young women of the community were moving away to take advantage of educational opportunities, while the men are left behind, living off hunting and trapping. The end result is a mostly male community with a low quality of life. These two views of reality exist concurrently within Indigenous society. In this chapter I will discuss how these two views find expression in Sápmi or Samiland.[1] I also discuss these views as they relate to gender and feminism within the Indigenous society.

### GENDER AND CHANGES

Enormous changes have taken place in Samiland within the last decade, from a way of life anchored in nature to one featuring modern and diverse lifestyles. A number of decades ago the vast majority of Sami people lived off traditional economies, using what nature provided. Women and men were each in their own way holders and purveyors of culture. The household, managed by the woman, was a central unit within the local community. Women and men made use of their own particular areas of expertise within the Sami landscape. The household was not confined "within the four walls" but extended far out into the wilderness. Women working in reindeer husbandry had a relatively strong position as they owned the reindeer they brought with them to the marriage. Agriculture in Samiland was primarily a woman's responsibility. Women were producers of food and clothing and were responsible for the raising of the next generation; they had the overall responsibility for caring in the community.

The men hunted, fished or raised reindeer in the mountains.

The integration of Sami agriculture and reindeer herding in Norwegian management regimes had serious consequences for Sami women. Norwegian regulations and laws contributed to undermining women's position in relation to production and competence. To make a long and complex history of Sami agriculture since 1945 very short, the Norwegian state communicated with Sami men, not the women, and the Sami men became the farmers and concession holders in reindeer husbandry, which came to be based on Norwegian farming systems and modern "scientific" knowledge of nature (Eikjok 1989).

There is now an ecological crisis in the North, connected to the colonial past of the northern territories, to the processes of modernization, to the integration of Sami land use laws into Norwegian law and to a global environmental crisis (Eikjok and Fyhn 1990). Marilyn Waring claims that the second wave of colonization over Indigenous peoples occurred after 1948, when states adopted the Gross National Product system. This system was based upon western norms, where men were assigned the role as the economic head and women were relegated to the position of "housewife" (Waring 1988). As a result, the central contributions of Indigenous women to the survival of Indigenous communities was undermined and rendered invisible. Women's knowledge lost its status. Societies that had understandings of the relations between the sexes that differed from the European model were thereafter defined as backward and primitive. The end results have been tragic for many Indigenous societies the world over.

## NEW CULTURAL EXPRESSIONS AND CONTRADICTIONS

In the wake of the new millennium, the Sami people have claimed themselves as "modern Indigenous people." Culture is no longer understood as being static and traditional. The Sami movement has defined itself within the context of global Indigenous peoples. Sami traditions have become integrated within global influences and trends, with new Sami cultural expressions coming to the fore. For example, the Sami *joik*[2] became blended with musical forms from other countries and continents, resulting in new musical expressions. A friend of mine who works in the reindeer industry makes a dish where she mixes smoked reindeer meat with lentils from India and coconut milk from Thailand, resulting in the transformation of a traditional Sami food product. Such cultural evolution occurs today within many areas of Sami society. Sami are a part of globalization. This has also made us far more conscious of our own identity and belonging than we were before. There is a general insight that through meeting others, we see ourselves. What we ourselves represent becomes clearer when contrasted with global trends and cultures.

Thus, within Sami communities there now exist many lifestyles and social orientations, leading to new formulations of male and female identities. Economic, cultural and social differences create different worldviews, lifestyles and practices. Contradictions and conflicts of interest have resulted. The traditional and the modern exist side by side within Sami community. The extent to which people are bound to these two aspects of Sami life is dependent upon education, occupation and generation. Older people are often more anchored within traditional values and lifestyles. Family connections and roots as well as place continue to be strong and dominant symbols of identity. Traditional society is characterized by individuals identifying themselves primarily as a member of a group or community. The ideal was to be useful in the society (Gullestad 1996).

The socio-cultural changes that have occurred have altered the relations between the generations. No longer can a person inherit the lifestyle and identity of her parents and live life the way earlier generations did. Each person is challenged to create her own "stories about herself," defining her identity from the many possibilities available.

Reality demands that we "find ourselves," that we be Sami in the contemporary conditions of modernity. Modernity creates pressures upon the old authorities and traditions. Previous values, traditions and meanings disintegrate and disappear. People are challenged by a wide spectrum of new choices, everything from hairstyling to childrearing, house décor/interior decorating, modes of living together and much, much more.

## GENDER AND MODERN SAMI SOCIETY

Gender roles are shaped by society or culture. At the same time we create culture — culture consists of an objectified expression of our collective experience. Gender constitutes both a framework for meaning and a code. We create notions about what is a man and a woman. Societal structures play a significant role: gender is shaped by the structural, cultural and personal conditions of the day. Thus, we find differences in the understandings of what is feminine or masculine between societies and historical epochs.

In traditional Sami society, there existed a strong gender-based division of labour, particularly for men. Women could, however, do both woman's work and men's work. An elderly Sami woman told me that net fishing for salmon in the Tana river was considered to be men's work. But since she was the eldest daughter in the house and they did not have any sons, "then I had to be a man" and participate in net fishing. Women's activities, particularly for those women without children, also consisted of raising reindeer along with men. Boys, however, were prohibited from sewing, with the warning that if they took up a needle, they would "lose their own needle." In other words, men were subject to strict sanctions if they in any way participated in women's work, as it would be perceived as "unmanly." The traditional ideals for women were to be *barggán* (a hard worker), *giedalaš* (have manual dexterity) and *doaimmalaš* (be good at organizing). These skills were necessary to the care and maintenance of the household. Elderly women who were raised with these ideals generally consider women today to be lazy. "A woman who cannot sew might as well just go live under a bush," an elderly women said to me once. For men it was important to be *searalaš* (have physical strength) and to relate to nature sensitively and holistically.

Modernization has reduced the need for these skills. Sami still have, however, environments where these skills are essential for survival and mastery. I was present when a number of young women discussed whether they should bake for Christmas, and how much. This task was no longer a given for them. The cultural expectations of creating warmth and enjoyment in the home are connected to the feminine. These young women questioned these expectations in relation to themselves as women. Modern Indigenous people today are daily confronted with negotiating new meanings and content in gender and gender relations.

Modernization processes have greatly influenced Sami gender relations over the generations (Eikjok 1989). Women and men now are faced with many, and sometimes contradictory, expectations. The Sami social scientist Vigdis Stordahl writes that the dividing lines within Sami society exhibit themselves on the basis of who has an education. Those who have an education have a command of both the dominant society's and Sami society's competence. In the new millennium Sami women obtain higher education in a variety of fields.

Clearly, women are a part of the new knowledge and information society. In some municipalities, twice as many women obtain college or university education as do men. When women have a higher education than men, dividing lines within the Sami society are drawn in relation to gender. In some municipalities women also earn higher average salaries than men.

The current discourses of resource management, defence of Indigenous peoples' landscapes and the use of nature and the environment are profoundly masculinized. In many small communities there still exists a tradition to harvest nature, and there is a need for motorized means of getting food home. Snowmobiles and all-terrain vehicles are not solely a means of food transport however, but have, just like nature, become new symbols for Sami masculinity. Within a number of Sami environments men are actively using these symbols to create the modern presentation of themselves and to express their masculine ethnic identity, despite the fact that the vast majority of them do not depend on nature for their own survival. A while ago I asked some young boys at what point did they feel most "Sami." They said: "When I drive snowmobiles and I *joik*." Debates have grown over the use of motorized traffic in the wilderness, with some wishing to protect nature.

One Sami man who represents the side for nature protection has received death threats.

These polarized positions on nature have created boundaries between the "manly" in the Sami context and those who are "unmanly," drawing on hegemonic masculinities in the dominant urban society. One result is that some aspects of Indigenous masculinity contradict trends of modernity, which in turn is reshaping Sami cultural expression, handled by women and men in different ways. Within modern society women have taken over in a number of arenas that were previously the domain of men. Men dominate in traditional trades. In Norway, only one third of the licences for reindeer herding belong to women, and one third of the owners of reindeer are women. In the Sami societies in Sweden, however, 11 percent of reindeer owners are women, with 7 percent owning licences (Government of Sweden 2001: 101). It has always been the cultural expectation that men must take care of families in Sami society. Women nevertheless subsidize reindeer husbandry and vocations in the traditional economy with their own incomes.

Women, to a much larger degree, are taking up the challenges of adjusting themselves to cultural changes and an evolving society. Earlier I mentioned that the historical socialization and gender codes in Sami society provide women a greater degree of freedom for their activities than it does men. Men are restricted by what is considered "manly." This limits the negotiating space for masculinity, and in light of rapid societal changes, the Indigenous man has become considerably weaker. Activities within traditional economies have been affected, as hunting, fishing and reindeer husbandry rights have been limited by increased state regulation and by influences in the global economy. This has resulted in high rates of unemployment and a significantly reduced quality of life, particularly for men, in many Indigenous societies in the Arctic (Williamson 2004: 126–76).

When Indigenous masculinity is so bound up with traditional activities, which in turn have become limited, the position of men in society becomes compromised and masculinity balances upon a knife's edge. Can this possibly explain the masculine symbolism of modern motorized transportation? The "male" space for negotiating self-realization in Sami society has become very narrow. Society cannot offer them anything else within this narrow space than traditional women's roles. The changes apply to generations as well as to genders. Men are now largely left out because masculinity is attached very narrowly to a particular expression of traditional activities and lifestyles. Thus, it is not just *between* men and women where these growing differences become apparent, but also within the genders, within groups of women and men. This can be conceptualized in the same way as class differences.

In one respect, the division between men and women within the Sami parliaments in those countries where Sami reside symbolizes the new gender divisions in Sami society as a whole. In the Sami Parliament in Norway, in the electoral period 2001–05, seven of the thirty-nine representatives were women, in other words 12 percent. In the elections in 2005 this was dramatically changed due to a campaign to vote for women. Nowadays 52 percent of the members are women. This is the highest rate of female political participation in the whole world! In Finland 21 percent are women, and in Sweden under one third of the popularly elected representatives are women. In administration, however, the trend is the opposite, where there is a significant overrepresentation of female employees, over 70 percent. This reflects a transfer of the traditional division of labour to modern society. Women are also active in industry and business at the local level, particularly in relation to culture and the raising of children and youth (Eikjok, Keskitalo and Pettersen: 2002). Their activity and experiences are not reflected in the daily running of the Sami Parliament, as women organize everyday aspects of life but lack political power. Men dominate the visible, popularly elected institutions and occupy the vast majority of the formal positions within it. This gender imbalance can be found within the political organizations of many other Indigenous peoples throughout the Arctic (Finland 2002: 126–76).

## GENDER IN INDIGENOUS SOCIETY

Let us turn back to the two different views of reality presented in the introduction. The male Indigenous leader attempted to establish a common and mutual understanding about gender relations and what "man" and "woman" mean today in Arctic Indigenous societies. The other view was presented by an Indigenous woman from East Siberia who noted that young women in many Indigenous communities are leaving their own societies and leaving the men behind. What notions of reality are these views based upon? I argue that the former roots itself in ideal notions of Indigenous society, while the latter reflects contemporary reality. Both views, however, present portions of a larger whole. The male Indigenous leader presented a picture of equality and harmony between the sexes, in contrast to the gender confusion and contestation in "the West." It reminds me of the 1970s in Samiland. The over-riding question at that time was whether Sami women were oppressed. The Sami movement claimed that Sami society was different from the larger Norwegian society, as equality between men and women has always existed. It also claimed that Sami women are strong and Sami women have power. This was an idealization of Sami society and Sami women in comparison to the "western" woman. In many ways Sami women were being used as a positive symbol for the difference between Sami and Norwegian culture.

"Women are valued as real human beings, making their contribution as real men do…. Gender equality issues have to be understood from a uniquely Arctic perspective, different from the typical power imbalance between males and females. Insisting on introducing southern styles of equity issues to the Arctic peoples will only reinforce colonial attitudes" (Williamson 2004). These statements articulate, in my view, a common theme found amongst both Indigenous leaders and the Sami movement, in that they perpetuate an ideal notion of what gender means and how gender relations manifest themselves in Arctic Indigenous communities. These expressions of gender in Indigenous societies are more preoccupied with differentiating Indigenous peoples from "the other" or "the western" than in actually dealing with what gender really means *within* Indigenous communities. Gender, "woman" and "man," are essentialized, or in other words, are concepts that are treated as given and unchangeable. Society and culture in the Arctic are portrayed as static, something to preserve. However, Indigenous societies of late modernity consist of a multitude of realities, within which gender produces additional complexities.

Indigenous peoples are not one homogenous group; they have significant cultural and societal differences, not least amongst Arctic societies. The rapid changes of modernity complicate this even further. I have shown some of the diverse gender identities that exist in Sami society. It is disturbing, therefore, that prominent Indigenous leaders choose to define Indigenous peoples and culture in a static and dogmatic manner. They represent the power that defines how Indigenous society is to be understood, including that such an understanding is associated with traditional ways of life. This is dangerous as, with such a definition, it becomes quite easy to exclude modern Indigenous people who no longer embrace traditional lifestyles. These spokeswomen and men exclude significantly large groups within the Indigenous world.

## FEMINISM AND INDIGENOUS PEOPLES

The women's movement and equal opportunity discourse have been present in the Sami community for thirty years. We initially took part, for a number of years, in the Sami ethno-political movement before we took up the fight for Sami women. The women's movement, which began in the West, was established in the 1970s and at that time rooted itself within the claim that all women were oppressed by men. The fight for equal opportunity and for equality for women were two sides of the same coin. Feminism, for its part, is an ideology not only connected to politics and policy but also to a theoretical foundation for analysis connected to science. Basic questions feminism raises include: How and to which degree are women oppressed and discriminated against? How is this oppression expressed? How can it be changed and eliminated? What roles shall women have in society and which relationships do we want to see between women and men? What are the differences and similarities between women and men?

The discourse of equal opportunity revolves around women's roles, and making both women and their rights visible. The ideology behind equal opportunity assumes equality between the genders, with the goal of eradicating unequal differences. At the same time, particularly within Indigenous societies, there exist deep rooted perceptions that there are in fact differences between genders. In Sami society we have traditional tools that represent the differences between masculine and feminine. The Sami language contains an abundance of nature concepts wherein gender differences are expressed, illustrating that men and women use nature in different ways. The feminist cause has been a difficult topic in Sami society, because introducing the women's movement in an Indigenous context creates animosity. It is not seen as proper to criticize "one's own" when they are already oppressed.

It has often been postulated that Indigenous women not only have to face oppression by dominant cultures, but that they face oppression from traditional and patriarchal practices in their own culture. This position is referred to by some as a double oppression:

> We were unpopular among our Sami brothers for introducing the women's cause into the struggle for our people's rights. We were unpopular among our fellow sisters in the wider community for bringing in our ethnic and culture identity as women. Our brothers ridiculed us because gender was irrelevant for them; our Nordic sisters rebuked and lectured us because the minority and Indigenous question was irrelevant for them. (Eikjok 2000: 18)

In contrast to the discourse of equal opportunity, which attempts to eradicate any differences between the genders, the position of "difference feminism" attempts to make the differences visible and express the "female difference" without sacrificing the "male difference" (Irigaray 1993; Birkeland 2002). I will employ difference feminism here, using the insights of the French feminist, philosopher and psychiatrist Luce Irigaray, as well as ecofeminism, to analyze the complexities and paradoxes of gender in Indigenous society today. Ecofeminists have shown that the discourse of nature itself is gendered and that nature has been given feminine attributes. Ecofeminists have also pointed to connections between the oppression of nature and the oppression of women, including the connections between violence against women and violence against nature (Merchant 1980; Plumwood 1993; Birkeland 1998, 2000, 2002).

Culture has been associated with the masculine and the European worldview. Non-European societies have been generically thought of as closer to nature, therefore feminine, and inferior to culture. The question is whether *both Sami women and men* can be said to be marginalized in the discourses on the use and management of Sami natural resources, but in *different ways*.

115

Women's particular and different knowledge and practices are not touched upon in the Sami legal commission's recommendations (Government of Norway 1997: 4), in the articulation of Sami customs (Government of Norway 2001: 34), nor in central publications pertaining to Sami customary law or legal practice (Svensson 1999). In this context, we may view existing notions of economy, law and justice as constructed categories resulting from a masculinist or androcentric worldview. This worldview is also referred to as the Law of the Father (see Irigaray 1993). An example of this, mentioned earlier, is the masculinist Norwegian reindeer management regime, which arrogated rights to the male, in practices that were strange to Sami custom and way of life.

When Sami society became integrated within the dominant society, it changed from one where women held a relatively strong position to one where the European masculine rationality prevailed. The technical, instrumental rationality represented by European masculinity held a higher status than the rationality of care, which was feminine and which had previously been part of Sami society. This explains why and how Sami women lost their position in relation to business practices and why Sami female knowledge lost its status. According to Waring (1988), this has also been the case in many other Indigenous communities.

In the discourse on women's oppression within Indigenous society it is often claimed that colonization is alone the cause of Indigenous women's oppression. In my view, this is a simplistic and superficial explanation and a repudiation of responsibility. The colonization of Indigenous societies strengthened the original patriarchal structures and, in introducing modern, masculine power, over-rode any non-patriarchal elements within Indigenous society.

According to Irigaray, in patriarchal societies, power becomes a masculine and phallic phenomenon. I argue that phallocratic power, masculinism[3] and masculine models (practices rooted in masculinism) are created by an alliance between colonial and Indigenous traditional and modern patriarchy These factors render the voices and realities of Indigenous women invisible. To mobilize phallocratic power, symbols of the feminine and feminine practices must be rejected and ridiculed.[4] Traditional masculinity in Indigenous societies is restricted because of the lost status of traditional industries. Modern Indigenous masculinity has limited room to manoeuvre. In reconstructing Indigenous masculinity, some have attempted to constrain women's power, restricting it to a narrow set of maternal and cultural roles.

Irigaray shows how women, through the role of mother, function as an underlying symbol for social order. Thus women take on the symbolic role as the *cultural mother of all* (Eikjok 2000). In many Indigenous societies women represent social order and are assigned responsibility to hold the society together. This becomes particularly acute when society undergoes profound changes. Traditional values crumble and disintegrate, networks are cut and gender roles change. Within a number of Indigenous communities, women take responsibility for holding the values and society together when masculinity loses ground.[5]

This does not necessarily change the power structures and relations between the sexes. When women are described as more caring and responsible than men, they are also conceptualized as closer to nature than men. When society values care and responsibility less than technical-instrumental rationality, it demonstrates a hierarchical organization of culture over nature. Such descriptions of Indigenous women articulate a patriarchal understanding of women's place in society. In combination with a static cultural understanding, the ideological presentation of the Indigenous woman is evidence of patriarchy (as a western phenomenon). This, then, contributes to the resistance and inability of some Indigenous communities to address social change.

## MOTHER EARTH IDEOLOGY AND THE NOTION OF THE FEMININE

A number of sources claim that Sami society was in fact traditionally matriarchal. No one, however, can describe such a society. The critique against theories of matriarchy is that a matriarchy cannot be the opposite of patriarchy since there have not been the same power dynamics as in patriarchy. Among many Indigenous peoples there is the notion of "the Mothers,"[6] Mother Earth or the feminine power (Kuoljok 1998). In Sami, earth is *"eana"* and mother is *"eadni."* There is a connection here, where the earth of old symbolized the motherly. Femininity had symbolic status and meant growth, fertility, life-giving and nourishing. In Sami visions of the world, the animals and all that live have their own *"mattaráhkku,"* Indigenous mother. There are, however, both feminine and masculine powers in nature, as well as notions of invisible female powers that functioned as helpers for many of life's situations. Amongst a number of Arctic Indigenous peoples, fire was associated with the feminine, and only women could touch fire. *Luondu* means nature in Sami but cannot be considered the equivalent of the European meaning of nature (Eikjok 1992). *Luondu* has an additional spiritual meaning, since one can speak of humans, relatives, places, animals and other living beings as having their own *luondu*. There are notions about which particular places in the landscape have a great deal of soul, and rules and rituals determine how one is to behave when one comes to such places. It is possible to claim that knowledge about human *luondu* means an association with the feminine in Sami culture. It is important to be aware that these symbolic constructions do not refer to individuals in everyday society. In the ethnographic literature these feminine powers are described by non-Sami as "female goddesses." In the Sami view it is very strange to refer to these mothers as goddesses, since goddess notions are connected to religion. Sami worldviews and religion are two very different things.

In parts of the Indigenous women's movement today one can find an ideological manipulation of the Mother Earth concept. At the United Nation's conference on women in Beijing in 1995, Winona la Duke delivered one of the main opening speeches on behalf of Indigenous women. Her message was that we, the Indigenous people, have Mother Earth, and we therefore do not need to attach ourselves to the woman's cause, which is western. She connected Mother Earth to the uterus. My own interpretation of what she said was that the uterus plays a central role in being an Indigenous woman, as it gives us the ability to give birth to Indigenous children. I would characterize this as "uterus feminism" — very reactionary!

"We Indigenous peoples have Mother Earth, we do not need to attach ourselves to the gender question. We know what we are. We know what are woman and man." This was stated by a distinguished Indigenous woman representative at an international conference not too long ago. Images of the Indigenous society as matriarchal, "mother-goddess," "the Mothers" and Mother Earth live side by side with colonial and patriarchal structures. I question whether there might be a connection between the Law of the Father and the Mother Earth ideology.

My contention is that the traditional and pre-Christian notion of "the Mothers" in Indigenous society deals with the realization of "mother's power." In Sami and other Indigenous societies, this is connected to the relatively strong position women had until a few decades ago. Where is the Mother Earth ideology in all of this? It is a reaction against colonization and a defence of Indigenous culture. We see once again that Indigenous women are using this imagery to establish a difference between Indigenous-ness and western-ness, and to reduce both Indigeniety and gender to simple categories. However, there are so many variations of gender categories in Indigenous society today that these simplistic notions of gender cannot function given the challenges we live with. "The Mothers" of Indigenous worldviews are being taken out of their original context and placed in the global political context of today in a show of resistance against "the western." The problem is that the definition of woman becomes narrow and loses any potential for change. This is not useful or functional for modern Indigenous women.

## A NEW RELATIONSHIP BETWEEN THE FEMININE AND MASCULINE

Ecofeminism greatly contributes to the analysis of the politicization of nature, taking as a starting point that discourses on both nature and women are connected to basic structures of power, including patriarchal power, and to the exercise of power in the production of knowledge. The alliance between colonial and Indigenous peoples and modern patriarchy has to be challenged.

It has contributed to the introduction of a socio-cultural, economic and political system that is destructive to humans and nature in Indigenous society. The scientific and liberal rationality of western modernity has marginalized the feminine (or feminist) and the Indigenous rationality of care, both for the earth and for all its creatures. This new rationality contributes to violence against nature and women, and oppresses feminine knowledge and resources in Indigenous communities.

Sami women's relatively autonomous status has been taken from them. If we continue to cooperate with patriarchy, the inequality in relations of power will never change. Yet, I am critical of equal opportunity feminism's perspective on equal rights for women and men, because that perspective is blind to meaningful gendered differences. Indigenous women must focus on the right to difference, both in relation to Indigenous men and to non-Indigenous women. The point is not to merely replace the male view or masculinist knowledge with a woman's view, but instead, to create knowledge that positively addresses both Indigenous men's and women's experiences, perspectives, forms of understanding and practices.

Mother power as a form of creation is a metaphor that extends itself well beyond the experiences of physical pregnancy, birth, breastfeeding and care for children. Mother's power is, for Irigaray, a creative, motherly dimension of love, desire, language, art, policy, religion, truth and knowledge. The spotlight needs to be focused upon Indigenous women's experience, ways of understanding and perspectives to encourage new knowledge about difference and change in Indigenous society. We must stop reproducing structures that are based upon masculine dominance and prevailing ideological and trade methods.

It is possible to see the Sami woman as the care provider of the social integration in Sami society. We must focus upon the rationality of care, which does still exist in Indigenous societies and amongst Indigenous women, and raise its status. We must begin to raise boys so that they integrate "mother as the first place" and value the rationality of care. Traditional women's roles or gender expectations should not create limitations for us. The female represents a powerful, life-giving and creative source for care, for humans, place and nature.

Irigaray challenges understandings of power as something necessary and given. Power as a phenomenon is not natural or predetermined but rather is cultural. Irigaray's utopia is a society where power assumes recognition of both genders' differences. In such a society gender differences are recognized as relevant, and human rights respect men's and women's differences.

In Sami society and other Indigenous societies where women have enjoyed a relatively strong position, we ought to take back this position on our own terms, without comparing ourselves to masculine structures and culture,

European male culture or the dominant culture's women. It is necessary to move away from any essentialization of culture and gender, and de- and reconstruct relations between nature, culture and gender. Ecofeminists claim that solutions to the environmental crisis are contingent upon feminist perspectives. Inspiration can be found in an ecologically oriented feminism, attentive to differences, which criticizes a gender-neutral concept of nature and reconstructs a special connection between women and nature that allows for culturally specific meanings. It is important to make visible gender's relationship to both nature and culture and to avoid approaches that prioritize culture over nature.

I see ecofeminist theory as relevant and useful in the empowerment of Sami women, especially by recognizing their relationship to landscape, to the development of ethno-ecological knowledge, and in regards to particular similarities and differences in traditional knowledge across gender and ethnic borders. In other words, it is necessary to establish new values that incorporate gender difference at all levels of society, both in private as well as public life. Irigaray argues both for legal rights that specifically address both genders, as well as for including the feminine in spiritual and symbolic life. Liberation for Indigenous women must avoid seeking equal footing with men but instead focus on the right to be different from men.

Women need to create their own space in society. Masculinism dominates the public domain today. Parts of Indigenous society are resistant to gender role and political change. Yet, the future of Sami societies may benefit from an analytical gender perspective that will strengthen Sami culture and social life rather than threaten it. Self-determination in Indigenous societies means that all components of the community must be represented in the creation of the community, and gender must be recognized as a central dimension in this.

## CONCLUSION

Colonialism and subsequent cultural impositions on Sami society have ensured that formal legal rights to industry and economic activity are now connected to men. The alliance between colonial patriarchy and patriarchal structures in Indigenous society contributed to the weakening of Indigenous women's position and knowledge. Contemporary views on change and on gender role difference in Indigenous societies are shaped by masculinist and colonial ideologies about gender and about colonized people.

Scientific and liberal rationality contributed to the marginalization of the Indigenous and feminine rationality of care. This has lead to violence against humans, women and nature. In our late-modern time we find a variety of gender identities in Indigenous society. Women demonstrate a flexibility and capacity to adjust to the modern. Masculinism is challenged by new critiques, even while it remains culturally dominant. In many contexts men are now becoming the losers. This is forcing women towards a role of the "mother of all." At the same time, women's experience and knowledge is not adequately reflected and respected in new systems, where men dominate. Society still relies upon masculinist solutions and models.

The discourse of gender is largely absent in Indigenous societies. There is a tendency to define Indigenous society as static, thus idealizing Indigenous gender relations. The gender perspective represents a central key to understanding cultural conflicts, societal changes and diversity, as well as equality and difference in our society. We must stop reproducing structures that build upon masculine dominance. Liberation for Indigenous women does not mean equality with men, but the right to be different. The spotlight needs to be focused upon Indigenous women's experiences, ways of understanding and perspectives to encourage new knowledge on difference and change in Indigenous society.

## NOTES

1.   The Sami live in northern Europe spread across four countries: Norway, Sweden, Finland and Russia. Sápmi means Sami homeland.
2.   *Joik*, pronounced "yoik," is a Sami form of music and song.
3.   By masculinism I mean those ways of understanding that claim to speak for everyone, but which in reality only take male experiences, positions and interests into consideration.
4.   Vigdis Stordahl (2000) says, "In the Samediggi the men need to put down their newspapers and look up when women address the Assembly, and stop meeting women's contributions with moody silence or undisguised sarcasm. They have to understand that women — particularly the younger generation — are not impressed by sexist male commentaries."
5.   This became clear after a number of presentations at the Arctic Council conference, Taking Wing: Conference on Gender Equality and Women in the Arctic, 3–6 Aug. 2002, Finland.
6.   According to Maria Eidlitz Kuoljok (s. 132) the movement makes use of "the mothers" as Arctic Indigenous peoples have had many concepts based on feminine power, such as Mother Sun, Mother Fire, Mother Water.

## REFERENCES

Birkeland, Inger J. 1998. "Nature and 'the Cultural Turn' in Human Geography." *Norwegian Journal of Geography* 52.

_____. 2000. "Mothers' Power." In Luce Irigaray, Iver B. Neumann and Inger-Johanne Sand (eds.), *Power's Strategies*. Oslo: Pax.

_____. 2002. *Stories from the North. Travel as place-making in the context of modern holiday-travel to the North Cape, Norway*. Report 2/2002. Department of Sociology and Human Geography, University of Oslo.

Eikjok, Jorunn. 1989. "Women and Men between Two Worlds: Sami Female and

Male Identities in Change." Masters thesis in Sami studies/ethnic relations. Tromsø: University of Tromsø.

_____. 1991. "Sami Women's Knowledge on Nature and People." In FOKUS (Forum for women and development questions). Volume 2. Oslo, Norway

_____. 1992. *Luondu is not the same as nature: Conflict between two rationalities in the Finnmark school.* Report. Kautokeino: Norwegian Sami Institute.

_____. 1992. "Environment and Sustainable Society from a Sami Perspective." Unpublished paper. Kautokeino: Norwegian Sami Institute.

_____. 2000. "Indigenous Women in the North: The Struggle for Rights and Feminism." *Indigenous Affairs* 3.

_____. 2004. "Gender in Sápmi — Sociocultural Transformations and New Challenges." *Indigenous Affairs* 1–2.

Eikjok, Jorunn, and Asbjørg Fyhn. 1990. "North Norway — Yesterday, Today and Tomorrow." *Nordlys* 19 (September).

Eikjok, Jorunn, Aili Keskitalo and Torunn Pettersen. 2002. "Do they not want to? Or do they not get the chance? An investigation into low representation of women in the Sami Parliament in Norway." Sami Parliament: Karasjok, Norway.

Finland, Government of. 2002. *Taking Wing: Conference on Gender Equality and Women in the Arctic.* Report from Ministry of Social Affairs and Health, Helsinki. August 3–6.

Gilligan, Carol. 1982. *In a Different Voice.* London: Harvard University Press.

Government of Sweden. 2001. *A New Political View on Reindeer Management.* Swedish Government Official Report (SOU). Stockholm: Prime Ministers Office.

Government of Norway. 1997, 2001. Norwegian Government Official Report (NOU). Oslo: Prime Ministers Office.

Gullestad, Marianne. 1998. *Everyday Life Philosophers: Modernity, Morality and Autobiography in Norway.* Oslo: Universitetsforlaget.

Haraway, Donna. 1991. *Simians, Cyborgs and Women: The Reinvention of Nature.* New York: Routledge.

Irigaray, Luce. 1993. *An Ethics of Sexual Difference.* London: Athlone Press.

Kailo, Kaarina. 2002. "From the Virile Discourse to Fertile Concourses: Ecofeminism and Northern Women." Paper presented at the conference Taking Wing: Conference on Gender Equality and Women in the Arctic, August 3–6, Finland.

Kuoljok, Maria Eidlitz. 1998. *Moder Jord hos arktiske folk* (translated from Swedish: Mother earth, in the concepts of Indigenous Peoples in the Arctic). Hannerzt: Stockholm, Sweden.

Merchant, Carolyn. 1980. *The Death of Nature.* London: Wildhood House.

Municipal and Regional Department. 1996–97. Parliamentary statement on Norwegian Sami policy. (st.meld) no. 41.

Myrhaug, May Lisbeth. 1997. *In the Mother Goddess's Footprints.* Oslo: Pax.

Nystad, Inger Marie Kristine. 2000. *Man between Myth and Modernity. Education and Mobility of Boys in Guovdageaidnu.* University of Tromsø, Department of Education. Davvi Girji: Karasjok, Sweden.

Paine, Robert. 1957. "Coast Lapp Society: A Study of Neighbourhood in Revsbotn Fjord." Tromsø Museum.

_____. 1982. *Dam a River, Damn a People.* International Working Group on Indigenous

Affairs (IWGIA) document no. 45. Copenhagen.

Plumwood, Val. 1993. *Feminism and the Mastery of Nature*. London: Routledge.

Sami Parliamentary Council. 2001. "Statement of Agreement." Presented to the Sami Parliament October 16.

Stordahl, Vigdis. 1996. *Sami in the Modern world*. Karasjok: Davvi Girjji.

_____. 2002. Keynote Speech. "The Sami Parliament in Norway: Limited Access for Women?" At the conference Taking Wing, Conference on Gender Equality and Women in the Arctic, Arctic Council, Finland, August 3–6.

Stordahl, Vigdis og Liv Østmo (ed.). 1979. "Sami Women's Situation in Previous Times and Nowadays." Seminar report, Norwegian Sami Association, Karasjok, Norway.

Svensson, Tom (ed.). 1999. "On Customary Law and Saami Rights Process in Norway." Tromsø, Norway: Centre for Sami Studies, University of Tromsø.

Thuen, Trond. 1995. *Quest for Equity: Norway and the Saami Challenge*. St. John's: OUT Books, Memorial University of Newfoundland.

Waring, Marilyn. 1988. *If Women Counted*. New York: Harper San Francisco.

Williamson, Karla Jessen. 2004. Arctic Council Human Development Report, *Gender Issues s.188*. Reykjavik, Iceland.

Chapter Seven

# PRACTISING INDIGENOUS FEMINISM
## Resistance to Imperialism

### Makere Stewart-Harawira

The writing of this chapter has challenged me in a number of ways, not the least of which has been to define for myself my own view of Indigenous feminism. The central question of this book is whether or not Indigenous feminism is a legitimate position. And if so, the corollary questions are: What represents an Indigenous feminist? What are they? What do they look like? Thus the first challenge for me has been to reflect on my own positionality in relation to Indigenous feminism.

I preface this discussion with a brief explanation of terms. In this chapter I have adopted the term "Indigenous" rather than "Aboriginal" because, while the term "Aboriginal" is applied to all Indigenous peoples, in the context of North America it is most commonly used to refer to First Nations, Métis and Inuit, all of whom make up the Indigenous peoples of North America. I am an Indigenous person from Aotearoa/New Zealand. Although we would argue that we are far from homogenous as people, the generic term most commonly applied to us since contact is Maori.[1] I am also of northern Scots descent. Hence I approach this chapter conscious of my dual heritage, yet positioning myself as neither hybrid nor of multiple subjectivities. I am simply both. Both descent lines were once strongly matriarchal. Neither can be described thusly today. Historical forms of imperialism and colonialism have contributed to the rewriting of Indigenous histories and the re-gendering of our societies.

Most generally today, I do not consciously engage in writing or speaking from a feminist position. This is not due to any deliberate decision. I simply am what I am — Indigenous woman, activist, grandmother. In earlier years my occasional foray into what some might conceive as a Maori feminist stance was met with derision from my late husband, who claimed that such a position merely demonstrated my lack of "Maoriness." This echoes a debate within Maori society whose roots begin in the re-inscribing of gender roles within Maori society by white anthropologists and historians and which has continued to disrupt the fabric of Maori society across many tribes and communities. Despite the evidence that Maori women had powerful leadership roles in pre-contact Maori society (c.f. Mikaere 1999; Pere 1994; Yates-Smith

1998), in today's post-colonial society (if today can be said to be post-colonial), the historical role of Maori women is frequently misinterpreted to have been secondary to that of males, a point that is further taken up elsewhere in this chapter.

The convictions that I hold are unquestionably shaped by my historical consciousness. Central to this chapter and to my stance with regard to Indigenous feminism is my conviction that both the project of decolonization and that of human survival and, ultimately, peace for a world hovering on the brink of self-destruction require, at the very least, the return of the feminine principle and, in the process, right balance and the compassionate mind to the centre of our political ontologies. An essentialist position? I hardly think so, as I argue later.

As the title suggests, I have chosen to situate this chapter within the complexities of the new forms of imperialism that characterize a world seemingly gone mad and the particular importance of Indigenous women in this situation. My thesis here is twofold: first, that Indigenous women have a vital role to play in the realization of alternative models of "being in the world" and, second, that this represent a particularly poignant paradox. On the one hand, Indigenous women are among the most deeply marginalized groups in the world, most especially in western countries, where, relative to other groups, they are over-represented in the worst social indices of poverty, health, unemployment and, as Amnesty International's (2004) report regarding Aboriginal women in Canada highlights, homicide. Yet by virtue of their historical role in pre-colonial Indigenous societies, large numbers of which were, as Paula Gunn Allen (1986) points out, gynocentric, through their ability to reconcile the political and the spiritual, Indigenous women have the power to facilitate a sea-change in the political ontologies of governance.

The reconciliation between the political and the spiritual is the primary task in the development of new and sustainable ways of compassionate co-existence on this planet. The political and the spiritual are, as Linda Hogan (cited in Allen 1986: 169) wrote, "the two wings of one bird and that bird is the knowledge of the interconnectedness of everything." In locating myself in the tensions that this discussion invokes for me at a personal level, I acknowledge the deeply political nature of the act of writing, as the discussion on contemporary imperialism that follows, bears out. The important point that these discussions preface is the urgency of the need for a new political ontology of governance and spiritually grounded, feminist-centred political ethics as one critical response.

## WRITING AS POLITICS

Like many other Indigenous academic women, my writing is the primary vehicle for my own participation in the global struggle to find a positive way forward out of the global morass of despair and frustration, and to bring to birth a politics of hope that has specific and particularistic relevance within a broad global ontology of being. The contradictions inherent in this positioning are obvious. One of the issues it brings into focus is the pitfall of essentialism and universalism. Another is the question of how I mediate the complexities of the self that I bring to my writing?

T. Minh-ha Trinh (1989) well articulates the struggle by feminist critics to bring reflexivity to bear upon the mode of writing and speaking, so that it is no longer possible to write or speak unthinkingly without being aware of the production of subjectivities that accompanies such activities. Trinh refers to the "triple bind" of women writers of colour, which is that no matter what position she takes, she will eventually be "made to feel she must choose from among three conflicting loyalties. Writer of color? Woman writer? Or woman of color?" (1989: 3). Maori women academics also engage the dilemma of as whom do we write, and for whom? (c.f. L.T. Smith 1992; Johnston and Pihama 1994). For Maori, the act of "writing back" is one of many important means for the recentring of Maori ways of being and knowing as central. Thus writing as a "Maori woman academic" becomes simultaneously an act of resistance and reclamation.

My own academic work is underpinned by what Gadamer (1998: 28) calls an "historically effective consciousness," a consciousness of the way that my own historical understandings and traditions, combined with particular sets of belief systems and values, shape both my interactions with the world and with others, and my interpretations. My understandings of events both past and present are always subject to my own conditionality. In my case, I write also as the daughter of a diasporic and ardently nationalist Scotsman with Highland Celtic roots. I come from two historical traditions in which women were both knowledge holders and decision-makers. Hence my understandings and interpretations of the past, present and future are tempered by an intentional *re*-membering, *re*-claiming, *re*-articulating which emerges from the political and cultural circumstance of being and knowing as a Waitaha woman academic who is also Celtic Scot, with a background of Maori activism, one who is simultaneously mother and grandmother and, above all, a daughter of *Papa-tua-nuku* (Mother Earth).

Such a politics of course carries its own risk. As Trinh (1989: 21) states, "writing constantly refers to writing and no writing can ever claim to be 'free' of other writings." One of my objectives in writing *The New Imperial Order* (2005) was to argue that traditional Indigenous ontological principles provide a framework and context for the development of a socio/politico/economic ontology of the possible, while at the same time endeavouring to avoid the pitfalls of essentialism and a romanticisation of the past, which presents Indigenous peoples as the non-violent, helpless victims of the marauding

West. As Trinh asks, "How do you inscribe difference without bursting into a series of euphoric narcissist accents of yourself and your own kind? Without indulging in a marketable romanticism or a naïve whining about your own condition?" — something I have struggled, I fear unsuccessfully, to avoid in my own writing. "Between the twin chasms of navel-gazing and navel-erasing," she pointedly remarks, "the ground is narrow and slippery. None of us can pride ourselves on being sure-footed there" (21).

Nevertheless, this chapter is written from the perspective of one Indigenous woman's endeavour to bear witness against the wanton violence that marks humanity's headlong slide into the abyss of self-destruction in the twenty-first century, and to call for a new model for being in the world, a political ontology grounded in spirit. And because it is my privilege to be the grandmother of six wonderful people, I further use this space to call for the voice of the grandmothers to be powerfully raised against systems of being that are founded in greed, consumption and corruption as they impel our world yet further into the abyss of genocide and destruction, and to demonstrate in its place a political ontology of compassion, love and spirit as the only possible remedy, the only way forward. This is, I claim, the most urgent decolonization project today.

At this point, I want to digress momentarily to address the accusations of essentialism that will undoubtedly be levelled at my arguments, in particular those based on a post-structuralist approach to feminism. Post-modernist and post-structuralist arguments are frequently invoked, most notably by white Anglo-American feminists, as justifications of the claim that the task of debunking justifications for women's oppression through her linking with nature is undermined by representations that link women and nature. These linkings are seen as functioning, to quote Alaimo (1997), to foreclose "the possibilities for agency" [by women] by "concealing the signification of 'woman.'" Alaimo draws here on Judith Butler's argument that the "immobilized," "paralyzed" referent of the category "woman" hampers feminist agency, and the "constant rifting" over the term "woman" is itself the "ungrounded ground of feminist theory" (Butler 1992, cited in Alaimo 1997).

I am bothered by post-modern, post-structuralist, post-colonial arguments of this nature. Here the category of "female" is deconstructed to the point where there are no longer categories of race, class and ethnicity but a nebulous state in which, as Grande (2004) suggests, the domain of the individual has superseded the arena of political struggle. In this arena of post-everything feminism, "woman" and "feminist" exist as endlessly abstract potentialities that encompasses the oppressed as well as the oppressor, so that there is no longer a space for the oppressed. I wonder about the effect of such approaches. If the goal of feminist politics is "to make visible the complexities of identity that have been made invisible by dominant discourses deeply invested in a knowable subject" (Butler, cited in Grande, 2004: 136), then it seems to me that these formulations represent yet another invisibilizing of the specific experiences of Indigenous women within the feminist democratic project.

In response to post-structuralist projects that ignore and thus conceal the effects of power and economics and instead inscribe difference as the new totalizing discourse, Third World feminist Eisenstein (2004: 183) writes, "Feminisms, especially of the West in the U.S., must be ready to speak against the cultural and economic domination of their home country that creates such impossible pain and sadness to people at home, as well as elsewhere." Eisenstein calls for a radicalization of feminism in which differences are neither "silenced in some hierarchically privileged order... or set up oppositionally against each other" (187). An inclusive feminism is one that not only recognizes difference but seeks to disrupt the privileging impact of the unequal structures of power.

While I concur with the view that deeply embedded discourses of the inter-linking of Woman and Nature have frequently invoked both as passive victim I am concerned about the effects of Indigenous delinking of these categories. The delinking of Indigenous from Nature, and by definition also the land, may undercut the arguments on which Indigenous peoples the world over base their claims to self-determination, that of place in relationship to the land. This relationship is one of the cornerstones by which peoples are identified as Indigenous. In response to accusations that the linking of land and women functions to re-inscribe Indigenous women as passive and subordinate, I argue that this evidences the ongoing inscribing of colonial interpretations onto Indigenous societies.

Unlike the societies of the colonizing countries, women and land were held in the highest regard in Indigenous societies. It is the case that some traditional Indigenous languages contain many textual keys that ascribe the feminine to the earth. One such key within Maori language is the term "Papatuanuku," Earth Mother. Another is "*whenua*," which means both land and placenta. There are multiple well-known references to land as the sustainer and provider of life. "*Ko te ukaipo, te whenua. Ko te whenua, te ukaipo*" — literally, "the earth is my breastmilk" — is interpreted as "the land is my nourisher and sustainer."

By no means do such sayings signify Maori women as historically passive or subordinate. For many Maori women, and I include here Rangimarie Te Uriki Rose Pere, Sana Murray and Del Wihongi as representative of strong, contemporary Maori women leaders and activists, our link to Papatuanuku, Earth Mother, is a source of our strength. This linking far from implies a weak-kneed, milly-molly-mandy view of the nature and role of Maori women as passive. On the contrary, despite the colonizing mythologies of early anthropologists and historians and in contradiction to oft-repeated arguments promulgated today primarily by Maori men, Maori women in at least some parts of Aotearoa/New Zealand fought alongside the men and paddled the war canoes. They were warriors and they were healers. They were spiritual leaders and political leaders. They were advisers and they were politicians.

The damaging effect of colonization on Maori women, which is most strongly evidenced in the exclusion of Maori women from the treaty settlement process and today's forms of tribal governance, is the basis for a treaty claim lodged with the Waitangi Tribunal in 1993.[2] This claim, led by a group of dynamic Maori women activists, asserts the powerful leadership role of Maori women in pre-contact societies while seeking redress from the Crown (Henare 1994). The exclusion of Maori women from the treaty settlement process gained further momentum in the 1980s, when the shift to a neoliberal treaty settlement process in response to the challenge to the state's privatization agenda by senior Maori males saw the emergence of a new breed of Maori male entrepreneurs, two of whom were awarded knighthoods for their negotiating acumen (Seuffert 2002). In her analysis of the silencing of Maori women, Seuffert points out that this process mirrored the reconstruction of the national identity from one of a caring community to the highly individualist, self-sufficient competitor in the global marketplace. These new Maori male entrepreneurs represented the new "civilized" Maori, one who was thoroughly incorporated into the global economy.

Almost without exception, Maori women have remained on the margins. In the context of corporatized post-settlement deals and the global economic imperative of imperialism, the on-going sale of Maori land (some of which is leased back) by some male-dominated corporate tribal trust boards is an impelling reason for arguing that the decolonizing of Maori society requires, at the very least, a recognition of and return to the role and function of Maori women within political and spiritual leadership. Yet this claim is not likely to have an easy passage. I turn here to the main context for this discussion, the imperative for responding to the new forms of global imperialism.

## IMPERIALIST TERRORISM IN OUR TIME

There is no longer any denial of the fact that today we are witnessing a new configuration of imperialism that has global ambitions. In the *New Imperial Order* I identified two competing and parallel conceptualizations of empire in the literature, one seen in senior state diplomat Robert Cooper's identification of the European Community as a postmodern empire; the other seen most strongly in the activities of the neoconservative cabal currently dominating the George Bush Junior administration of the U.S. Government. In the case of Cooper, his solution to what he refers to as a global crisis precipitated by the harbouring of agents of terror in "premodern" or "barbaric" states is "postmodern imperialism," represented by what he calls a "new configuration of states" (1998: 42). Accordingly, for Cooper the European Union (EU) is "the most developed example of a postmodern system," its twin principles being transnational cooperation and openness pertaining largely to issues of order and security (10–18). In this "more highly developed" form of state, the defence of regional borders against the nationalisms of "less developed" states is paramount. Its chief characteristics are mutual interference in traditionally domestic affairs coupled with mutual surveillance; the breaking down of the distinction between domestic and foreign affairs; the growing irrelevance of borders; and the rejection of force for dispute-solving. In stark contrast to the concept of collective rights, which characterize Indigenous peoples' political, social and economic formations and aspirations, the putative end-product of this process was given as "the freedom of the individual; first protected by the state and later protected from the state" (2003: 76).

Since the conclusion of that writing, a second imperialist state model with similar hallmarks has emerged. It is identifiable in the Council for Foreign Relation's (CFR) proposal for a North American Community of which the new Security and Prosperity Partnership of North America (SPP), publicly announced through the media in March 2005, is the precursor. The catchwords for this new postmodern state endeavour are again security and economic prosperity. The SPP international framework for trilateral and bilateral cooperation between Canada, the U.S. and Mexico is designed to strengthen North American competitiveness, particularly in the face of increasing economic competition from China, India and the EU. The twin agendas of national security and economic prosperity are supported by three key principles: "improved security from external threats to North America; strengthened internal measures; and bolstered economic growth for the region as a whole, particularly in the face of increased global competition" (Ackleson and Kastner 2005). The CFR, however, has a wider-reaching agenda, that of establishing a North American Community by 2010. Recommendations for achieving this include: a common security perimeter; a dispute tribunal; a review of previously excluded sectors of NAFTA; a North American energy strategy; the restructure and reform of Mexico's public finances; the full development of Mexico's energy resources and a North American inter-parliamentary group (Council for Foreign Relations 2005). The inherent characteristic is capitalism's twin logics of expansion and accumulation.

As Samir Amin wrote, "capitalism has always been... by nature, a polarizing system... the concurrent construction of dominant centers and dominated peripheries, and their reproduction deepening in each stage" (Amin 2004: 1). In the current phase of U.S. imperialism, the Monroe Doctrine is expanded to encompass not just the entire globe but space as well. The unequivocal objective of American empire in the twenty-first century is explicit in the 2002 U.S. National Security Strategy document. Throughout the entire world there is one only economic and political system that is viable, it declares, and that is the American model of liberal democracy and free enterprise. And this model would henceforth be promoted and defended through the unilateral use of force, pre-emptively if necessary.

Lest there should be any doubt, the link between the imposition of "endless war" in the Middle East by western powers and the intention of the U.S. to assert ownership and domination over the world's largest sources of energy resources is unequivocally laid out in Brzezinski's *The Grand Chessboard*, published in 1997. The escalating violent civil war that has encompassed Iraq in the face of the West's intervention on behalf of "freedom and democracy" and which is in danger of becoming the downfall of both the British and American elected state heads, is but a harbinger of things to come.

In a world in which militarism and endless warfare have become the signifiers for a civilization in which westernization is the legitimizing ideology for what can only be described as a bloodbath, in which the disfigurement and murder of young children, the wanton and deliberate murder of civilians fleeing in obedience to orders from their attackers, targeted attacks on hospitals and places of worship, the deliberate murder of U.N. peacekeepers, the destruction of thousands of years of knowledge and historical records as in the case of Afghanistan and Iraq, and other horrific casualties of war are sanctioned as a geopolitical strategy to exert domination over the Middle East. In the case of Israel's unholy U.S.-sponsored war of terror on Lebanon, Chossudovsky (2006) notes that the world's largest strategic pipeline, one which will channel to western markets over a million barrels of oil, was inaugurated on the same day and "at the very outset as the onset of the Israeli sponsored bombings of Lebanon," July 13, 2006. Today most of the world stands in silent complicity as the U.S.-Israel alliance ensures that no other power will emerge to challenge U.S. supremacy in that region by razing cities and villages, shooting down fleeing women and children, and bombing helpless children sheltering in terror in underground basements.

Hardt and Negri's argument that one of the defining characteristics of Empire is crisis and decline (2000: 386) is some cause for hope. That the American version of neo-imperialism is in decline can hardly be in doubt. The world watches in increasing cynicism as U.S. foreign policies unravel; as its Straussian politics of fear become increasingly hollow and the polemics of its elected president lurch further into incredulity; as trillions of dollars of U.S. debt skyrockets and U.S. health and welfare policies sink to the lowest in the western world; and as the rest of the world becomes increasingly exhausted or alternatively, incensed, by its strident insistence on bombing "undemocratic" countries and those unwilling to align with its policies of destruction into submission. Yet we stand by while America and now Britain readies itself for the next phase of the escalating "war on terrorism," this time in Iran. Next, Syria.

The obvious question that begs to be asked is this: if global domination supported by militarism and the alignment of economic policies with security, including over the energy resources, is required for dominance, if all this is not the answer to the world's ills, then what are the alternatives? And, for the purposes of this chapter, how does this connect with Indigenous women? As a preface to my response to this question, I return briefly to the historical impact of imperialism on Indigenous women.

## CAPITALISM, DOMINATION AND THE SUBJUGATION OF THE FEMININE

The impact of historical forms of imperialism and colonialism on women and in particular, women in Third World countries has been well recounted (c.f. Eizenstein 2004). Maori feminist scholarship has documented the re-ordering of the gender relationship of balance and reciprocity that characterized Maori social structures, the demoting of the status of Maori women and the undermining of their considerable power as a direct result of colonialism in Aotearoa/New Zealand (c.f. Irwin 1992, Pihama and Johnston 1994, Pere 1990; Yates-Smith 1998).

Maori mythology acknowledges the powerful role of *atua wahine*, or Maori goddesses, within Maori cosmology, including the ability of Maori women to control the forces of the universe (Yates-Smith 1998). Although the force of that power is still invoked in ritual practices today, these practices are often misunderstood and the power that they contain thus hidden. It is commonplace for non-Indigenous women to decry what they see as the subordination of Maori women in ritual practices through sheer lack of understanding of the power and meaning of the practices that they observe. Wikitoria August's work (2005) uncovers some of the ways that such misunderstandings have been applied. She demonstrates that what has been seen as the historical exclusion of Maori women from certain spaces during particular times, such as menstruation or pregnancy, is instead an acknowledgement of their sacredness and importance. In an earlier work, Ani Mikaere (1999) argued that notions of unclean, impure and cast-out were introduced for consistency with the Christian Bible and have no foundation at all in traditional Maori society.

Earlier feminist post-positivist critiques of androcentric models in social and material sciences emphasized the relationship between the domination of women and the domination of nature (e.g., Merchant 1980; Griffen 1978; Starhawk 1982, 1999, 2004; Daly 1990, 2006; Waring 1984, 1996). The major role played by the Christian Church in perpetuating patriarchal ideologies of dominance has also been well documented. In the early centuries of Christianity, ancient belief systems and religions that celebrated the Mother

Goddess and the fecundity of Earth Mother became incorporated into the Marian doctrines of the Catholic Church. The Celtic Church also became known for its celebration of Nature and for the ecclesiastical leadership of women. Despite the Church's attempts to discredit doctrines such as the St. John tradition of the love of creation and the essential goodness of humanity, the influence of Celtic spirituality continued, at least in pockets, well into the eighth and ninth centuries. Ultimately, however, the dominance of patriarchal ideologies led to the dogmas responsible for the marginalization and oppression of both women and Nature. By the mid-sixteenth century, Marian doctrines and the recognition of Earth as the Primal Mother had been driven out of European religious and spiritual practice by the patriarchal austerity of the Calvinist Reformation (Roszak 1999).

As Christianity and capitalism spread throughout the world, recognition of the sacred and political roles of Indigenous women was one of the greatest casualties. Yet many Indigenous women have continued to exercise significant political and spiritual leadership. Outstanding Maori women such as the late Irihapeti Murchie, Dame Whina Cooper and Dame Mira Szazy come immediately to mind. Indigenous women are in the forefront of the multi-fronted battle to save the remnants of biodiversity and have waged holy war in the hallowed halls of the World Trade Organisation to prevent and reverse the profiteering and plundering of Indigenous fauna. Here I pay tribute to the work and contemporary leadership of Indigenous women such as Vandana Shiva of India, Del Wihongi, Sana Murray and Aroha Mead of Aotearoa/New Zealand and Winona La Duke, an Ojibwe of the U.S., to name but a tiny handful of the numerous Indigenous women whose leadership provides outstanding role models today.

The re-inscribing of women as weaker and inferior to men has longer historical antecedents, however, than is generally recognized. Rianne Eisler's work demonstrates that the overthrow of gynocentric societies by patriarchally driven models has origins that extend far back into pre-recorded history. Her work has relevance today. In her book *The Chalice amd the Blade: Our History, Our Future* (1995), originally published in 1987, Eisler drew on historical and pre-historical data to demonstrate a correlation between societal models in which the masculine and feminine principles were equally valued and which were based on what she termed "partnership" models of social organization and societies in which the masculine principle was dominant and which was reflected in a "dominator" model of social relationships and organization. Although in all cases societal models were in many respects widely divergent, there were distinctive shared characteristics. Societies that were based on the partnership model gave birth to new material and technological advances that were used for purposes that celebrated life. On the other hand, societies based on the dominator model, as is the case today, were characterized by the use of technology for purposes of domination, including the taking of life. The central thesis of Eisler's work is that, allowing for periods of massive regression, these two models of social organization follow very different paths of cultural evolution.

Eisler, like other evolutionary change theorists (c.f. Wallerstein 1998), sees evolution as being punctuated by moments of "critical systems branching or bifurcation," points at which "critical transformation can occur" (Eisler 1995: xxii). In arguing that the dominator model of social organization is at least in part responsible for the increasing global crisis, her contention is that we are now at a critical point of bifurcation in which there is immense possibility for evolutionary transformation and for the development of a new global ethic (203). I follow Eisler with respect to this moment as one of critical bifurcation. In the wake of the most recent damning report on global climate change and on the eve before the anticipated declaration of a nuclear war on a non-nuclear country, Iran,[3] we are perilously close to the point of no return. To return to the point about decolonization, I am convinced that the most critical decolonization agenda goes beyond the reclaiming of Indigenous self-determination to the reclaiming of the whole globe from the grip of insanity fuelled by ruthless greed and ambition.

## ALTERNATIVE POLITICS

The most fundamental principle in the search for a new political ontology for being together in the world is the relationship between "self" and "other." The work of developing alternative models of governance that are centred on our interrelationships with one another has been addressed by a number of feminist scholars. Some of these take an eco-centred approach (c.f. Warren 1991). Feminist philosopher Marilyn Frye, in her work entitled "In and Out of Harm's Way: Arrogance and Love" (1983), emphasizes the importance of the "loving eye," which she describes as not an invasive, coercive eye which annexes others to itself, but one which "knows the complexity of the other as something which will forever present new things to be known" (cited in Warren 1991: 28). McAfee (2000: 125) suggests that we are coming into a time when it is possible to create a new imaginary in place of the politics of triumphing over the other, a politics instead of "inclining toward." I am reminded of our late and much-loved Waitaha matriarch who consistently exhorted us to recognize the "other" as also ourself, a concept that I balked against at the time, enmeshed as I was in tribal struggles over land settlements. Yet surely, in the deepest meaning, she was right. As I now understand her words, this means at the very least to honour the sacredness inherent in all things and all beings, to recognize the truth of our inherent interconnectedness and to act in the world and towards each other appropriately. "All my relations."

Iris Marion Young emphasized the contribution of the Iroquois system of federalism towards the "project of rethinking democracy in a post-colonial age" and noted in particular the role of the Council of Matrons (Young 2006). In traditional Iroquois societies the Council of Matrons was the dominant executive body that determined and instituted general policies. Accordingly, Allen writes, it was the matrons who were the ceremonial centre of the system and also the prime policy-makers (1993: 592). This demonstrates that historically, as also within Maori societies, spirituality and politics were inseparably bound together. It also demonstrates the centrality of the grandmothers in the political structures of many traditional Indigenous societies.

## STANDING AT THE JUNCTURE

It seems logical to extrapolate from that to the role of contemporary grandmothers in this "transformational timespace," as Wallerstein (1998) names it. It is the case that millions of Indigenous women and grandmothers today are not only over-burdened but suffer the most horrendous forms of oppression, and the statistics and reports from countries across the globe bear witness to the tiniest tip of the iceberg. However some of us are in positions of privilege. We are policy-makers, academics, community activists and home-makers, while others of us are dispersed around the globe. It is to those of us in positions of relative privilege that I speak as we stand at the intersection of the politics of the local, represented by our families, communities, cities and of the global, the terrain of empire and capitalism.

At this moment in time, the global has become represented by a new imperialism with an old name — that of Greed. Imperialism's objective is total, ultimate power over every natural resource and over each and every human life. It is exercised through data mining, iris scanning and digital chips. Its power is deployed internationally through the military machine. This power is maintained by the racialization of the Other as terrorist, measured by racial profiling, and by the surveillance and disciplining of domestic citizens deemed a hindrance to the politico-economic wellbeing of the state acting on behalf of the global financial/military/complex. This power is experienced in the military dominance over space, land and sea by an imperial power and by the subjugation of democratic freedoms and citizenship rights to economic interests. This power is exercised in the return to a previously illegitimate doctrine of pre-emptive strike. Most certainly, it is demonstrated in the view of the treasures of the universe as resources to be commodified, mined and controlled, and in the representation of children's deaths as collateral damage in war.

There are, however, alternatives, and there are interventions to be made. If we are in truth in a moment of tremendous bifurcation, then some of those alternatives and interventions must be made by us, by the Indigenous women of the world, the grandmothers of the world. On another occasion I wrote,

> As a race of beings, we have lost touch with the sacred. We have lost touch with the deep spiritual essence of our "being"ness. We need to reclaim our own histories; we need to reclaim our true reality. As more and more women are doing. More and more women are re-membering that there was a time when the societies of human beings that lived on this planet our home, were much more matriarchal in nature, when the values by which existence was ordered were based on a spirituality which connected us to Mother Earth, to each other and to the universe. Those histories are today being rediscovered, being brought forth. Indigenous women, Celtic women, the healers and the gatherers in whom the genetic memory is stored, all women everywhere are re-membering, re-envisioning, re-weaving, re-turn-ing the ancient knowledge, the ancient epistemologies towards the re-construction of a different political and economic paradigm for co-existence. (Harawira 1999)

That this is our most urgent role, our most critical responsibility, is for me inarguable. Indigenous women who are in positions of privilege are called upon to vigorously refute capitalism's excesses and greed; to refuse the domi-nator politics of power-over; to refuse to give up our sons and daughters, our children and grandchildren to the warmongering that is now called democracy; to reject the greed that is now called freedom; and to stand firmly in the intersection of the politics of local and global. It is from that intersection that we must decolonize the local and transform the global. As Indigenous women warriors, we are called to re-weave the fabric of being in the world into a new spiritually grounded and feminine-oriented political framework and process of "being together in the world." In that process, we are invited to deeply embrace the Other, who is after all, the Elders teach us, Ourself. This, I argue, is the urgent decolonizing project of Indigenous feminism today.

## NOTES

Some of the material in this section previously appeared in Stewart-Harawira, M. (2005). *The New Imperial Order: Indigenous Responses to Globalization*. New Zealand and Australia: Huia Books; London: Zed Books.

1. "Maori" is a generic term that was developed post-contact and applied to all Indigenous tribes of Aotearoa/New Zealand.

2. The Waitangi Tribunal is a Crown body established to hear Maori grievances stemming from violations of the 1840 Treaty of Waitangi, signed between the leaders of some Maori sub-tribes and the British Crown.

3. The likelihood of an imminent nuclear strike against Iran by Israel supported by the U.S., is demonstrated in numerous articles and commentaries and evidenced by the buildup of U.S. warships in the Mediterranean. Among other things, it has given rise to an urgent letter signed by twenty-two senior physicists, which urges the U.S. Congress to forbid nuclear strikes on non-nuclear countries (http://ucsd-news.ucsd.edu/newsrel/science/22physicists07.asp [accessed April 2007]).

## REFERENCES

Ackleson, A., and J. Katsner. 2005. "The Security and Prosperity Partnership of North America." Submitted to *The American Review of Canadian Studies*. Available at <http://www.k-state.edu/projects/fss/research/conference/AcklesonKastnerACSUS-ARCS20051206.pdf> (accessed July 10, 2006).

Alaimo, Stacey. 1997. "Feminism, Nature and Discursive Ecologies." *EBR 4, Critical Ecologies*. Green special edition. Available at <http://www.altx.com/EBR/EBR4/alaimo.htm> (accessed January 30, 2007).

Allen, Paula Gunn. 1986. *The Sacred Hoop: Recovering the Feminine in American Indian Traditions*. Boston: Beacon Press.

———— 1993. "Who Is Your Mother? Red Roots of White Feminism." In Patrick Williams and Laura Chrisman (eds.), *Colonial Discourse and Postcolonial Theory: A Reader*. London and New York: Harvester Wheatsheaf.

Amin, Samir. 2004. "U.S. Imperialism, Europe, and the Middle East." *Monthly Review* 56, 6. Available from <http://www.monthlyreview.org/1104amin.htm> (accessed July 14, 2006).

Amnesty International. 2004. *Stolen Sisters: Rights Response to Discrimination and Violence Against Indigenous Women in Canada*. Available at <http://www.amnesty.ca/stolensisters/amr2000304.pdf> (accessed September 2004).

August, Wikitoria. 2005. "Maori Women: Bodies, Spaces, Sacredness and Mana." *New Zealand Geographer* 61.

Brzezinski, Z. 1997. *The Grand Chessboard: American Primacy and Its Geostrategic Imperatives*. New York: Basic Books.

Butler, Judith. 1992. "Contingent Foundations: Feminism and the Question of 'Postmodernism.'" In Joan W. Scott and Judith Butler (eds.), *Feminists Theorize the Political*. New York: Routledge.

Chossudovsky, M. 2006. "The War on Lebanon and the Battle for Oil." Available from <http://www.globalresearch.ca/PrintArtilce.php?articleID=284> (accessed July 27, 2006).

Cooper, Robert. 1998. *The PostModern State and the World Order*. [1996] London: Demos.

————. 2003. *The Breaking of Nations: Order and Chaos in the Twenty-First Century*. New York: Grove.

Council for Foreign Relations Taskforce. 2005. *Report of the Independent Taskforce on the Future of North America*. Briefing Transcript. Available from <http://www.cfr.org/publication/8138/building_a_north_american_community.html?bread...> (accessed July 10, 2006).

Daly, Mary. 1990. *Gyn/Ecology: The Metaethics of Radical Feminism*. Boston: Women's Press.

_____. 2006. *Amazon Grace: Recalling the Courage to Sin Big.* New York: Palgrave Macmillan.

Eisenstein, Z. 2004. *Against Empire: Feminisms, Racism, and the West.* Melbourne: Spinifex Press; London and New York: Zed Books.

Eisler, Riane. 1995. *The Chalice and the Blade: Our History, Our Future* [1987]. New York: HarperCollins.

Frye, M. 1983. "In and Out of Harm's Way: Arrogance and Love." In *The Politics of Reality.* Trumansburg, New York: Crossing Press.

Gadamer, H-G. 1998. *The Beginning of Philosophy.* Trans. Rod Coltman. New York: Continuum.

Grande, Sandy. 2004. *Red Pedagogy: Native American Social and Political Thought.* Oxford: Rowan and Littlefield Publishers.

Griffin, S. 1978. *Woman and Nature: The Roaring Inside Her.* New York: Harper and Row.

Harawira, M. 1999. "Women and Economic Globalisation in Aotearoa/New Zealand." Presented at the Women's International League for Peace and Freedom Consultation, Women Meeting the Challenge of Economic Globalisation. Tokyo, October 18–22.

Hardt, M., and A. Negri. 2000. *Empire.* Cambridge, MA: Harvard University Press.

Henare, D. 1994. "Carrying the Burden of Arguing the Treaty." In Witi Ihimaera (ed.), in conversation with Rosalie Capper and Amy Brown, *Kaupapa New Zealand: Vision Aotearoa.* Wellington, New Zealand: Bridget Williams Books.

Irwin, K. 1992. "Towards Theories of Maori Feminism." In R. Duplessis et al. (eds.), *Feminist Voices: Women's Studies Texts for Aotearoa/New Zealand.* Auckland: Oxford University Press.

Johnston, P. and L. Pihama. 1994. "The Marginalisation of Maori Women." In *Hecate* 20, 2, Queensland: Australian Council for the Arts.

McAfee, N. 2000. *Habermas, Kristeva, and Citizenship.* Ithaca: Cornell University Press.

Merchant, C. 1980. *The Death of Nature.* New York: Harper and Row.

Mikaere, A. 1999. "Colonisation and the Imposition of Patriarchy: A Ngati Raukawa Woman's Perspective." *Te Ukaipo* 3.

Pere, Rangimarie. 1990. "Tangata Whenua." In *Puna Wairere: Essays by Maori.* Wellington, New Zealand: New Zealand Planning Council.

_____. 1994. "Mother Energy." In Witi Ihimaera (ed.), *Vision Aotearoa Kaupapa New Zealand.* Wellington: Bridget Williams Books.

Roszak, T. 1999. *The Gendered Atom: Reflections on the Sexual Psychology of Science.* Berkley, CA: Conari Press.

Seuffert, Nan. 2002. "Race-ing and Engendering the Nation-state in Aotearoa/New Zealand." *American University Journal of Gender, Social Policy and the Law* 10, 3.

Smith, L.T. 1992. "Maori Women: Discourses, Projects and Mana Wahine." In S. Middleton and A. Jones (eds.), *Women and Education in Aotearoa 2.* Wellington, N.Z.: Bridget Williams Books.

Starhawk. 1982. *Dreaming the Dark: Magic, Sex, and Politics.* Boston: Beacon Press.

_____. 1999. *The Spiral Dance.* Harper SanFrancisco

_____. 2004. *The Earth Path: Grounding Your Spirit in the Rhythms of Nature.* Harper

SanFrancisco.

Stewart-Harawira, M. 2005. *The New Imperial Order: Indigenous Responses to Globalization*. Wellington, N.Z.: Huia Books; London: Zed Books.

Trinh, T. Minh-ha. 1989. *Woman, Native, Other: Writing Postcoloniality and Feminism*. Bloomington: Indiana University Press.

Wallerstein, Immanuel. 1998. *Utopistics or, Historical Choices of the Twenty-first Century*. New York: The New Press.

Waring, Marilyn. 1984. *Women, Politics, and Power: Essays*. Wellington, N.Z.: Unwin Paperbacks-Port Nicholson Press.

_____. 1996. *Three Masquerades: Essays on Equality, Work and Hu(man) Rights*. Auckland: Auckland University Press with Bridget Williams Books.

Warren, K.J. (ed.). 1994. *Ecological Feminism (Environmental Philosophies)*. London and New York: Routledge.

Yates-Smith, G.R. Aroha. 1998. "Hine! E Hine! Rediscovering the Feminine in Maori Spirituality." Unpublished PhD thesis, University of Waikato, New Zealand.

Young, I.M. 2000. "Hybrid Democracy: Iroquois Federalism and Postcolonial Project." In D. Ivison, P. Patton, and W. Sander (eds.), *Political Theory and the Rights of Indigenous Peoples*. Cambridge: Cambridge University Press.

Chapter Eight

# BALANCING STRATEGIES
## Aboriginal Women and
## Constitutional Rights in Canada

### Joyce Green

Constitutional change in Canada has, for most of the country's history, been a cautious process driven by white male elites within colonial and federal-provincial relationships, in a context driven by capitalist rather than democratic interests. Occasionally, women have used law and politics to secure a measure of equitable justice, as in the 1929 Judicial Committee of the Privy Council (then the highest appeal court) Persons decision,[1] which held that Canadian women were persons for the purpose of Senate appointments. This decision did not, however, translate then or since into an equitable or even significant number of female appointments to the Senate, itself an unrepresentative, unaccountable and highly problematic vestige of a more anti-democratic historical period. Legal action has also produced decisions like the infamous 1974 *Attorney-General* v. *Lavell* and *Isaac* v. *Bedard* decisions, in which the Supreme Court of Canada confirmed the racist, sexist status quo of the pre-1985 *Indian Act* as *de jure* equality, as all Indian women were equally subject to the offensive provisions.[2]

However, in 1982 the patriation[3] of the *British North America Act of 1867* (now re-named *Constitution Act 1867*), together with constitutional revisions and the adoption of the *Charter of Rights and Freedoms*, signalled a change in both constitutional vision and in federal and democratic engagement in constitutional politics in Canada. Constitutional and federal politics subsequently would be contested by citizens, especially through social movements. Citizens would henceforth have rights guarantees under the Charter, including protection from sex and race discrimination and recognition of Aboriginal and treaty rights. This democratic challenge to the Canadian tradition of constitutional politics as a preserve for the administrative engagement of federal and provincial governments is still being worked out.

The fact of citizens engaging elected politicians and governments over constitutional visions and practices is an emerging phenomenon in Canada. Democracy has developed over the span of the country's existence, from a class-, sex- and race-limited franchise, to the more thorough engagement of diverse citizens in matters far from the political intentions of the "Founding

Fathers." White women gained the federal vote in 1918; Canadians of Asian background were disenfranchised until after World War II; status Indian men and women only got the right to vote in 1960. The franchise, however, has not translated into equitable representation in political and economic institutions, nor has it resulted in representative governments that, in turn, produce policy favourable to marginalized groups of Canadians. Pending possible changes to the existing plurality ("first past the post") electoral system and the hoped-for improvement of democratic representation, many activists prefer social movements to political parties as vehicles for democratic engagement.

Of the citizens' groups that emerged in the 1970s as powerful political and constitutional actors, none were more prominent and compelling than mainstream women's and Aboriginal women's organizations, and Aboriginal[4] organizations. Women forced the political elites to place equality rights into the Charter. Aboriginal organizations forced consideration of the constitutional implications of pre-existing, unsurrendered political and land rights onto the Canadian constitutional table, despite the hostility of most provincial premiers and the federal government. Consequently, the 1982 patriation of the Canadian constitution, accompanied by the *Charter of Rights and Freedoms* and the *Constitution Act 1982*, confirmed recognition of the undefined Aboriginal and treaty rights of Indian, Inuit and Métis peoples.[5] During subsequent national constitutional debates, including the failed Meech Lake Accord of 1985 and the failed Charlottetown Accord of 1992,[6] women's groups such as the National Action Committee on the Status of Women, the Féderation des Fémmes du Québec, the Native Women's Association of Canada and the malestream Aboriginal organizations all contributed to Canadians' understanding of constitutional change and democracy. Aboriginal disapproval, voiced by the strategically placed Aboriginal member of the Manitoba legislative assembly Elijah Harper (then sitting as a New Democrat), was central to denying the passage of the Meech Lake Accord.

Again, in 1992, in the Charlottetown Accord process and subsequent referendum, settler women, Aboriginal women and malestream Aboriginal organizations injected questions of representation, citizenship, inclusion, identity, democracy and colonialism into the constitutional debate. This is remarkable because women of all ethnicities and Aboriginal people of both genders constitute historically marginalized people in Canada. While changes to the Canadian Constitution have not erased the consequences of state-sponsored sex and race discrimination and colonialism, constitutional changes have gone some distance to identifying these matters and creating legally enforceable rights.

Most significantly, the constitutional enumeration of protected rights created space for meaningful contestation of certain kinds of oppression. While this is laudable, it must also be remembered that incremental successes occasionally obtained by using a legal and political system designed by and for race, class and male privilege will not secure profound institutional and cultural changes any time soon. However, social movement activism continues to till the fields of social justice, creating the conditions for solidarities, political activism and public education.

All political communities are acts of imagination. "Project Canada" is the realization of the colonial imagination, now infused with liberal democratic settler populations' visions. Project Canada is not yet, however, a realization of Indigenous imagination. This reality sustains the colonial and subsequently settler assumptions, values, cultures and practices in the apparently neutral apparatus of the state. Because of this, all women, but especially Indigenous women, must use the state apparatus and liberal democratic practices cautiously, while remaining aware of their inherent limitations and preferences.

Prior to 1982, the bulk of constitutional litigation involved courts arbitrating jurisdictional disputes concerning governments. Since 1982, the courts are constitutionally directed to arbitrate tensions between government action and citizen rights and freedoms, and to hold government actions accountable to constitutional human rights obligations. Since 1982, Aboriginal peoples have existed in the constitutional declaration of the vision of Project Canada in an uneasy and undefined relationship with the colonizing state. The judiciary has an important role in defining the parameters of that relationship.

Post-1982, citizens are recognized as necessary and legitimating agents of constitutional life. Subsequent efforts to change the Constitution have been characterized by the desire of many Canadians to be involved. Indeed, the legitimacy of mega-constitutional politics may now be dependent on the inclusive nature of consultative processes leading to new agreements. A democratic imprimatur is now implicitly necessary for constitutional change, while prior to 1982 it was assumed to be conferred by the participation of first ministers in the elite space of executive federalism. In all of these transformations, activist Aboriginal women have been and continue to be agents for democratic, inclusive justice for all Aboriginal people.

On April 17, 2007, the patriated Constitution, its new 1982 components and the Charter turned twenty-five. Youthful in constitutional terms, it is nevertheless time to consider how the record is shaping up. Attention has been paid primarily to the Charter articulation of the rights and freedoms of citizens and to the 1982 constitutional amendment acknowledging Aboriginal and treaty rights. These are indeed important historical moments, with significant consequences. They are, however, only steps on the journey toward ideals of justice. As we celebrate the indubitably important constitutional elements and their social and legal consequences, it is also important to remember that the ideal of justice has not been attained and will not be attained with the constitutional tools at our disposal. Justice requires not only transparent, accountable and representative democratic political processes but protection and implementation of minority rights relative to majority interests. In particular, in Canada, justice requires a gendered decolonization process that inscribes Indigenous peoples, institutions and processes into Project Canada (Green 2003).

Throughout the constitutional debates, Aboriginal women were central to challenges to the undemocratic, sexist, unrepresentative and colonial impulses in the Canadian constitutional and political processes. Aboriginal feminism motivated some of these women, and their contributions have, in turn, embedded Aboriginal feminism in Canada's critical political repertoire.

## CONFRONTING COLONIAL POWER RELATIONS

As the aphorism says, where you stand depends on where you sit: location matters. All Canadian citizens have not benefited equally from the Constitution and from the Canadian political regime. For some, emancipatory objectives are frustrated by the ideological assumptions embedded in law and concretized in state institutions. For others, especially Aboriginal women, there is a chronic tension between the laudable protections guaranteed by the Constitution and the limitations of law and policy. Finally, while freedom and equality are celebrated in the Constitution, the barriers that hinder their attainment are not taken into account, and those barriers are primarily economic, including the economic practices of colonialism. This is consistent with western liberal democratic theory and ideology and compromises legal and political gains for all.

Colonialism is both an historic and a continuing wrong. A term that encompasses economic and political practices, it refers to the appropriation of the sovereignty and resources of a nation or nations, to the economic and political benefit of the colonizer. The practices by which colonialism is normalized and legitimated include racism, which is encoded in law, policy, education and the political and popular culture of the colonizer. Thus, the subordination and immiseration of the colonized are understood as the inevitable consequence of their deficient civilization, lack of technological development and innate moral and intellectual incapacity (Said 1979, 1994; Blaut 1993; Green 1995; Anaya 1996: 20).

Aboriginal peoples in Canada have endured colonialism in its different forms during the evolution of Project Canada. While there is solidarity among Aboriginal peoples because of this, men and women have not had identical experiences. The reality of gender role distinction and especially of the imposition of European-derivative and Christianity conditioned patriarchy has constructed Aboriginal women's specific experiences with colonialism. For Aboriginal women, then, resistance to sexism, racism and colonialism is complicated by the intersecting allegiances with Aboriginal men and by the reality that settler women and men are complicit in and benefit from the colonial policies of their government. Sexism within Aboriginal communities is often minimized as only a consequence of colonialism, while Aboriginal women's resistance is often done within the context of Aboriginal male-dominated politics confronting settler Canada's political regime. Further, when Aboriginal women adopt feminist analyses, they are often criticized for being culturally inappropriate and politically maladept (Silman 1987; Green 1997; LaRocque 1997). All of this complicates political solidarity, and thus constitutional politics are fraught with difficulties.

Liberation from colonialism, then, is not simply tied to a formula for equality with the colonizer, on terms dictated by the ideology of the colonizer. Liberation includes the possibility of traditional or contemporary institutions and practices chosen by the colonized. It includes reparations for the damage wreaked by colonial practices, which have not coincidentally enriched the complacent and historically oblivious colonial or settler populations. Truly liberatory constitutional and legal strategies must be able to advance these political and cultural objectives, and not simply reduce Aboriginal and women's claims to simple equality with the not-so-neutral white male norm in the colonial state. Both human rights and decolonization are entitlements of Aboriginal women.

Instructionally, at the Beijing Fourth World Conference on Women in 1995, in the Declaration of Indigenous Women, Indigenous women demanded recognition of both their Aboriginal rights and their equality rights, unfettered by tradition.[7]

> We, the women of the original peoples of the world have struggled actively to defend our rights to self-determination and to our territories which have been invaded and colonized by powerful nations and interests. [We demand]... That Indigenous customary laws and justice systems which are supportive of women victims of violence be recognized and reinforced. That Indigenous laws, customs, and traditions which are discriminatory to women be eradicated.... That all internally displaced Indigenous peoples be allowed to return to their own communities and the necessary rehabilitation and support services be provided to them.

Aboriginal women have suffered from colonialism similarly to Aboriginal men, but also in gender-specific ways, including the loss of culture, traditional territories, identity and status, children and culturally respected gender roles (Sayers and MacDonald 2001: 11). Most Aboriginal women's organizations identify colonialism as the cause of their social, economic and political inequality, and many suggest that the solution lies in reclaiming Aboriginal cultural traditions and political autonomy. Colonialism also inflicted European patriarchy and sexism on Aboriginal women. It fused with racism, creating a social scourge that affects Aboriginal women today. The most notorious (but not the only) case of legislated sex discrimination involves the membership provisions of the pre-1985 *Indian Act*. These provisions faithfully reflected colonial assumptions that women took on the identity and status of their most proximate patriarch — father or husband. Therefore, Indian women who married non-status men were stripped of their status; non-status or non-Aboriginal women who married status Indian men gained status. These sex discriminatory provisions were amended in 1985, but were replaced with provisions that arguably continue sex discrimination and which permit sex and race discriminatory band membership codes to determine band membership (Green 1985, 1997). As a prime example of this continuing discrimination, the continuing experience of Jeannette Lavell and her family, and of Sharon McIvor and her family, are cited later in this chapter.

While there is no consensus on whether sexism in Aboriginal communities is an entirely colonial creation or whether it preceded colonialism in some communities, sex discrimination is now a reality for many Aboriginal women. Some Aboriginal women suggest that Aboriginal political elites and governments must be accountable for sexism and that Aboriginal governments must guarantee women's equality rights, human rights and political participation along with women's Aboriginal rights (LaRocque 1997; Sayers and MacDonald 2001; McIvor this volume). Arguably, political institutions and practices emerging from decolonization have a duty to international human rights law (Green 2003), and Aboriginal women are entitled to benefit from both decolonization and human rights.

## ENGAGING THE CONSTITUTION

The political process leading to patriation of the Constitution in 1982 and the creation of the Charter galvanized politically aware constituencies of citizens who had not previously been taken account of in the practice of executive federalism (the high level political and bureaucratic interactions of both orders of government on matters of mutual concern) nor of constitutional governance (Cairns 1988, 1995; Russell 1993:115, 134; Trimble 1998). While white women and Aboriginal women had certainly been politically active through self-conscious organizations prior to 1982 (Silman 1987; Sawer and Vickers 2001: 12–28), it is in the constitutional process that then emerged, and subsequently, that both have come to be perceived, and to perceive themselves, as legitimate collective political actors in federal and constitutional politics.

Indeed, it is certain that without the collective activism of women and of Aboriginal peoples, neither would be explicitly protected in the Constitution. The Charter's section 28 explicitly guarantees constitutional protection to women and men: "Notwithstanding anything in this Charter, the rights and freedoms referred to in it are guaranteed equally to male and female persons." The first ministers were uncomfortable with sex equality guarantees (Kome 1983; Sawer and Vickers 2001: 24–8) and with an acknowledgement of Aboriginal and treaty rights, and had to be forced by political and legal pressure to acquiesce to the very limited constitutional sections on these categories. A constitutional amendment in 1983 extended Aboriginal and treaty rights protection to modern land-claims settlements and required that a first ministers conference be held with Aboriginal representatives prior to any future constitutional amendment directly affecting Aboriginal rights (Russell 1993: 130–31; see also Eberts, McIvor and Nahanee 2006).

Most significantly, and only because of organized political pressure by Aboriginal peoples, is the recognition in the 1982 Constitution of those whom the colonial state has colonized. To appreciate the significance, consider the history of Canadian colonial and settler relations with Indigenous peoples.[8] Prior to 1982, the single reference in the *British North America Act* was section 91(24), which gave to the federal government sole jurisdiction over the subject matter of "Indians, and Lands reserved for the Indians." This section gave the federal government jurisdiction to pass and enforce the incarnations of the *Indian Act*, a fundamentally racist piece of legislation that injured all "Indians," though not in a gender-neutral fashion. By defining "Indian" consistently with colonial patriarchal social assumptions, and then bureaucratizing and enforcing this definition, the federal government stripped generations of women of their status as Indians, simultaneously depriving them of the right to live in their communities, raise their children in their cultures and participate in the social, economic and political life of their communities. This was a violation of fundamental human rights guaranteed in the International Covenant on Civil and Political Rights and was condemned by the United Nations Human Rights Commission (Green 1985).[9]

The loss of the human capital of these women and their children to Indian communities is inestimable; the loss to the individuals who were exited from these communities is serious and more quantifiable (Jamieson 1978; Green 1985, 1993, 1997; Silman 1987; Weaver 1993). By defining "Indian," the federal government identified those Aboriginal people who would be acknowledged for the purposes of the *Indian Act*; legislatively unrecognized Aboriginal peoples were ignored as subjects of targeted public policy. Simultaneously, they were subjected to the racism endemic in colonial societies (for analyses of this phenomenon, see Memmi 1965; Said 1979;

1994; Blaut 1993). As the language of rights was deployed in resisting colonial oppression, the state refused to recognize those without status as genuine claimants of Aboriginal and treaty rights. Too often, those with status also rejected the rights claims of Aboriginal people who were not recognized by the state as status Indians.

The practical result of the relevant Charter and Constitution sections was that courts could be asked to consider cases where women's and Aboriginal rights were alleged to be violated and could declare remedies. Thus, the government could be held accountable by citizens, through the courts, for infringements of rights named in the Constitution (and more recently, for equality rights that are analogous to the protected section 15 subjects). Obviously, however, the litigation remedy is most available to those with education, wealth, information, time and a sense of political efficacy. And, section 15 equality rights[10] were not in force until 1985, three years after the rest of the Charter was operative, a tactic intended to permit governments to bring discriminatory legislation in line with the Charter's equality guarantees.

The 1982 Constitution, then, promised not just the possibility of confronting colonialism but the necessity of confronting sexism; and of doing so not only in relation to colonial institutions but also in relation to Aboriginal ones. These confrontations were to occur in a political environment made more porous to citizen activism by the great degree of citizen interest in and activism around constitutional change.

Quebec, alone of the ten provinces, had not accepted the 1982 patriation and *Charter of Rights and Freedoms*. The 1985 Meech Lake Accord, designed by then Prime Minister Mulroney to bring Quebec into the Constitution "with honour and enthusiasm," was rejected by a majority of Canadians outside of Quebec, partly because of its process — it was the product of executive federalism and was seen to be antidemocratic and secretive — and partly because of opposition to what was seen to be "special status" for Quebec (see Cairns 1988 for a discussion of this process). The Accord was also opposed by Aboriginal peoples because of anger that the first ministers were able to cobble together a unanimous agreement for constitutional change to accommodate Quebec, while the majority of those same First Ministers had, at three constitutional conferences held after 1982, refused to come to a similar consensus to accommodate the definition of "self-government."[11]

Chastened by the rejection of the Meech Lake Accord but still committed to repairing the constitutional rift with Quebec, Prime Minister Mulroney initiated the discussions that would culminate in the Charlottetown Accord. (Eberts, McIvor, and Nahanee [2006] provide an excellent summary of these initiatives.) These discussions were far more inclusive and representative than any constitutional process had ever been in Canada, and the resulting package was taken to the electorate in the 1992 referendum. It was narrowly rejected, because of its complexity and because the public was by then thoroughly disenchanted with and mistrustful of its government and with constitutional processes.

Legitimacy of new political, constitutional and administrative arrangements with Aboriginal elites and communities was also dependent on democratic consensus, and that meant involving Aboriginal women and taking account of their interests in meaningful ways. This is evident when, for example, Judith Sayers and Kelly MacDonald (2001) suggest that Aboriginal gender analysis is essential in assessing policy that falls under the rubric of "governance." Male elites did not automatically include gender analysis and women activists in the constitutional initiatives, the 1985 Meech Lake and 1992 Charlottetown accords, and have yet to demonstrate much willingness to incorporate gendered analysis into political and policy debates.

The democratic impetus that emerged in the patriation process impelled self-conscious collective actors such as the National Action Committee on the Status of Women (NAC) and the Native Women's Association of Canada (NWAC) to insist, with differing degrees of success, on voice in subsequent constitutional negotiation processes (Green 1993; Dobrowolsky 1998). Importantly, it also impelled women's organizations to educate each other on different perspectives, political agendas and the tentative and conditional nature of women's solidarity (Kome 1983; Dobrowolsky 1998: 737–38). This is a continuing challenge and one that destabilizes assumptions about a unitary women's movement, agenda or identity. The differences in the agendas of the Aboriginal participants, including status Indians, Métis, nonstatus Indians, Inuit and women-focused Aboriginal organizations such as the Native Women's Association of Canada, the National Métis Women of Canada and Pauktuutit, the Inuit women's organization, forced Aboriginal people, and settler Canadians, to consider how to constitutionally accommodate this diversity.

Aboriginal women have been visible and active in constitutional negotiations and have dramatically increased the public space for Aboriginal women's voices and participation. Unsurprisingly, Aboriginal women don't have a unified political analysis, either on decolonization strategies or on feminism. NWAC, long considered the national voice of Aboriginal women, has found itself sidelined by the federal government from controversial discussions in 2001–04 on First Nations governance. The then Liberal federal government began funding a new organization, the National Aboriginal Women's Association (NAWA), apparently to replace NWAC in its First Nations Governance Initiative consultations (Boisard 2002). The federal government has historically used the power of funding and recognition to cultivate certain groups and leaders, and to marginalize others, and NWAC could be forgiven for thinking this was happening in the above instance.

Diversity, factored by class, gender and other social markers, also places the fact of intersectional identity before political actors and theorists: we are all, always, all of our identities simultaneously, and that makes identity claims conditional and contextual in ways that we are still exploring. For Aboriginal women, then, identification as only *woman* is not possible in the context of a racist colonial society, where white women unconsciously enjoy race privileges while they seek gender solidarity from those injured by that privilege.[12] Many Aboriginal women activists "interacted with the constitutional order through a paradigm of nationalism and highlighted continuing colonialism" (Sawer and Vickers 2001: 25). For white women, the identification as *only* woman is possible only by being oblivious to the race privilege of their location in a racist settler society. And yet, in the constitutional alliances of the late 1980s and early 1990s, women's solidarity across organizations, ethnicities and analyses created a powerful lobby. However, while NAC and NWAC appreciated their diversity and their common ground, male political elites were unable and unwilling to engage women's organizations speaking for diverse constituencies.

## CHARTER LITIGATION FOR ABORIGINAL WOMEN

While the Charter has produced some important litigation on women's rights generally, there is no new precedent on Aboriginal women's rights specifically. Supreme Court decisions on First Nations rights have addressed self-government, restorative justice, fishing and hunting, all pursued under section 35 of the Constitution, not under the Charter. As noted earlier, these cases strengthen Aboriginal women's rights as Aboriginals, though they are not gender-specific nor gendered in their application. Some cases may potentially produce significant benefits for Indian women who have regained their status since 1985; for example, in *Corbiere v. Canada* [1999][13] *Indian Act* "provisions barring off-reserve band members from voting in band elections were found to be unconstitutional" (Cornet 2001: 123). This affects many off-reserve women, who are now able to vote in reserve elections. (However, reserve residency remains a requirement for running for office. Many women who have regained status have been unable to acquire reserve residency, and it is likely that the residency provision also will be challenged as unconstitutional in the future.)

While arguably Aboriginal women benefit from an expansion of and concretization of Aboriginal rights, there is little new law pertaining to Aboriginal women's rights or to a requirement for gendered policy analysis in the development of Aboriginal and treaty rights, or equality rights and social processes.[14] Nor has there been any sustained effort by any government to grapple with the extraordinarily high rates of male violence against Aboriginal women. Indeed, the United Nations Committee on the

Elimination of Racial Discrimination urges Canada to take steps to provide adequate services for "victims of gender-based violence," and particularly names "the specific vulnerability of aboriginal women and women belonging to racial/ethnic minority groups" (CERD 2007: 6). Personal security is arguably an essential precondition to the enjoyment of other rights. The following examples provide an indication of the ways in which Aboriginal women's rights have been sustained or thwarted by politics and Charter law.

Immediately prior to the conclusion of the Charlottetown Accord, NWAC attempted to use the courts to declare that Aboriginal women had a right of representation by Aboriginal women's organizations in constitutional negotiations that were constitutionally mandated and in which the government of Canada was required to consult with representatives of Aboriginal people on matters affecting their rights. NWAC criticized the consultative processes leading up to the ill-fated Charlottetown Accord because they did not provide space for the participation of Aboriginal women through women's organizations, while they did provide space and funding for the malestream Aboriginal organizations. Central to NWAC's position was the issue of sex discrimination and lack of gendered analysis within Aboriginal communities, in political elites and in constitutional proposals and the need to protect Aboriginal women's human rights against real or potential abuse by Aboriginal and settler governments. Along with other women, NWAC took the view that representation of women's interests, especially when they were oppositional to dominant interests, required the voice of the affected constituency.

While some (Russell 1993: 194–95) have argued that women were already represented by malestream organizations, NWAC took its stand after a series of protracted and unsuccessful negotiations with especially the Assembly of First Nations (AFN) on inclusion on the constitutional agenda of a range of issues of particular interest to NWAC. In short, the AFN and others refused to represent NWAC on terms acceptable to NWAC and most importantly, would not agree to Charter application, and hence equality rights guarantees, to future Aboriginal governments.

Some Aboriginal women, especially NWAC, wanted the protection of the Charter, including having it apply to Indian governments. The Assembly of First Nations opposed Charter application to Indian governments on the argument that the Charter was a colonial imposition that could violate cultural practices (Green 1993; Cairns 2000). NWAC lost at trial, won on appeal and then lost again, ultimately, in the Supreme Court of Canada.[15]

Following the 1985 revisions to the *Indian Act*, a number of Indian bands drafted membership codes, pursuant to the revised Act. Some of these codes are racist and sexist in their effect, and some seem to resurrect the discriminatory formula of the pre-1985 *Indian Act*, now presented as "custom." Yet, the 1982

Constitution prohibits discrimination and guarantees Aboriginal and treaty rights equally to men and women. In order to prevent exited women and their children from being reinstated to their bands of origin, several bands initiated a legal action arguing that Aboriginal tradition legitimated the exclusion of women where they married anyone other than a band member and that this tradition was itself protected by the Constitution's recognition of Aboriginal and treaty rights. The case, *Sawridge* v. *The Queen*, lost at the Federal Court (Appeal); however, the comments of the judge were considered to be sufficiently inflammatory to create a "reasonable apprehension of bias" and so the case was bounced back through the court hierarchy to trial and is now on its way back through the system (Green 1997, 2001; Dick 2006).[16] This case may make an important precedent for all women, if it settles the question of whether "tradition" can trump women's human rights to equality.

The continuing discrimination in *Indian Act* membership provisions is also evident in the life and family history of Jeannette Lavell.[17] In 1970, before the patriation of the constitution and the adoption of the Charter of Rights and Freedoms, Lavell lost her Indian status when she married a non-Indian man. She got $30 from the federal government, representing her "share" of her band's wealth and notice of "disenfranchisment" — that is, she was stripped of her membership. The noted civil rights lawyer Clayton Ruby took her case forward, alleging sex discrimination in the membership provisions of the *Indian Act*, contrary to the Canadian Bill of Rights. Lavell won at the Federal Court in 1972. However, the Attorney General for Canada appealed the case to the Supreme Court in 1973. The National Indian Brotherhood (now the Assembly of First Nations) intervened against Lavell, and, in a deeply problematic decision that compromised the authority of the Canadian Bill of Rights, the court held that, as all Indian women were treated equally by the *Indian Act* (that is, as all were potentially discriminated against) there was no inequality in the application of law.

When Lavell attempted to lobby then Prime Minister Pierre Trudeau, now remembered as a great civil libertarian and the premier Charter advocate, he told her to get her chief and men onside before approaching him on the issue, that is, an Indian woman was being told to speak through "her" men, rather than directly to the government that putatively represented her and all Canadians. Trudeau did not amend the *Indian Act* and was evidently more concerned with the political relationship between his government and the National Indian Brotherhood than with the violation of rights (which he must have understood) of Indian women.

In 1985, following the inclusion in the Constitution of the Charter of Rights and Freedoms and the amendments to the *Indian Act*, Lavell was reinstated, along with her three children. However, the amendments structure continuing discrimination by differentiating between section 6(1), 6(2) and

6(3) categories of membership — framing a status hierarchy prejudicial to reinstated women and their children and thus perpetuating the sex discrimination of the pre-1985 Act. These new forms of discrimination, which differentiate between children with status parents, one status parent or a status grandparent, now play out in the lives of Lavell's grandchildren. Her grandson has status, as he is the child of Lavell's now-status son and a status Indian woman. However, Lavell's granddaughter does not have status: she is the child of Lavell's status son and a woman who does not have status. Thus, within the same family, children are labelled differently, with legal, political, economic and identity consequences. Children are still being affected, differentially, by *Indian Act* discrimination.

On the same issue, Sharon McIvor (the former vice-president of NWAC) and her children are mounting a Charter challenge to the Indian Act, R.S.C. 1985.McIvor was born in 1948. Because her Indian lineage was acquired through her grandmother and her mother, she was, under the pre-1985 Indian Act, not entitled to registration as a status Indian at birth. McIvor subsequently married a non-Indian man, and consequently, their children were not entitled to be registered. Under the 1985 Indian Act "C-31" amendments, McIvor has been granted Indian status under section 6(1)(c) but not under section 6(1)(a). This means that, while her children may be registered, they cannot pass Indian status to their children. However, the 1985 Act entitles McIvor's brother, his wife, his children and his grandchildren to status, although his wife is non-Indian.[18]

These instances show that constitutional rights guarantees may require successful litigation to secure their implementation. Law, political culture and bureaucratic practices are still being reshaped by constitutional changes, and much of that reshaping is driven by litigation. However, not all decisions are favourable, so legal strategies are uncertain; and even favourable decisions are occasionally resisted by governments and elites who are charged with changing social, bureaucratic and political practices to implement rights guarantees. Furthermore, class factors mean that the likely litigants, marginalized Aboriginal women, are least likely to have the money, confidence and expertise to pursue legal remedies. Finally, while the Charter has provided some important support for equality and anti-discrimination claims, it has been an inadequate tool for obtaining social and economic relief from poverty, a condition that, for Aboriginal people, is a consequence of colonialism and is systemic in its perpetuation. The Charter's focus on rights and freedoms is not matched by attention to equality of opportunities, nor to social and economic minimums for basic human needs. However, if the political will to address this can be marshalled, international law provides some direction on how that lacuna could be addressed domestically.

International law is increasingly reflective of normative claims to justice, with the United Nations Charter affirming the centrality of states and the promotion of "equal rights and self-determination of peoples," "respect for human rights and for fundamental freedoms" and "conditions of economic and social progress and development" (Anaya 1996: 40–42). The Charter, of course, is drawn extensively from international law, to which Canada is also committed. Yet it is devoted to only part of this corpus, particularly the individual equality rights found in the Universal Declaration of Human Rights and the Covenant on Civil and Political Rights. The guarantees in the Covenant on Economic, Social and Cultural Rights have been largely neglected. Thus, in Canada, following the liberal ideological adherence to formal but not to actual equality, the prince and the pauper are still equally entitled to sleep under the bridge. Aboriginal peoples are disproportionately poor and suffer from poor health and low education relative to Canada's first world norms. Sarah Lugtig and Debra Parkes (2002: 14) argue that "the Charter will not be a success until it is interpreted and applied in a way that meaningfully addresses the growing social and economic inequalities in Canada." Constitutional rights should surely include basic human needs.

There is also the possibility that a Canadian government may eventually be willing to exercise some political leadership and demonstrate commitment to the rights of Aboriginal women and children by implementing legislation intended to eliminate legislative discrimination. Indeed, repeating an earlier 2003 criticism of Canada under the Convention on the Elimination of Discrimination Against Women[19] in 2007, the United Nations Committee on the Elimination of Discrimination urged Canada to "reach a legislative solution to effectively address the discriminatory effects of the Indian Act on the rights of aboriginal women and children...." (CERD 2007: 4).

## CONCLUSION

Aboriginal women have obtained a theoretical benefit, along with white and other women, from the equality guarantees in the Charter and from the emerging convention that constitutional change requires democratic participation of even marginalized groups for its democratic legitimacy. Yet, this has not translated into equitable treatment or representation as *Aboriginal women* in either Aboriginal or settler political institutions or policies.

For Aboriginal women, many of whom suffer from the kinds of oppression that the Constitution is designed to address, there remains the paramount problem of colonialism and the difficulty of entertaining the prospect of liberation via the colonial state and its imposed Constitution. Even when the Constitution serves as an instrument to contest particular cases of oppression, some of which are generated within Aboriginal communities, many Aboriginal women are often deeply uncomfortable with using the colonial Constitution and legal system to defend their rights as Aboriginal women and most acutely uncomfortable when this involves using colonial institutions to challenge Aboriginal men, organizations and governments.

Contemporary treaties and the sets of inter-governmental agreements called "self-government" do not take a gendered view of decolonization. Without suggesting that Aboriginal regimes are any more likely than colonial ones to violate women's rights, it is arguably a "best-practices" matter to explicitly name protection of women's rights in these agreements. After all, Aboriginal liberation must be linked to compliance with international human rights regimes if Indigenous governments are not to run the risk of replicating the abuses they seek to transcend through decolonization.

Activist Aboriginal women, however, have not only focused on constitutional and legal strategies for combating sex discrimination and colonial immiseration. Aboriginal women's groups have emerged at especially the local level, sometimes around a particular issue and sometimes around clusters of issues or objectives. While not often claiming to be feminist, the initiatives of these groups are nevertheless consistent with feminist objectives. The following examples are illustrative. The Aboriginal Women's Action Network (AWAN) of Vancouver is very active in an urban setting, combating poverty, violence and discrimination, especially on the downtown Eastside, the most impoverished urban area in Canada (see also Blaney 2003). AWAN works in solidarity with other social movements and performs a public educative and advocacy function as well as developing its members' political and related skills. The Liard Aboriginal Women's Society, of Liard, Yukon, is focused especially on ensuring women's participation in the constitutional development of the Kaska Dene. In 2005–07, NWAC, founded in 1971 and originally focused on the issue of status under the *Indian Act*, has been conducting a national campaign to draw attention to the high numbers of missing and murdered Aboriginal women in Canada. In Nunavut, where Inuit form a majority, Qulliit, the status of women branch of the Nunavut government, includes Inuit and non-Inuit women in its mandate. In Quebec, the Quebec Native Women's Association, created in 1974, has consistently advocated for Indigenous women, children, and communities.

And yet, the federal government and Aboriginal organizations have resisted the participation of Aboriginal women's organizations in democratic processes. FAFIA writes: "Aboriginal women's organizations suffer from poor funding and exclusion from critical political processes. ... Aboriginal women's groups continue to receive less funding than other Aboriginal organizations, and groups like the Metis National Council of Women and the Pauktuutit continue to be excluded from meaningful political participation."[20]

Clearly, many Aboriginal women and women's organizations are important political and social forces in Canada. Their advocacy and litigation enhance human rights, of which Aboriginal rights and women's rights are important components. Their political interventions can only broaden and deepen our understanding of human rights, of which Aboriginal rights and governance and women's rights are a part; Canadian decolonization; and democracy.

## NOTES

1. Henrietta Muir Edwards and Others v. Attorney General for Canada and Others (Olmsted 1954).

2. The *Indian Act*, a piece of federal legislation passed under the constitutional aegis of s.91(24) of the *Constitution Act 1867*, governs most aspects of life on Indian reserves in Canada. "Status" is the term used to refer to those who are recognized by the federal (national) government as "Indian" for the purposes of the *Indian Act*. Prior to 1985, the Act's membership provisions stripped status from any Indian woman who married anyone other than a status Indian man. Their children were not recognized as Indian, and non-status Indians could not reside on reserves or participate in the political life of reserve communities. Status Indian men, however, retained their status upon marriage and conferred it upon their wives; thus, non-Indian women acquired status upon marriage to status Indian men, and the children of these marriages were recognized as Indian. Pressured by the guarantees of sexual equality in the 1982 *Constitution Act's Charter of Rights and Freedoms*, the federal government amended the *Indian Act* in 1985. However, the amendments have not eliminated sex and race discrimination from the Act, as I discuss later in this chapter. See Green 1985 and Green 1993 for a discussion of these issues.

3. The *British North America Act* was enacted by the British Parliament and was only amendable there. In 1982 the Canadian constitution was patriated, or "brought home," and expanded, and a domestic amending formula was included.

4. The term "Aboriginal" refers to Indigenous peoples, including Indians, Inuit and Métis. Section 35 of the *Constitution Act 1982* acknowledges this. The term "Indian" refers to those Aboriginal peoples who are recognized under the *Indian Act*, and also includes non-status Indians. "Status" refers to those Indians who are recognized under the *Indian Act*; they may be treaty or non-treaty. "Métis" is used to refer to persons of both settler and Indigenous ancestry, though some Métis communities and the Métis National Council prefer a definition based on historical connection with the early Red River Community, and with association with Métis communities and culture(s). The Inuit are distinct from Indian and Métis peoples and historically are from the circumpolar arctic. "Indigenous," the preferred international term, refers to people who are descended from communities that preceded settlement by colonial populations; they are connected to particular lands by culture, economics and history. In this chapter I use the terms Aboriginal and Indigenous interchangeably.

5. Section 35 of the *Constitution Act 1982* reads:
   (1)  The existing Aboriginal and treaty rights of the Aboriginal peoples of Canada are hereby recognized and affirmed.
   (2)  In this Act, 'Aboriginal peoples of Canada' includes the Indian, Inuit and Métis peoples of Canada.

(3)   For greater certainty, in subsection (1) 'treaty rights' includes rights that now exist by way of land claims agreements or may be so acquired.

(4)   Notwithstanding any other provision of this Act, the Aboriginal and treaty rights referred to in subsection (1) are guaranteed equally to male and female persons. Section 35 must be read together with section 25 of the Charter of Rights and Freedoms: 25. The guarantee in this Charter of certain rights and freedoms shall not be construed so as to abrogate or derogate from any Aboriginal, treaty or other rights or freedoms that pertain to the Aboriginal peoples of Canada....

6.   Both the Meech Lake Accord and the Charlottetown Accord were attempts at amending the Canadian constitution. The former was intended to acquire the support of the Province of Quebec for the 1982 *Constitution Act* by making certain guarantes to Quebec for politically and constitutionally significant measures of recognition as a "distinct society." It was the product of elite political consensus (by premiers of provinces and the Prime Minister of Canada), further to constitutional amending formulas in Canada. However Canadians objected to the lack of democratic participation. The latter accord was intended to secure Quebec's support, but was expanded to include economic, Aboriginal and institutional transformations and was the result of democratic consultations throughout the country. It was, however, rejected in a national referendum.

7.   See <http://www.ipcb.org/resolutions/htmls/dec_beijing.html> (accessed March 2007).

8.   The term "settler" refers to those descended from the colonial population, together with contemporary immigrant Canadians. For discussions of this relationship, see Cardinal 1977; Green 1995; Jamieson 1978; Manual and Posluns 1974; Miller 1989; Silman 1987.

9.   Re Sandra Lovelace, United Nations Human Rights Commission 6-50,M 215-51 CANA. The case was brought against Canada by Sandra Lovelace, a Maliseet Indian woman deprived of status by the discriminatory membership section of the pre-1985 *Indian Act*. The decision held that Lovelace was deprived of her right to live in her cultural, religious and ethnic context in her community, contrary to section 27 of the Convention on Civil and Political Rights.

10.   Section 15 (1) Every individual is equal before and under the law and has the right to the equal protection and equal benefit of the law without discrimination and, in particular, without discrimination based on race, national or ethnic origin, colour, religion, sex, age, or mental or physical disability. Section 15 (2) Subsection (1) does not preclude any law, program or activity that has as its object the amelioration of conditions of disadvantaged individuals or groups including those that are disadvantaged because of race, national or ethnic origin, colour, religion, sex, age or mental or physical disability.

11.   First ministers conferences (FMCs) routinely involve the provincial premiers and the prime minister of Canada. At the FMCs in question, the male-dominated Aboriginal organizations were at the table, while the Native Women's Association of Canada and the Quebec Native Women's Association were relegated to observer status.

12.   For a useful discussion of white privilege and the politics of inclusion, see Olson (2001).

13. [1999] 2 Supreme Court Reports, 203.
14. I am indebted to Kelly MacDonald, L.L.M., for her discussion of these matters. Personal communication, September 16, 2002.
15. Native Women's Association of Canada v. Canada [1994] 3 S.C.R. 627 (S.C.C.) reversing (1992), 95 D.L.R. (4th) 106 (F.C.A.). Citation taken from Sawer and Vickers 2001: 27. For a feminist analysis of the decision and for a discussion of NWAC's position in the case, see Eberts, McIvor and Nahanee, (2006).
16. *Sawridge Band v. Canada* [1995] 4 Canadian Native Law Reporter 121 (Federal Court Trial Division); [1997] 215 National Reporter 133 (Federal Court of Appeal).
17. Presentation by Jeanette Lavell to *Moving Toward Equality*, a conference held by Le reseau DIALOG and Quebec Native Women, February 22–24, 2005, Montreal.
18. Sharon Donna *McIvor and Charles Jacob Grismer* v. The *Registrar, Indian and Northern Affairs Canada and the Attorney General of Canada*. Statement of Claim, Written Submissions, filed in the British Columbia Supreme Court in 2002, No. A941142. Thanks to Gwen Brodsky, plaintiffs' counsel, for this reference. The Charter challenge in this case was heard in the BC Supreme Court in October-November 2006 by Carol Ross J. in the BC Supreme Court. The decision is on reserve at the time of writing.
19. The 2003 Convention on the Elimination of Discrimination Against Women (CEDAW) *Concluding Observations of the Committee: Canada* (2003) (A/58/38), paras. 361, 362, stated that: "the Committee is seriously concerned about the persistent systematic discrimination faced by aboriginal women in all aspects of their lives.... The Committee urges the State party to accelerate its efforts to eliminate de jure and de facto discrimination against aboriginal women both in society at large and in their communities, particularly with respect to the remaining discriminatory legal provisions and the equal enjoyment of their human rights to education, employment and physical and psychological well-being."
20. Feminist Alliance for International Action (FAFIA) submission to the United Nations Human Rights Committee on the occasion of its review of Canada's 5th report on compliance with the *International Covenant on Civil and Political Rights*, September 2005, page 15.

## REFERENCES

Anaya, James. 1996. *Indigenous Peoples in International Law*. New York: Oxford University Press.

Blaney, Fay. 2003. "Aboriginal Women's Action Network." In Kim Anderson and Bonita Lawrence (eds.), *Strong Women Stories: Native Vision and Community Survival*. Toronto: Sumach Press.

Blaut, James. 1993. *The Colonizer's Model of the World: Diffusionism and Eurocentric History*. New York: Guildford Press.

Boisard, S. 2002. "Reforming the *Indian Act*: Implications for First Nations Governance?" Unpublished paper, Dept. of Political Studies, University of Saskatchewan.

Cairns, Alan. 1988. "Citizens (Outsiders) and Governments (Insiders) in

Constitution Making: The Case of the Meech Lake." *Canadian Public Policy* (Supplement).

_____. 1993. "The Embedded State: State-Society Relations in Canada." In D.E. Williams (ed.), *Reconfigurations: Canadian Citizenship and Constitutional Change.* Toronto: McClelland and Stewart.

_____. 2000. *Citizens Plus: Aboriginal Peoples and the Canadian State.* Vancouver: University of British Columbia Press.

Cornet, W. 2001. "First Nations Governance, the *Indian Act* and Women's Equality Rights." *First Nations Women, Governance and the Indian Act: A Collection of Policy Research Reports.* Ottawa: Status of Women Canada.

Dobrowolsky, Alexandra. 1998. "Of Special Interest: Interest, Identity and Feminist Constitutional Activism in Canada." *Canadian Journal of Political Science* 31, 4.

Eberts, Mary, Sharon McIvor and Teressa Nahanee. 2006. "The Women's Court Decision in the Appeal of *NWAC* v. *Canada.*" *Canadian Journal of Women and the Law* 18.

Green, Joyce. 1985. "Sexual Equality and Indian Government: An Analysis of Bill C-31." *Native Studies Review* 1, 2.

_____. 1993. "Constitutionalising the Patriarchy: Aboriginal Women and Aboriginal Government." *Constitutional Forum* 4, 4.

_____. 1995. "Towards a Détente with History: Confronting Canada's Colonial Legacy." *International Journal of Canadian Studies* 12 (Fall).

_____. 1997. "Exploring Identity and Citizenship: Aboriginal Women, Bill C-31 and the Sawridge Case." Ph.D. dissertation, University of Alberta.

_____. 2001. "Canaries in the Mines of Citizenship: Indian Women in Canada." *Canadian Journal of Political Science* XXXIV, 4.

_____. 2003. "Decolonisation and Recolonisation in Canada." In Wallace Clement and Leah F. Vosko (eds.), *Changing Canada: Political Economy as Transformation.* Montreal and Toronto: McGill-Queen's University Press.

Jamieson, K. 1978. *Indian Women and the Law in Canada: Citizens Minus.* Ottawa: Queen's Printer/

LaRocque, Emma. 1997. "Re-Examining Culturally Appropriate Models in Criminal Justice Applications." In M. Asch (ed.), *Aboriginal and Treaty Rights in Canada.* Vancouver: UBC Press.

Lutig, S., and D. Parker. 2002. "Where Do We Do From Here?" *Herizons* 15, 2.

Memmi, Albert. 1965. *The Colonizer and the Colonized.* Boston: Beacon Press.

Olmsted, Richard A. (ed.). 1954. "Henrietta Muir Edwards and Others v. Attorney General for Canada and Others." *Decisions of the Judicial Committee of the Privy Council 2.* Ottawa: Queen's Printer, 1954.

Russell, Peter. 1993. *Constitutional Odyssey.* Second edition. Toronto: University of Toronto Press.

Said, Edward. 1979. *Orientalism.* New York: Random House.

_____. 1994. *Culture and Imperialism.* New York: Random House.

Sawer, M., and J. Vickers. 2001. "Women's Constitutional Activism in Australia and Canada." *Canadian Journal of Women and the Law* 13, 1.

Sayers, Judith and Kelly Macdonald. 2001. "A Strong and Meaningful Role for First Nations Women in Governance", *First Nations Women, Governance and the Indian Act: A Collection of Policy Research Reports.* Ottawa: Status of Women Canada.

Trimple, Linda. 1988. "Good Enough Citizens: Canadian Women and Representation in Constitutional Deliberations." *International Journal of Canadian Studies* 17.

Weaver, S. 1993. "First Nations Women and Government Policy, 1970–92: Discrimination and Conflict." In S. Burt, L. Code and L. Dorney (eds.), *Changing Patterns: Women in Canada*. Toronto: McClelland and Stewart.

# Chapter Nine

# LOOKING BACK, LOOKING FORWARD

## *Shirley Green*

We are creatures of context: our identities are formed in the context of history, family, community, gender, culture and so on. All my life I've struggled with the elemental question: Who Am I? and come to several answers, each contextual, each authentic. In this chapter I explore some of the challenges and the necessity of owning our identities.

It was a lovely, sunny morning in August 2002 when I rode out of Regina on my Harley Davidson 1200 Sportster headed for El Paso, Texas, where I would join other riders for the start of the Annual Three Flags Classic Ride from Mexico to Canada. It had been a busy two weeks and I was glad to be "On the Road Again." I love riding. It gives me a feeling of peace and joy and the time to think about problems and issues in my life.

The Three Flags Classic "begins" from the rider's home, to the start point of the race and because it had been my home for several years (and because I wanted to try for the longest distance) I decided to enter the race from Whitehorse, Yukon. I had left Golden, British Columbia, to ride the 3000 or so kilometers to Whitehorse. I rode southeast for about another 3,000 kilometers, for a week-long stopover in Regina, Saskatchewan, to visit my daughter and to attend the Aboriginal Feminism Symposium held August 21–22, 2002. The ride to El Paso would give me time to reflect on the Symposium, to try to absorb the information presented and to remember the women I had met there: passionate, dedicated women who spoke knowledgeably and articulately about their different lives, issues and concerns. It would also give me time to reflect on my own presentation to the Symposium, "Looking Back, Looking Forward," and to ponder the question: How did I get here from there?

When I was first asked to attend the Aboriginal Feminism symposium, I quickly accepted. I did not know what to expect but I had long been interested in both my Aboriginal heritage and in the concept of feminism. I think the seeds of feminism had always been with me, although it had taken them awhile to grow. But over the years grow they did, as I observed and experienced the struggles for acceptance and equality by myself and by my sister as single parents following divorces, as well as by other women. Some of these other women had faced bitter struggles, to the point of being killed by the husbands who had promised to love, cherish and protect them. The words "until death do us part" became their brutal reality.

The casual acceptance by many men but also by many women, of the male right to dominate and control women, caused me to question the society we had created. When Crystal Senyk of Whitehorse, Yukon, was shot by her best friend's husband because she had helped his wife by driving her to a women's shelter, I was horrified by a comment made by a woman co-worker: "She shouldn't have interfered."

Another incident, which also happened in the Yukon, involved an Aboriginal woman who was shot in the back and killed by her husband, as she walked down the road. A few short weeks later, a cow moose, pregnant with twin calves, was shot and left beside the road, near the same community. This created an avalanche of letters to the editor, castigating the person who had committed such a heinous crime and demanding prosecution to the fullest extent of the law. I wrote my own letter, pointing out the disparity in the public reaction to each incident and stating that it was open season on women in the Yukon. I asked the newspaper to withhold my name, as I feared for my safety for expressing these opinions. Incidents such as these served to strengthen my feminist beliefs, and I realized that I could not be a feminist without also becoming an activist. So I looked forward to attending the Symposium. This was an opportunity to further my education as a feminist, and I thought diligently about what I wanted to say as I rode the Alaska Highway from Whitehorse to Regina.

My name is Shirley Green. I was born on May 29, 1935, in the East Kootenay, the southeastern corner of British Columbia, near a place called Flagstone, in a log cabin on the property belonging to my Great Aunt Alice Phillipps Parnell. Flagstone no longer exists but the log cabin is still standing. The East and West Kootenays are part of the traditional territory of the Ktunaxa people (known as the Kootenay in English), and part of my ancestry is Ktunaxa.

My mother, Elizabeth (Bessie) Harriet Sinclair Totten, was also born near Flagstone, and her mother's family had lived in the Tobacco Plains area for too many generations to be counted. Her mother, Mary Rowena Phillipps Sinclair, was a daughter of Michael Phillipps, an Englishman, and Rowena David, the daughter of Chief David, of the Tobacco Plains band of the Ktunaxa nation. Chief David's wife, Rowena's mother, is recorded as "Mrs. Chief David" on her grave marker. Her name, as told me by a cousin, was "Aneas Antiste," which could have been a version of Agnes Baptiste. She was my great-great grandmother.

In 1884, when the Ktunaxa were being forced onto tiny reserve lands by the government, Chief David originally asked for the entire continent for

Indian peoples. Michael Phillipps, his son-in-law, who had been appointed translator for these negotiations, explained that this was not possible. Chief David then named a southern boundary in the U.S. and a northern boundary at the loop of the Columbia River, identifying the traditional territory of the Ktunaxa nation. However, when the existence of the international boundary between Canada and the U.S. was explained to Chief David, he exclaimed: "White man say that line runs right through the middle of my house. Why should you, without asking me or considering me, divide my property and also my children?" (Miller 2002: 23–24).

The Ktunaxa Nation is, at the time of writing, negotiating a treaty with the governments of Canada and British Columbia. The Ktunaxa Nation communities include Columbia Lake, near Windermere, B.C.; Lower Kootenay, near Creston, B.C.; Shuswap, near Invermere, B.C.; St. Mary's, near Cranbrook, B.C.; Tobacco Plains, near Grasmere, B.C.; the Kootenai Tribe of Idaho, near Bonner's Ferry, Idaho; and the Confederated Salish and Kootenai Tribe, near Elmo, Montana. The traditional territory of the five Ktunaxa communities in southeastern British Columbia includes the east and west Kootenays, ranging from north of Golden, to the south into Idaho and Montana, and east of the Rocky Mountains into what is now Kainai and Peigan (Blackfoot) territory.

The Hudson's Bay Company (HBC) played a major role in the colonization of Canada, or Rupert's Land, as it was known then. Hundreds of Bay employees, recruited mainly in Britain and Scotland, arrived in North America to spend years working for the Company. Many took Aboriginal women as wives, sometimes with the legal ceremony of marriage but often, in the phrase used in those days, as "country wives." The well-to-do men, or those who ranked higher in the organization of the Hudson's Bay Company, would often later return to the British Isles to seek a wife from among those of their own social and economic class. Sometimes the country wife and her children would be passed along to another Bay employee. This was a common practice as women and children were viewed as chattels and were at the mercy of the male head of the family unit, be it husband, father, brother, uncle, son: whoever was deemed to be in charge. Sometimes the woman and her children were simply abandoned and left to fend for themselves, often far from their families.

The Hudson's Bay Company was the epitome of a patriarchal corporation and ran its operations with an iron hand. The "Company of Adventurers," as it was known, had a main objective of profit. The colonization of the country and the domination of the Indigenous peoples were wholly connected to the profitability of the fur trade. Many of the Bay employees were recruited from the Orkney Islands, off the northeast coast of Scotland, where the climate was harsh and so too were the economic conditions.

My great-great grandfather, William Sinclair, left from Stromness, Orkney, to sail to North America, to enter the employ of the Hudson's Bay Company. He married Nahooway (her gravestone records her as both Margaret Sinclair and Nahovway, but Cree speakers suggest Nahooway is the more likely formulation), a Cree woman from the Moose Factory area of northern Manitoba, and together they had eleven children. James Sinclair, my great-grandfather, was born at Oxford House in 1806, in what was then the North-West Territories and is now part of Manitoba. As a young Cree and English speaking teen, James was sent to Pomona, Orkney Islands, near East-on-Quay, where he attended the village school for four years, until 1822, when, aged seventeen, he was ready to enter the University of Edinburgh (Lent 1963: 42–45). Most of the male children were sent back to Scotland for their education, and many entered into service for the Bay, as did James upon his return to Rupert's Land. In 1829 he married Elizabeth Bird, daughter of Chief Factor James Bird and his Cree wife (whose name is not recorded). Their youngest child, Colin, born at Fort Garry, was my grandfather.

While there is considerable information available about the men, little is known or recorded about the women they married. The girls of the family were taught practical skills, such as how to sew clothing of cloth and buckskin, how to make moccasins and how to cook and clean, by their mother. Most married young and most married influential Métis or white men, some of them traders for the Hudson's Bay Company. Many were abandoned by their husbands or assigned to another Hudson's Bay employee. That's how it was in the deeply racialized society of Red River: Métis women were married off and generally were ignored in the annals of white man's history. Yet, without the help of these and other Aboriginal women, many of the white men who came to our country would have perished or at least had a much more difficult life.

James Sinclair fell out with Sir George Simpson and the Hudson's Bay Company, largely because of his support for "free trade" and his efforts in lobbying for the Métis and Half Breeds, who wanted to be able to sell their furs, hides and pemmican on the open market and for the best price. The Hudson's Bay Company maintained a Crown-supported monopoly on trade, both on the buying and selling of goods, and punished those who stepped out line by not renewing contracts, by refusing to purchase or transport their goods and by the application of taxes. As Merk (1967: x) writes, "The British Government was a monarchy, much interested in the profits of colonialism. It did not scruple to employ methods which a democracy would not toler-ate. One of these was the creation of colonizing corporations armed with monopolistic privileges, such as were given the British East India Company and the Hudson's Bay Company." So, capitalism and colonialism came to-gether, as the British Crown granted not only a corporate monopoly to the

Hudson's Bay Company, but also empowered it to claim sovereignty for the Crown against Aboriginal nations and other colonial competitors, wherever the HBC would set up shop.

The impact of these colonizing corporations on the Indigenous peoples throughout the world was profound and the legacy of their policies continues to affect the descendants of these peoples. Most especially affected were the women who were taken as "wives" and the children resulting from these unions. As documented in D. Geneva Lent's *West of the Mountains* (1963) and Sylvia Van Kirk's *Many Tender Ties* (1980), they were often discarded or passed on to another Bay employee. Sir George Simpson made such arrangements (actually, he had a friend make these arrangements) (Lent 161-62) when he tired of his "bit o' brown," "article" and "his commodity" (his words), Elizabeth (Betsey) Sinclair, William and Nahooway's daughter, James' sister and my great-aunt. His treatment of the Aboriginal women he formed alliances with illustrates the contempt he had for them, which must have done much to influence the behaviour of the men under his command. And, while Betsey had little power to determine her relationships, she was (mis)characterized as "wild" for the failed dalliance, though it is probable there would have been little criticism had Simpson not cast her off. Nor was her daughter and Simpson's, born in 1822, acknowledged or supported. "Handed off" to Robert Miles, Chief Accountant at York Factory and allegedly under an "obligation" to Simpson, she then vanished from official history (Van Kirk 1980: 161).

While the Hudson's Bay Company and its development of the fur trade had an enormous impact on the colonization of Canada and its Native peoples, the American policy of "Manifest Destiny," coupled with their policies of exploration and development, meant open season on the American Indian. These genocidal policies of warfare and displacement, which included the attempted extermination of Indians and of their economic mainstay, the buffalo, did much to affect the Canadian Government's treatment of Native people. While not as overtly harsh as the American policies, Britain's and then Canada's patriarchal vision of the Indians as "children," who needed to be placed under the care and protection of the Great White Queen, resulted in the mythology that Canada protected Indian people and their best interests by another genocidal policy, assimilation.

My grandmother, Mary Rowena Phillipps, the eldest daughter of Michael Phillipps and Rowena David, married Colin Sinclair, a Métis business associate of her father's, on April 4, 1893, at Fort Steele, B.C., when she was twenty-two and he was forty-nine. Colin and Mary Rowena had eight children, who he insisted be raised as white. They were never registered as Indian and so they were not recognized as "status Indians" under the federal *Indian Act* nor as members of the Tobacco Plains band (of which their maternal grandfather was chief) of the Ktunaxa Nation. That same racism also isolated Mary Rowena and her children from half of their family and from the community they were part of. Colin Sinclair died in 1910 when his team of horses ran away, throwing him from the wagon. Mary Rowena was left a widow at a young age, her youngest child just a year old. There was no public safety net for the poor in 1910, and survival became a real challenge for the family, a challenge made worse by their alienation from the very community that might have supported them — the Ktunaxa community.

Colin was the youngest son of James Sinclair and Elizabeth Bird, both originally from Fort Garry, Manitoba. Both James and Elizabeth were Métis, of Scottish and Cree origin. As a young boy, Colin had travelled from Fort Garry to Fort Walla Walla, Oregon, as part of the 1854 expedition led by his father. The difficult journey took almost seven months and took them to Ktunaxa territory, over Kananaskis Pass and White Man Pass through the Rocky Mountains, to the Kootenay River, which they followed up the Kootenay Valley near Columbia Lake. The party of about one hundred persons camped at Canal Flats and also camped for three days at Tobacco Plains, an area to which Colin would return and live until his death.

Mary Rowena had inherited land from her husband, but through chicanery, she and we were deprived of a portion of it. She is alleged to have signed away some of her land to a government surveyor, marking the sale with her "X." Our family history recounts how her sons, two young Indian boys, approached the white man, busy with his survey instruments. "You're in the wrong place," they said. "This land belongs to our mother." He told them to go away: what did they know — just two Indian kids. He surveyed thirty-five acres of land that belonged to my grandmother for sale to a private third party. Subsequently, to cover up his mistake, she was offered one thousand dollars, to sell it to a man from Alberta. She knew how to sign her name but she didn't want to sell the land and she didn't want to sign the white man's papers. Her name is written on the paper, which I have, under it is "X Her Mark." We consider this to be questionable. They took her land from her, a young Indian woman, a widow with eight children. It is then recorded that the man from Alberta sold it to another man for one dollar. Nothing was ever done with the land. My uncle, a reclusive man who never married, lived there until he died, alone in his small cabin, on a corner of the land that had belonged to his mother.

Colin Sinclair senior had accumulated land — by colonial alchemy, the same land that the Ktunaxa were losing — and my mother, Bessie Sinclair, inherited a quarter-section of land from her mother. However, this land was sold and no longer belongs to the family. My mother married a white man, Harry Totten, and had four children: Harry, Bob, me and Genevieve. We moved to Rock Lake, near Elko, B.C., when I was three, and I lived there until I left home at the ripe old age of seventeen.

My grandmother Mary Rowena lived with us for a time, until her death when I was five. I remember her well. I recall one Easter when I would have been almost five years old. I came out of the bedroom where I slept with my mother and younger sister and saw Grandma sitting on the edge of her bed, with two Easter eggs beside her pillow. "Grandma," I said, "how come you have two eggs and I only have one?" She laughed softly and told me that the Easter rabbit had left one beside her pillow and that, when he came out of our bedroom and hopped by her bed, "I reached out and took another egg out of his basket." I have only a few memories of my grandmother but I cherish them all. I remember her as a wise and gentle women, who told the Easter egg story with humour and compassion, so that a little girl would not feel left out. She died in 1940.

My parents ranched, logged and ran Rock Lake as a small summer resort, with cabins and tent sites for rent and a small store, selling mainly candy, soft drinks and ice cream. The ice cream was delivered to the end of the road leading to the lake in an insulated pack. There was a cool room at the store, also insulated, where the ice cream stayed frozen for a few days. Soft drinks were kept cold by putting them into a tub of ice water. The ice was cut in blocks from the frozen lake during the winter and stored in sawdust in an ice house, for use during the summer. There was a rodeo ground and a dance hall, and my parents made and sold hamburgers. It was apparently idyllic, but there were also awful dysfunctions and abuses that tainted that paradise for my mother and we children, and for other children. I will not speak more of this at present; suffice it to say I believe my life has been threatened for "knowing" and for trying to speak of these matters of long ago.

The lake was small and warmed early in the spring, so my birthday, May 29th, was the unofficial first day of swimming. It was idyllic for us children and it seemed as if we lived in our bathing suits during the summer. Many campers came year after year, and there were usually lots of children to play with and campfires to attend, with storytelling and singing during the warm summer nights. There were chores to do too, such as feeding the chickens and gathering eggs, hauling wood and water and weeding the vegetable garden. There was no electricity or running water so oil lamps had to be filled and the chimneys cleaned and ashes cleaned out of the wood cook stove. Laundry day meant carrying and heating the water and, for many years, using a scrub board to get the clothes clean, wringing the water out of them by hand after washing and rinsing them, and then hanging them on the clothes line to dry. It was a lot of work to do during the summer, but was even more difficult in the winters. It was not an easy life.

Rock Lake was fairly isolated as it was located a mile off the highway and the road was not plowed during the winter unless my father plowed it himself, using a team of horses and a wooden vee-shaped plow or a plow fixed to the front of the old truck. It was a mile to the nearest neighbour, five miles to the small town of Elko and twenty-five long slow miles to Fernie, where the nearest hospital and medical attention were located, as well as banks and the major grocery stores

*It was very dark. My father stopped the truck and got out to listen. There was a Pow Wow, near Edwards Lake and he needed to hear the drums to find the location. There was a very big fire, throwing sparks into the dark sky. I remember an open shelter made of upright posts and it seemed that the roof was covered with branches. I would have been about three years old and this is my earliest memory. Most of all, I remember the sound and feel of the drums, beating, beating, beating their way into my heart.*

My mother must have found it extremely difficult when my father joined the army in late August 1940, to serve in World War II, leaving her with four children, the eldest nine years old and the youngest two and a half. She did not drive and had no way to keep the road open during the winter. I remember one winter when our food supplies were almost completely depleted. Mom decided that she would have to take the train to Fernie, where she would arrange to have the road plowed and purchase a large supply of groceries. We got up early and started the mile and a quarter walk through the deep snow towards the train station at Caithness Siding. The station was an empty, unheated wooden shed, holding only the flag on a pole that my mother would use to signal the train engineer that there were passengers waiting to be picked up. It was hard for her to walk through the unbroken snow. She had to carry my sister Genevieve, because if she put her down the child would disappear in the snow. Imagine our despair when we were still about a half mile from Caithness and we heard the train whistle blow and knew we had missed the train. So we trudged back home and tried again the next morning, after a meager breakfast of the last of the dried currants, which were almost all that there was left to eat. This time we made the train, thanks to an earlier start and to the fact that the trail was broken part of the way.

Staying in town was pretty exciting for us at first. The hotel room was always warm and the inside bathroom was a convenience that we did not have at home. But after the first few days, we longed to be back in our own home, so after Mr. Rahal, the owner of the grocery store, had made arrangements to have the road plowed, he drove us back in a van, loaded with groceries and other purchases.

Getting to school was another problem, as there was no school bus service. I started grade one at the Elko school. I can still remember the excitement and anticipation I felt at the thought that I was going to learn to read and write and do all of the wonderful things that make up Learning. The first day of school, my mother put me on Red, her roan horse, for the mile-long trip out to the highway. There she flagged down the Greyhound bus and explained to the driver that I would be catching the bus each day and also returning after school was out.

My two brothers rode their bicycles or walked, as there was not enough money for all of us to ride the Greyhound bus. That meant a ten mile round trip each day they went to school and chores for them to do in the morning and after they got home each night. After my oldest brother was caught in a blizzard and suffered frostbite, my mother home schooled us, with the help of the Department of Education's Correspondence Courses. This was not ideal: it was hard for us to apply ourselves to the lessons. They were often not completed on time and we fell further and further behind. Our schooling was pretty erratic and was a mixture of correspondence lessons and attendance at schools at Elko, Galloway and Waldo.

The Galloway school was pretty primitive, even by the standards of the day. There was no electricity. Water was carried from a nearby creek by the older boys and the one room was heated by a large oil drum converted into a wood heater. The teacher would make hot cocoa or soup on the stove, which was a welcome addition to the sandwiches made of home baked bread, usually carried to school in a metal syrup or honey pail.

We then went to school at Waldo, a small community on the Kootenay river. You can't find it now, as it was flooded decades later when the Libby dam was built on the Kootenay River in Montana. There was no school bus service so my oldest brother Harry was granted a special drivers licence by the Department of Motor Vehicles so that he could drive us to school in the old green model T, which we affectionately christened Matilda. It was seldom that we arrived at school on time, for much could happen on the six or seven mile drive each morning. I remember running the last half mile when the drive shaft dropped out of the truck, trying to get to school before the bell rang. And the despair of hearing the last bell ringing and knowing that I was going to be late yet again.

It was at this school that I had some of my best and worst teachers. Mr. John Clarkson was the best. He knew how to inspire and encourage the students and encouraged my love of books, reading and learning. The worst teachers shall remain unnamed, though they too made their own contribution and were a source of influence through their conduct and actions. We missed a lot of school, even when bus service started, sometimes purposely missing the bus, walking slower and slower and finally waiting just before rounding the last bend of the road. Waiting to hear the familiar whine of the bus as it came up the hill before our stop and then waiting while the driver stopped and opened the door and looked for us before continuing on his route. Then we would go home to tell our mother that we had "missed the bus."

School had become unpleasant: I felt awkward and self-conscious, and I was so poorly prepared that I couldn't cope well with the demands. This is a feeling that persisted for most of my life and is tied into the issues around identity, knowledge and self-acceptance. We four children hated school by then, or rather hated the part where we had to associate with the other students. Everyone else seemed to have a "best friend" to share a seat on the bus or to chum around with during recess or lunch hour. We always felt left out, different, on the sidelines and not knowing why or what to do about the situation. This feeling of difference and of not being accepted has stayed with me all of my life.

As children, we had to depend on each other for companionship. We spent a great deal of time outdoors, exploring the land and creeks on the 320 acres of land we lived on. Many of our games centred on practising what we viewed as "Indian" skills, as we searched for the missing part of ourselves. We so much wanted to be who we are — but we had no one to teach us. Without any role models, we were left to practise what we could piece together from romantic stereotypes. My oldest brother tried hard to teach himself Native skills: he dug spruce roots and tried to fashion a framework for a canoe but it was too heavy and awkward. He then tried to make a dugout canoe from a log but it, too, ended up too heavy and poorly balanced. One time, he wanted to tan a deerskin and immersed it in the lake to soften the dried hide and loosen the hair. When he took it out a couple of days later, he found that it had turned green and, without anyone to help him or to teach him the traditional skills, he gave up in despair.

Coming from a rural hunting family, we worked on learning to walk through the brush without making a sound. This involved sweeping our eyes ahead of us to see what lay on the trail, such as a stick or some leaves, then glancing from side to side to watch for deer or grouse while we walked forward, using the memory of the trail to avoid stepping on sticks or leaves. The one in front had the responsibility to stop the follower. A hand gesture meant an immediate stop, even in mid-step, to listen intently for the real or imagined sound. A hand cupped behind the ear while turning the head in the direction of the sound helped to amplify whatever it was that we heard. It was also important to know the wind direction, and this was done by sticking your finger in your mouth and then holding it up. The wind would make your finger cold on the side it was blowing from. Or you could let a little bit of grass fall and watch to see what way it fell. Hunting was a way of life and provided meat for the table all year round, regardless of the game regulations.

*My mom and I were standing on Baker Street in Cranbrook. I think I was about twelve years old. An Indian lady, wearing Native dress and moccasins and carrying a baby in a papoose board on her back, came along and spoke to my mother in her language. My mom answered her using the same language. After she had left, I asked my mother what she had said. She said the woman had said "Hello, how are you?" in the Kootenay language. I asked her to tell me how to say that and she told me. But a few days later, I could not remember so I asked my mother to tell me again. She refused and when I asked her why she would not tell me. She said, "You can't look back, you have to look forward."*

My mother could but would not speak Ktunaxa, and with her decision, she deprived her children of that knowledge and of the possibility of connection with who we are. The missing part of my identity has had a profound affect on me, my siblings and later, on my children. I am sure my mother, and perhaps her mother before her, thought they were doing the right thing for their children in turning their backs on their Ktunaxa heritage. I also know that they were under intense pressure from the men they were married to — and in a patriarchal society, male opinion about women's choices also determines what is possible. I am sure my mother and grandmother thought they were giving their children an advantage in a racist, sexist society where being an Aboriginal, and especially an Aboriginal woman, was not an advantage. We four children shared the feeling of being different, of never fitting in, and we all shared a sense of loss that we were not able to articulate. We passed that feeling on to our own children.

It is interesting to consider the idea of "heritage," defined as "what is, or may be handed on to a person from her ancestors" — "a birthright." A birthright. The idea is profound, the responsibility immense and includes not only the ancestors but parents, relatives and indeed, the entire community relating to one through cultural heritage. Why is it that persons of mixed blood are deemed to not be worthy of their heritage or that their birthright can be determined by the pressures and demands of a dominant white society? Who makes the decision that a person does not have the correct amount of the "right" blood to be accepted into the culture and traditions of their society? It is important for us to reclaim our heritage in order that we may become who we are and to heal the psychic wounds left by racism and exclusion.

*I was working during the summer at a small general store and motel near where we lived. A woman came into the store while I was there. After she left, the owner's wife asked me why I had not spoken to her. I said that I did not know who she was, and she told me that the woman was my mother's aunt — my grandmother's sister. I felt embarrassed and ashamed, because I had not known who she was. I often wondered why my family did not visit some of our relatives. My mother did not like to be asked questions like this and would become angry and upset. So I learned to not ask questions.*

It still makes me angry to know that I had a large extended family: aunts, uncles, cousins — girls my age who could have been my friends and playmates. I feel sorrow as well that I never had the opportunity to know these people to whom I was related. There were aunts who knew how to tan hides and make beautiful dresses, jackets, moccasins and gloves and decorate them with beading or quill work. Uncles who could have shown my brother how to make a canoe.

When I lived in Whitehorse, Yukon, I took classes at the Skookum Jim Friendship Centre to learn how to measure and cut out moosehide and to bead and sew moccasins. I found a great deal of satisfaction in practising these skills, and I felt a sense of peace during the sessions, while we sat and beaded, discussed and shared patterns and designs and admired each other's work. I liked to listen to the stories that some of the women would tell as we worked. One told of how her mother taught her and her sisters to bead, starting at quite a young age. She told how, if they dropped a bead on the floor, their mother would make them find it. She told them that each bead was precious and made them pull out any work that was not to her standard and do it over again. She wanted them to learn how to do beautiful work and to have pride in their skill, as she knew they could support their families in the future by selling the items they made. She also wanted them to be able to teach their daughters the traditional skills.

Another woman told us that our work could not be perfect, as only the Great Spirit could make something that was perfect. She told us to make sure to place one bead so that the design was not perfect. There was much laughter at these lessons and sharing of knowledge and supplies. One woman told us of how she would get up early in the morning so that she had an hour or two just to sit and bead before she went to work. Beading was like meditation, soothing to the spirit.

One thing that I have always enjoyed immensely is my relationship with the land. During the fifties and sixties I had become an ardent hunter of big game and spent many hours from dawn to dusk in the bush. This often meant getting up at 3 a.m., in order to drive the fifty or sixty miles to be in the area I wanted to hunt at first light. I loved getting to know an area: the ridges, the draws, the open spaces and the game trails. Sometimes something magical would happen and I would become a part of the land. When this happened, time ceased to exist, and it seemed that my hearing and seeing became sharper. I remember one day when I was able to move right to the edge of a feeding herd of elk. It was still early in the season and I did not want to shoot an animal, so I remained quietly watching them until they moved away, unaware of my presence. Another time I felt that there were animals nearby and stayed quiet. Three whitetail deer came down the ridge and one approached to within ten feet of me, feeding just the other side of a small fallen tree. Again, I did not shoot. It would have shattered the peace and quiet that I felt, both within myself as well as of the moment.

In later years I spent more time hiking and walking in the mountains and seldom hunted, as I did not need the meat. I enjoyed the feeling of independence and self sufficiency that came from packing all my needs on my back, often setting up a small tent or lean-to shelter and sleeping overnight. Though there was always a feeling of peace and joy at being in the bush, I never again experienced the magical feeling of being part of the landscape. To achieve this state of being requires that one be able to empty one's mind of everyday stresses and concerns and to be able to be completely in the moment. There is a sense of oneness that defies my ability to describe.

How does one define identity? Is it the way we view ourselves or is it the way in which we are viewed by others? How can we reclaim our heritage when who we were or who we were supposed to be has been denied us during our most formative years? My mother denied her heritage and ours because of the pressures of a racist, sexist society, where to be Indian was to be viewed as being a lower-class person, with few opportunities for education, employment, growth or progress within the dominant white society.

In order to reclaim our heritage we must look back. We must examine and acknowledge both the good and the bad and remember the injustices done to the women of this country by the colonizers, by society and by our own families, for the parts they played in denying us our birthright and the opportunity to know our own identity. It is only by reclaiming our heritage that we can gain an understanding of who we are and enable us to achieve our full potential, as Aboriginal women.

Samantha Sam says that she feels like a stranger in her Native land. "I don't have that feeling of belonging because I was raised in foster homes. I'm not accepted in the white community because of my skin color and I'm not accepted in the [First Nations] community because I never grew up in it" (2004: 1). Her story reflects that of so many other persons, who for many different reasons, grew up without a knowledge of their Aboriginal culture and heritage. She writes: "Many grow up with a sense of being displaced and of not fitting in properly to society."

Richard Wagamese (1989) speaks of the positive influence he experienced from elders and other spiritually centred people he met as a young adult. He credits those influences with rescuing him from cultural anonymity and giving him back "an appreciation of my culture, my heritage and myself." He also speaks of his search for knowledge and understanding as an incredible journey. He is fortunate in that he had guides to assist him on his journey.

During the on-going process of attempting to reclaim my heritage and define my identity, I explored a relationship with different groups, associated with either the First Nations background of my grandmother or the Métis background of my grandfather. While there were areas of satisfaction, there was also pain, because of the politics of inclusion and the politics of exclusion, based on who you were and who you knew.

I relate closely to the women from whom I am descended. Through these women, I am Ktunaxa and Cree-Scottish Métis. Many of these women, their spouses and other family members — aunts, uncles, cousins to the second, third and more degree — are buried in the little cemetery at Roosville, B.C., overlooking the valley. The cemetery is part of traditional Ktunaxa territory, which pre-exists Canada and the United States and is imposed on by the Canada-U.S. border, which, as my great-great-grandfather claimed, runs through his territory and family. My youngest son, David James Green, dead at the age of twenty-two as the result of a car accident, is there as well, and I wish to be buried there too when my time comes.

It seems as if I have spent a lot of time looking back but I think it is important to remember both the good and the bad happenings in our lives, the positive and the negative, the kind and the cruel, so that we can reach some kind of acceptance and understanding. Only when we are able to hold onto the good and let go of the bad will we be at a place where we can be at peace and can begin our own journey towards our cultures, our heritages and our identities. All of them. Only then can we be whole.

## REFERENCES

Lent, D. Geneva. 1963. *West of the Mountains: James Sinclair and the Hudson's Bay Company.* Seattle: University of Washington Press.

Merk, Frederick. 1967. *The Oregon Question: Essays in Anglo-American Diplomacy and Politics.* Cambridge, MA: Belknap Press of Harvard University Press.

Miller, Naomi. 2002. *Fort Steele: Gold Rush to Boom Town.* Surrey, B.C.: Heritage House Publishing, B.C. Arts Council.

Sam, Samantha. 2004. "Caught Between Two Cultures." *Aboriginal Peoples Family Accord (APFA) Newsletter* Spring.

Van Kirk, Sylvia. 1980. *Many Tender Ties: Women in Fur-Trade Society, 1670–1870.* Winnipeg, MB: Watson and Dwyer Publishing.

Wagamese, Richard. 1989. "Touching the Circle." *Windspeaker* September 1.

Chapter Ten

# MAORI WOMEN AND LEADERSHIP IN AOTEAROA/NEW ZEALAND

*Kathie Irwin*

## TOI WAHINE: THE WORLDS OF MAORI WOMEN

I returned to my office one day having collected my phone messages and prepared myself to respond to them as usual. There was one message that made my heart leap — "Would you please ring Robyn Kahukiwa." Would I what!

She is one of my all-time favourite "sheros." To say that I would run barefoot over broken glass to work for her communicates something of the regard that I have for her work and for the way that she walks her journey through life. I've learned to celebrate sheros; they contribute so much. I also celebrate heros and have lots of them. It's just that we're much better at recognizing and celebrating our heros in this country than we are our sheros. More is the pity. Celebrating sheros seeks to bring a more balanced ensemble into the spotlight.

Yes, I would ring Robyn, and did, immediately. She was home. She had a project she wanted me to look at. Irihapeti Ramsden and Robyn had worked on putting together a book of Maori women's work. Robyn had created a new series of paintings of Maori women; Irihapeti had gathered a new selection of Maori women's writing about aspects of Maori women's lives. The paintings are a collection of images of our women, young and old, some capturing modern images, some traditional. In the collection of written pieces was a wonderful new short story by Patricia Grace called "Something Important," about a young teenage Maori girl, poetry by Bub Bridger and a short story by Mereana Pitman called "Broken Peace/s," which describes the impact of domestic violence on a *whanau*.[1] Keri Kaa wrote a delightful piece called "Dear Mrs Government." It is written from the viewpoint of a *kuia* (woman elder) on the East Coast who writes to the wife of the Government seeking help for her *whanau*. She writes to the wife having assessed that the husband (Mr Government) isn't listening! To this day the piece is a classic.

The view of the collection was that something was missing, that it didn't quite work. Robyn asked me to read the pieces, to look at the paintings and to see if I could make any suggestions about how to proceed.

When I saw the material I was stunned by it. It was so real, so raw and so direct. I sat with it for a while before my sense of what was happening with this collection emerged. The writing was all in the genre of fiction and I knew what was wrong. That they were fiction was hiding the truth of the stories, making them seem unreal. Yet I knew that they were real; they were stories I'd experienced, seen and could connect to in many contexts. The solution seemed easy: mix the genres. Put non-fiction pieces that spoke of facts and figures and actual policies with the fiction pieces, so that the "truth" of our lives as a group of women could not be denied. We gathered a series of academic essays, papers and speeches that addressed the themes relevant to our worlds as Maori women. We added a university graduation speech by Dame Mira Szaszy, the address Hinemoa Awatere gave to the Second World Indigenous Youth Conference in Darwin and academic papers on policy (Liz McKinley), gender, race and the politics of difference (Trish Johnston and Leonie Pihama) and goal setting (Everdina Fuli).

Added to the paintings and fictional pieces already written we now had a new dimension. What the publishers were reflecting in their initial response was the fact that people seem to find it hard to believe the realities that Maori women live. The publishers loved what we proposed to do, and the book was produced as *Toi Wahine: The Worlds of Maori Women* (Kahukiwa, Ramsden and Irwin 1995). *Toi Wahine* provides a series of powerful lived insights about *mana wahine*, which enables readers to look again at the women, the *whanau*, the communities and the country they live in. Maori women have made a huge contribution to the Maori renaissance, the programs of Maori development and the models of transformative social and educational practice that have led Maori in this country from the wretchedness of colonization to the hope of new futures (Fanon 1967; Freire 1994; Irwin 2002).

## THE MAORI RENAISSANCE

Maori in Aotearoa have been engaged in what has been termed a "renaissance" for over three decades now (Black, Marshall and Irwin 2003). Since perhaps 1975, when Dame Whina Cooper led the *Hikoi*, the Land March, from Te Hapua in the north to Parliament, highlighting the impact of the alienation of Maori land from *iwi* Maori, Maori have been on the move, creating new futures. Key features of the new initiatives were expressed in programs that resulted from the reform of the Department of Maori Affairs in the late 1970s (Puketapu 1982). Known as the Tu Tangata programs, the approach inspired Maori to stand tall.

The aims of Tu Tangata were to improve educational attainment; provide opportunities for self-fulfillment within the community; raise the socio-economic status of the Maori people; and *kokiri*, "to advance" (Puketapu 1982: 3). Three features of the approach were identified as: Tu Tangata, to recognize the stance of the people; Whaka Whaiti, to harness the resources and strengths of all the people; and Ko tou rourou, to increase the contribution each of us can make to the advancement of the Maori and to New Zealand as a whole (Puketapu 1982: 10). The Tu Tangata programs were designed to enable Maori "to stand tall" again by reclaiming Maori knowledge as the theoretical framework that informed them and by adopting *te reo* Maori, *tikanga* Maori and the rituals and protocols of the *marae* as the means of operationalizing them. This inspired Maori to find the nexus between Maori epistemology, ontology and methodology and to celebrate this in new and exciting ways.

Maori women were at the forefront of these developments advocating change and transformation through traditional concepts (e.g., *whanau* development) and knowledge (*matauranga whanau/hapu/iwi*). Maori women contributed to these programs of Maori development in the following ways: Maori women were consulted extensively in the formulation of Maatua Whangai, Tu Tangata and Kohanga Reo programs. They also participated on a voluntary basis in their implementation. Indeed, were it not for the unpaid effort of the women none of these programs would have got off the ground (Ministry of Women's Affairs/Department of Statistics 1990: 20).

## MAORI WOMEN LEADING MAORI EDUCATION

One of the strategies to learn about the big picture in this country has been to study the little picture. Through this I discovered for myself why the integration of herstories is such a critical component of theorizing *mana wahine*. So often our women have walked against the grain of history and created opportunities where none were supposed to exist. I want now to turn to the stories of women who have provided profound leadership to our people. In doing so I am clear that many, many women will be left off this list and that some may be offended by these omissions. I apologize in advance. The project is a long-term one and will include more vignettes as it grows.

### Makareti Papakura

Makareti Papakura was born in Whakarewarewa, Rotorua, in 1872. Her schooling included a three-year period at Hukarere. She returned to *whanau* in Whakarewarewa and to the burgeoning tourist industry and became one of the famous guides of Whakarewarewa, mixing with guests from around the world. In 1912 she travelled to England to marry and settle (Te Awekotuku 1986).

Makareti obtained her bachelor of science degree in anthropology at Oxford University. Her research was published in 1938 under the title *The Old Time Maori*. The text is "the first comprehensive ethnographic account by a Maori scholar" (Te Awekotuku 1986: ix). Dr Ngahuia Te Awekotuku noted that "Makareti saw her own work as an attempt: to show to the western academic a unique and challenging view — that of the Indigenous person, disciplined, but certainly not shaped, by the niceties of western education" (ibid). Whereas non-Maori scholars rose to international fame through their writing on Maori at about this time (e.g., Elsdon Best), Makareti and her work did not. Te Awekotuku reflects on why this might have been:

> *The Old Time Maori* emerged not from the erudite pondering of an amateur historian writing within the kauri walls of his villa on raupatu land; rather this work came, quizzically, from the faraway cloisters of prestigious Oxford — and the pen of a Maori woman who "should have known her place." (x–xi)

## Te Puea Herangi

Te Puea Herangi led a life of exemplary service to her people. There are many stories from Te Puea's life that show her innovative and profound leadership: her nursing through the influenza epidemic and her care and provision for children orphaned through it; her leadership in doing what needed to be done herself, not calling on others to do what she would not do. The story of Turangawaewae is one that has national significance. It tells of her work to achieve what King describes as "the turangawaewae prophecy" (1977: 103). Tawhiao is recorded as having stood in front of his father Potatau's burial tomb saying: "Alexandra will be a symbol of my strength of character, Cambridge a washbowl of my sorrow, and Ngaruawahia my turangawaewae" (ibid).

King identifies the prophecies of Tawhiao as a source of power for Te Puea (105). Creating a settlement at Ngaruawahia was about working to "re-establish the mana of the King Movement," as she put it, "to make Waikato a people again" (104). Te Puea had planned a range of strategies to implement this goal: "model settlements, helping people become economically self reliant through farming, building new meeting houses, obtaining Pakeha recognition of the movement" (ibid). King describes her paramount strategy in this way: "the one that had to precede all others to make what she was doing auspicious and spiritually valid — was the creation of a pa at Ngaruawahia" (ibid). In August of 1921 Te Puea told her people that they were to shift to Ngaruawahia. King reports that she said, "We are going to build a marae there that will be suitable for everybody throughout the country; a marae that, one day, people will visit from all over the world. And we're going to do it for Waikato and for our king." Then she repeated Tawhiao's *whakatauaki* about his *turangawaewae* and said it was the guarantee of their success (108). The land selected for purchase was on the banks of the Waikato River across from Ngaruawahia itself. The land "had been used over a long period as the town's unofficial rubbish tip" (105).

## Dr. Rangimarie Rose Pere

Rangimarie Rose Pere has provided a rich source for research and scholarship in *matauranga* Maori with the publication of her monograph, *Ako* (1982). The work was based on a career in both the Maori and western traditions in which she has held every position from a scale-A teacher to university fellow. An ancestral speaker of our language, she was socialized into the traditional worldview of our people, and she has travelled all over the world working with Indigenous and non-Indigenous peoples in their quest for a new humanity. She has always described herself as a child of the universe and her work as universal, based on principles that are relevant to any culture in any context.

The paper "Te Wheke," published in Middleton's ground-breaking *Women and Education in Aotearoa* (1988), outlines and explores principles of child development in the Maori worldview. It has enabled research and scholarship to be theorized from the nexus between Maori epistemology, ontology and methodology.

## Iritana Tawhiwhirangi

Iritana Tawhiwhirangi led the team that brought us the concept of *te kohanga reo*, which has not only brought the revitalization of *te reo* Maori into the new millennium in Aotearoa but has also created a model for educational transformation that is portable across cultures (Tawhiwhirangi et al. 1988). *Kohanga reo* were part of the Tu Tangata programs, which emerged from the reform of the Department of Maori Affairs in the mid-1970s. The aim of those programs was "to enhance the social, cultural and economic well-being of Maori people in a way which reflected their cultural strengths and aspirations" (Tawhiwhirangi et al. 1988). The objective of the movement was described in this way by the then Hon. Koro Wetere, Minister of Maori Affairs: "The ultimate objective of te Kohanga Reo is nothing less than the rebirth of the Maori Nation as an equal but separate element contributing to the common good of New Zealand society" (Fleras 1983).

The model was profound, implementing what Banks (1988), theorizing in America (and writing about schools), identified as the crucial aspect of transforming education, namely that "the total school environment" had to be the unit of change. This was the *kohanga* way: the *kohanga* was an immersion program, in *te reo* Maori *me ona tikanga*, at the early childhood level, run by the *whanau* for the *whanau* (Tawhiwhirangi et al. 1988). In 2003 it was the subject of an invited presentation to the First Permanent United Nations Forum on Indigenous Issues (Black, Marshall and Irwin 2003).

## Dr. Patricia Grace

Patricia Grace was our first Maori woman novelist, fitting her writing career around her roles as secondary school teacher, wife and mother of seven.

She has published numerous novels, collections of short stories and children's books. Amongst her works are her first novel *Mutuwhenua* (1978), her
first collection of short stories, *Waiariki* (1975) and the children's books *The
Kuia and the Spider* (1981) and *Watercress Tuna and the Children of Champion Street*
(1984). The 1984 text is written by her with paintings by Robyn Kahukiwa.
Her books have been translated into a number of languages and are taught
in universities around the world, opening the world up to an understanding
of the Maori worldview. Her stories are the stories of our people; she has
enabled people from the four corners of the globe to walk in our footsteps
and see a little of the world through our eyes.

### Dr. Katarina Mataira
Katarina Mataira has worked for decades on the promotion and retention
of *te reo* Maori. Her work has included both academic research and community-based Development, as well as service on the boards of Te Mangai
Paho and Te Taura Whiri I Te Reo Maori. She completed an M.Ed. thesis
at Waikato University (1981) on the methodology of second-language teaching, entitled "The Effectiveness of the Silent Way Method in the Teaching
of Maori as a Second Language."

The research in this work informed Te Ataarangi, the community-
based Maori language learning program, which has become a focal place
for adult second-language learners of Maori. The Te Ataarangi Society was
formed in 1982 and has amassed many years of service to thousands of New
Zealanders, providing Maori language classes to adults raised without their
ancestral tongue.

### Merata Mita
Merata Mita started her career as a secondary school teacher and became
an internationally recognized filmmaker. *Bastion Point Day 507* and *Patu* are
two of her outstanding documentary films that have captured watershed
events in our history (Myers 1986). The story of her work to bring us *Patu*,
the documentary about the Springbok Tour, should leave no one in any doubt
about what is at stake when Maori women try to bring the truth about our
society to the public eye. I read Merata's account of this in *Head and Shoulders*
(Myers 1986). She was threatened with the sack if she was "seen anywhere
near the demonstrations" (1986: 58). She was working in television at the
time. Of particular impact were the insights she gained about our society
through the making of this film. In her words:

> I completely underestimated the viciousness in New Zealand society.
> Like many people I'd been sold the myth that we are all really very
> nice people…. the underbelly of New Zealand society showed up,
> and it was pretty ugly. It was vicious, it was violent, it was racist,

and that was a shock to me. But it was a good shock to me because it taught me never to underestimate what I was up against. (Myers 1986: 59)

## Robyn Kahukiwa

Robyn Kahukiwa has created a huge portfolio of images of Maori women, which enables us to see ourselves in art work of the highest calibre. Her work hangs in esteemed galleries all around the world. In *Wahinetoa* (1984) Robyn completed a series of paintings that bring us the stories of the women in our creation stories. The book provides a number of images for each of the women and their *korero*. Black and white sketches as well as glorious full colour photos fill the book.

Robyn has painted a particular set of images that provide powerful insights into the theorizing of Maori feminists. For each woman she has created a painting that shows the whole story of that woman in context, with the relevant men also included in the image. The lesson of this is useful, in making the woman visible, the *mana* of the context and the other people around her are left intact. Robyn has also created the visual images in a number of children's books. One was *Taniwha* (1986), which she worked on with Keri Kaa.

## Professor Ngahuia Te Awekotuku

Ngahuia Te Awekotuku was the first Maori woman to obtain a Ph.D. in Aotearoa/New Zealand, graduating from the University of Waikato with a doctorate on the impact of tourism on her people, Te Arawa (Irwin et al. 1991). Ngahuia has been a published academic writer of international renown for at least three decades. *Maori Women: An Annotated Bibliography* begins her citation with a 1971 publication in *Craccum*. The citation for a 1989/1990 paper in which she reflects on herstory is catalogued as follows:

Of particular importance is her analysis of the political thinking of the Maori university-based groups which were prominent in the early seventies. Her reference to the need to develop an Indigenous theory of Maori oppression, rather than import theories from the black civil rights movement of the United States is significant, foreshadowing the time when Maori sovereignty would make a case for a similar theoretical position in the 80s. (Irwin et al. 1991: 35)

Ngahuia is credited as being one of the founders of the gay liberation movement in Aotearoa (Dann 1985). When refused a visa to enter America to take up a scholarship that she had won because of her lesbianism, she led a national gay rights campaign in protest. She has since then been a champion of many issues relating to gay and lesbian rights.

## Dr Irihapeti Ramsden

Irihapeti Ramsden, initially a trained nurse, later became a nurse educator and involved in the development of Kawa Whakaruruhau (Brown 1994), a program based in anti-racist education that aims to facilitate decolonization in nursing education. By teaching basic cultural knowledge rather than focusing on the specifics of cultural awareness, this program moves to an analysis that teaches about the cultural locatedness of any education or training program within a socio-political context.

The program has been the subject of much debate and critique and has transformed the nature of nursing education in this country (Ramsden n.d.). Through her international networks the research has also had an impact on nursing education globally. The work is the subject of her doctoral thesis and is available online, through the Massey University website.[2]

## Donna Awatere

In the early 1980s Donna Awatere provided a gripping political analysis in *Maori Sovereignty* (1984) that challenged the women's movement directly to face decolonization as a project of feminism. One of the very few trained Maori psychologists at the time, her work had tremendous impact as she deconstructed the institutionalization of power and privilege that has benefited the non-Maori signatory to the Treaty of Waitangi since its signing.

The text became compulsory reading in many university courses. Donna became a shero and role model for many Maori women coming through the university system and looking for cutting-edge analyses informed by research and scholarship located in *kaupapa* Maori.

## MAORI WOMEN AND LEADERSHIP

The "wretched" aspects of Maori women's lives, at the group level, can be understood against the larger historical, political and structural context of "wretchedness" as articulated by Fanon (Fanon 1967, 1990; Mead 1994). That wretchedness cuts through every dimension of life, from the macro, global level to the most personal, micro level; without choice, without invitation, without consent. An invasion of the complete kind, it is institutionalized into the very fabric of society, so that there is no escaping it. The past is steeped in its grip, the present grapples with its legacy, and the future awaits its impact. The only response available is to deal with it: to confront and manage the wretchedness of colonization. The responses to this vary among peoples, institutions and countries. The stories of these women, and their work, reveal to us a range of responses from Maori women that defy oppressive history.

Far from being doom and gloom revisited, there are now exciting horizons of hope as new futures are created. The new leadership taking us forward is revolutionary. Each one of these *wahinetoa* took a stand against the wretchedness of colonization and gave back to us as Maori not only our hope to dream again but the capacity to build those dreams in many and varied ways (Irwin 2002). We have watched our women achieve success where others thought that this was impossible. Their courage is compelling, as are the stories of the successes they achieved.

## CONCLUSION

"Shero worshipping" is a positive strategy of reclaiming the human spirit and is accomplished simply in telling the herstories of our women. The shero emphasis lets us stand a little taller about the contributions our women have made. It is utterly oppositional to the "tall poppy syndrome" in New Zealand, which seeks to cut down anyone who dares to rise beyond the expectations society has for them.

Gathering such herstories is a powerful exercise. It enables us to see that what is written and said about our society does not always match up with what is experienced by those living in Maori communities and working in programs of Maori development. Maori women are demonstrating what Covey (1989) calls the Character Ethic. They are taking a "principle centred, character based, 'inside out' approach to personal and interpersonal effectiveness," and implementing The Seven Habits of Highly Effective People.

Herstories, when integrated with structural, institutional and personal analyses, add a powerful experiential dimension to educational analysis: they highlight where the gaps are. The strategy of reclaiming herstories, shero worshipping, contributes to theorizing about Maori feminisms and development in a very grounded way, from the bottom up, rather than the top down. We have suffered at the hands of top-down theory much as we have from economic development premised on the same approach. Our realities are rarely integrated into the thinking of those designing the "big picture." Baer Doyle (1988) argues that the events in our lives provide a foundational aspect of the development of any philosophy/worldview.

The Maori social structure of *whanau/hapu/iwi* locates Maori women in a collective social configuration. It is towards the strengthening of this social structure that the programs of Maori development are being directed. Maori women take our political analysis and action beyond the "individualistic" mode characteristic of the western tradition. The slogan from feminism, "the personal is political," becomes something else for Maori women: "the personal is political, the personal is collective, the collective is political." The change has significant implications for the nature of the work that Maori women undertake. Simply put, the political nature of the projects is about survival in authentic terms: decolonizing our community and the wider society, so that we can find new futures, "unmasking" in the sense taken from Fanon (1967).

Dame Mira Szaszy (1995: 134) has suggested that "what we... need... is a new Maori humanism — that is a humanism based on ancient values but versed in contemporary idiom." The vignettes presented in this paper suggest that the leadership Maori women are providing is helping to create just that: a new Maori humanism. *Kia maumahara koe I tou mana ake:* Remember your absolute uniqueness (Pere 1988).

## NOTES

1.  The following translations of Maori words to English is kindly provided by Makere Stewart-Harawira.

    *hapu* – usually taken to mean sub-tribe, *hapu* were the primary social organization of Maori societies

    *hikoi* – means to step, to march. In this case it refers to the Maori Land March of 1975 when Maori from all corners of the country marched from the top of the North Island to the Parliament Buildings in Wellington to protest against the ongoing confiscation of Maori land and to demand control, retention and management of Maori land by Maori.

    *iwi* – tribe, usually referred to a confederation of *hapu* or sub-tribes. *Iwi* also means "bones," so can be loosely interpreted as the bones of the ancestors from whom you came

    *kaupapa* Maori – Maori philosophy, also used to describe an intervention strategy in the Maori renaissance, which is based in the Maori worldview, which privileges Maori knowledge and seeks to re-normalize it in a contemporary context

    *kauri* – a native tree

    Kawa Whakaruruhau – *kawa* means cultural customs, *whakaruruhau* means to be aware. Kawa Whakaruruhau refers to a set of cultural guidelines that have been established for nursing, midwifery, etc.

    *ko tou rourou* – *rourou* means, literally, baskets. This refers to one section of a Maori proverb and means "your contribution." The entire proverb is *Ko tou rourou – ko taku rourou – ka ora ai te iwi.* "With your contribution and my contribution the people flourish."

    *kohanga reo* – literally meaning "language nests," refers to the Maori immersion preschool programs first developed during the early 1980s by Maori, for Maori, partly in response to concerns that the language was facing imminent extinction. Originally begun in people's homes, these programs spread rapidly and became the foundation of the Maori language revitalization movement, which now includes immersion primary schools and secondary schools.

    *kokiri* –to advance

    *korero* – their stories

    Maatua Whangai – a Maori not-for-profit community-based social service provider in the areas of justice, health and youth

    *mana wahine* – refers to the status, dignity, spiritual power of Maori women

    *marae* – literally means the meeting house and the attached buildings such as the *whare kai* – dining hall, the courtyard and surrounding area

    *matauranga whanau/hapu/iwi* – the specific forms of Maori knowledge and ways of doing things that are held by those groupings.

*pa* – fortified village

Pakeha – a generic term referring to non-Maori New Zealanders, usually those who are the descendants of the settler societies. Similarly, the term Maori is a generic term that was applied post-contact to all the Indigenous tribes of Aotearoa/New Zealand.

*Patu* – the name of one of the films by Merata Mita refers to a traditional Maori hand club carved out of bone, wood or pounamu (greenstone)

*raupatu land* – confiscated land. Land that was confiscated by the colonial government because of the resistance of the people to invasion by the British and their desire to retain their own sovereignty.

Tawhiao was the second Maori king and leader of the Ngati Mahuta tribe in the central Waikato region. He reigned for thirty years and was for many Maori the figurehead of the Maori nation-wide movement, which sought a Maori government alongside the colonial government. The movement was eventually defeated by the colonial government, and huge land losses were incurred through confiscation. Tawhiao died in 1894.

Te Hapua – the name of a Maori community in the Far North of the North Island

Te Mangai Paho – Maori Broadcasting Service

Te Puea was a high-ranking Waikato leader who became famous throughout the entire country for the work she did on behalf of her people. This included the establishment of the carved meeting houses at Turangawaewae and land development to provide an economic base for her people, who had suffered enormous land losses through the confiscations that resulted from Tawhiao's movement.

*te reo* Maori – the Maori language

*te reo* Maori *me ona tikanga* – Maori language and customs

Te Taura Whiri ITe Reo Maori – the Maori Language Commission

*tikanga* Maori – Maori cultural protocols

*tu tangata* – literally, to stand

*turangawaewae* literally means "the planting of my feet" or "place to stand." Turangawaewae is the name of the *marae* that is the headquarters of the Maori King Movement of the Waikato tribes at Ngaruawahia, a small town of a mostly Maori community in the centre of the North Island. Hence "*Ngaruawahia my turangawaewae*" means this town, this community, is where I will place my feet.

*wahinetoa* – literally means "warrior women" and is also the title of a book by Robin Kahukiwa

Whaka Whaiti – *whaiti* means to be cautious

*whakatauaki* – proverb

*whanau* – extended family in the very broadest sense

An excellent article of which Kathie Irwin is a co-author and which provides more detail regarding some of the concepts can be found at <http://www.kohanga.ac.nz/docs/UNAddressMay21.pdf> (accessed March 2007).

2.  <http://www.massey.ac.nz> (accessed March 2007).

# REFERENCES

Awatere, D. 1984. *Maori Sovereignty*. Auckland: Broadsheet Books.

Baer-Doyle, T. (1988). "To Learn or to Know: What is the Quest?" In S. Middleton (ed.), *Women and Education in Aotearoa*. Wellington: Allen and Unwin Books/Port Nicholson Press.

Banks, J. 1988. *Multiethnic Education: Theory and Practice*. Boston: Allyn and Bacon.

Black, T., P. Marshall and K.G. Irwin. 2003. "Te Kohanga Reo: Twenty Years On, Address to United Nations Permanent Forum on Indigenous Issues." New York. Available at <www.kohanga.ac.nz/docs/UNAddressMay21.pdf> (accessed March 2007).

Brown, A. 1994. *Mana Wahine: Women Who Show the Way*. Auckland: Reed Books.

Covey, S. 1989. *The Seven Habits of Highly Effective People*. Melbourne: The Business Library.

Dann, C. 1985. *Women and Liberation in New Zealand: 1970–1985*. Wellington: Allen and Unwin/Port Nicholson Press.

Fanon, F. 1967. *Black Skins, White Masks*. London: MacGibbon and Kee.

_____. 1990. *The Wretched of the Earth*. New York: Grove Press.

Fleras, A. 1983. "Te Kohanga Reo: Preparation for life or preparation for school." A preliminary report on the organisation, objectives and implication of Maori language nests presented to the Department of Maori Affairs. Unpublished paper. University of Waterloo, Waterloo, Ontario.

Freire, P. 1994. *Pedagogy of Hope*. New York: Continuum.

Grace, P. 1975. *Waiariki*. Auckland: Longman Paul.

_____. 1978. *Mutuwhenua*. Auckland: Longman Paul.

_____. 1981. *The Kuia and the Spider*. Auckland: Longman Paul.

_____. 1984. *Watercress Tuna and the Children of Champion Street*. Auckland: Longman Paul.

Grace, P., and Kahukiwa, R. 1984. *Wahinetoa*. Auckland: Collins.

Irwin, K.G. 2002. "Maori Education: From Wretchedness to Hope." Unpublished Ph.D. thesis. Victoria University.

Irwin, K.G. et al. 1991. *Maori Women: An Annotated Bibliography*. Wellington: Learning Media.

Kahukiwa, P. 1986. *Taniwha*. Auckland: Penguin.

Kahukiwa, R., I. Ramsden and K. Irwin (eds.). 1995. *Toi Wahine: The Worlds of Maori Women*. Auckland: Penguin.

King, M. 1977. *Te Puea*. Auckland: Hodder and Stoughton.

Mataira, K. 1981. "The Effectiveness of the Silent Way Method in the Teaching of Maori as a Second Language." Unpublished M.Ed. thesis, University of Waikato.

Mead, A. 1994. "Maori Leadership: The Waka Tradition." Proceedings of the Hul Whakapumau, Maori Development Conference. Department of Maori Studies, Massey University.

Middleton, S. (ed.). 1988. *Women and Education in Aotearoa*. Wellington: Allen and Unwin Books/Port Nicholson Press.

Ministry of Women's Affairs/Department of Statistics. 1990. *Women in New Zealand*. Wellington: Department of Statistics.

Myers, V. 1986. *Head and Shoulders*. Auckland: Penguin Books.

Pere, R. 1982. "Ako: Concepts and Learning in the Maori Tradition." Paper No. 17, Department of Sociology, University of Waikato, Hamilton, New Zealand.

_____. 1988. "Te Wheke: Whaia te maramatanga me te aroha." In S. Middleton (ed.), *Women and Education in Aotearoa*. Wellington: Allen and Unwin.

Puketapu, K. 1982. *Reform from Within*. Wellington: Department of Maori Affairs.

Ramsden, I. (n.d.). "Kawa Whakaruruhau." Unpublished Manuscript.

Szaszy, M. 1995. "Seek the Seeds for the Greatest Good of all People." In Kahukiwa. Ramsden and Irwin.

Tawhiwhirangi, I., K.G. Irwin, R. Renwick and F. Sutton. 1988. *Government Review of Te Kohanga Reo*. Wellington: Government Printer.

Te Awekotuku, N. 1986. "Introduction." In M. Papakura, *The Old Time Maori*. Auckland: New Women's Press.

Chapter Eleven

# YES, MY DAUGHTERS, WE ARE CHEROKEE WOMEN

## Denise K. Henning

Every colonizer is privileged, at least comparatively so, ultimately to the detriment of the colonized. (Memmi 1965: 11)

The slow rhythmic beating of the drum and singing of the Gourd Dance pulsed in time with the familiar sound of the gourd rattles that more than fifty men shook while honouring the songs of warriors. As a young mother with three daughters, I regularly attended weekend powwows, or "doins," in what became our homeland after the *nunna dual tsunyi* (literally translated, "the trail where we cried") in southeastern Oklahoma. I recall this particular event because it was the time when "Baby Girl," my youngest daughter, asked me during the Gourd Dance, "Mom, why can't girls dance inside the circle with the men instead of only dancing on the outside?"

This was my signal that the time had come to ensure that the teachings of the women who had gone before me were passed on to my daughters. They needed to learn about the roles of Cherokee women, our place, where we fit within our society and our worldview, and how our ways had been forcibly changed by the European colonizers, who saw only their way as civilized and entitled. It was the time to be certain that my daughters knew and understood that the *Ani yun wiya*, "Principal People," are still here and in many ways still intact.

Let me start at the beginning with the story of Selu, the Corn Woman:

> Selu lived with her husband, Kanati, and two sons. Every day, she would go away from the house and return with a basket full of corn. The boys wondered where the corn came from, so they followed her one day. They saw her go into a storehouse, and they got where they could peek in and watch her.
>
> There they saw her place her basket and shake herself. The corn started falling from her body into the basket. They then thought that their mother must surely be a witch!
>
> Selu could read the boys' thoughts. She told them that after

they put her to death, they would need to follow her instructions so that they would continue to have corn for nourishment.

"After you kill me, you must clear some ground in front of our house. Then drag my body in a circle seven times. Then, you must stay up all night and watch."

The boys did this, but they got the instructions backwards. They cleared seven areas of ground and drug her body twice in a circle. Where her blood dropped, corn began to grow.

Because the boys were careless in listening to the instructions, corn must now be planted and taken care of in order for it to grow. And to this day, it only grows in certain spots and not the entire earth.

Selu brought the gift of corn to the Cherokee; it fed our people, which created harmony born from death. This story reflects the importance of women as the givers of life. It also speaks to forgiveness and second-chances — even though the two sons did not respect Selu, through her death she provided life.

## WOMEN AS HISTORY AND FEMINISM

Every Aboriginal nation in North America has its own unique creation story. The story of Selu is still told today; she can be understood as the giver of life to the Cherokee, her children. For thousands of years my people have lived in a matriarchal, matrilineal and matrilocal society. This female-centred society kept our nation grounded; our nuclear and extended families were related, traced and identified through the mother. Even though some of our cultural knowledge and oral history has been lost, it is clear that our Nation relied on and was nurtured by the feminine principle.

"We are a revitalized tribe," says Wilma Mankiller, in her book, *Wilma Mankiller: A Chief and Her People* (Mankiller and Wallis 1993: xix). Wilma is and has been, for me and many others, the embodiment of the "feminine principle." In her youth she acknowledged the stirrings to fight against injustice directed toward "Indian people" in the U.S. She stood for civil rights for the many nations of "Indian people" across North America in the face of a federal government that still wanted to make the "Indian problem" disappear. Her numerous trials and hardships were met with dignity and humility. She became the Principal Chief in 1983 and represented the "Cherokee *Agehya* way," present amongst my people before the forcible assimilation processes of the white man began. She wrote:

It is certain that Cherokee women played an important and influential role in town government. Women shared in the responsibilities and rights of the tribal organization. Our Cherokee families were traditionally matrilineal clans. In general women held the property, including the dwelling and garden. (Mankiller and Wallis 1993: 19)

Women were held in the highest regard amongst our villages, played critical roles within decision-making processes and had access to and wielded many forms of power — all a direct result of the bonds of the matrilineal inheritance. In particular, there was always one very powerful woman in the communal configuration, who was called the *Ghigau*, or Beloved Woman. According to Mankiller, "The name [*Ghigau*] may be a corruption of *giga*, or blood, and *agehya* or woman. If so, the title might be phrased more accurately as 'Red Woman' or 'War Woman'" (19). The last documented *Ghigau* before the *Indian Removal Act* was Nancy Ward, born in 1738. She presided over the powerful Cherokee Council of Women, participated in the Treaty of July 20, 1781, and the Treaty at Hopewell, November 28, 1785, as a principal speaker. Along with many other extraordinary deeds before her death in 1822, Nancy Ward is held up as the embodiment of a traditional Cherokee woman. In many ways, contemporary feminists see Indigenous matriarchs like Nancy Ward as early forerunners of modern feminism.

Twenty-first-century models of feminism risk a certain amount of anachronism and inaccuracy in describing a society that in many ways is the predecessor of so-called more "modern" and "progressive" concepts of social and cultural infrastructures without gender biases. These models arise primarily out of and as a reaction against long-standing western or predominantly European patriarchal traditions. Rosalind Delmar states,

> Many would agree that at the very least a feminist is someone who holds that women suffer discrimination because of their sex, that they have specific needs which remain negated and unsatisfied, and that the satisfaction of these needs would require a radical change (some would say a revolution even) in the social, economic and political order. (cited in Herrmann and Stewart 1994: 5)

This definition has its place in speaking to (as well as taking its meaning from) the predominant cultural practices and beliefs that have characterized the "conqueror" societies of North America for the last several centuries. However, for generations prior to the colonization of the Cherokee people, Cherokee women had political, economic and social rights equal to those of Cherokee men. Therefore, utilizing contemporary feminist perspectives can help us to elucidate only the extent to which the European influence resulted in the "de-volution" and "dis-order" of a highly equitable worldview and lived experience.

Prior to contact with the colonizers and the rapid change within Cherokee society, women and their children were the primary members of a household, which included extended family members. Husbands were always from a different clan and therefore considered outsiders. In the case of a new marriage, the man moved from the household of his mother into the household of his wife, although the husband continued to maintain responsibilities to his mother, sister and sister's children. Exogamy, marriage outside of clan membership, was vital to upholding the taboo of marrying inside one's extended family, making kin relationships critical to the selection of appropriate mates.

Political ties, class, economics and/or position had no bearing on status within Cherokee society. Only through matrilineal kinship within the Bird, Blue, Deer, Long Hair, Paint, Wild Potato or Wolf clan was one's existence acknowledged:

> Cherokees distinguished themselves from others not by skin color or political allegiance but by their membership in a Cherokee clan. Any person, regardless of ancestry or nationality, who was born or adopted into one of the seven clans, was a Cherokee; any person who did not belong to a Cherokee clan was not a member of the tribe. (Perdue 1998: 49)

In fact, clan relationships had great bearing on how all Cherokees identified and behaved with one another. Clan membership and kinship were achieved only through birth or through the ceremony of adoption. Since the ability to give birth, literally or by ceremonial re-creation, was the province of females, Cherokee women were the sole determiners of kin relationships and clan identity.

Balance and harmony, the most precious and respected aspects of the Cherokee belief system, were reflected in male and female roles in Cherokee society and mirrored as well the masculine and feminine principles within the natural world. The balance between male and female, as well as the importance of kinship, was used to positively characterize an outsider's behaviour. Historical records acknowledged this practice: "He had behaved like a True Brother in taking care to conduct their squaw home" (Perdue 1998: 47). Kinship was also used in describing our relationships to the winged, crawling, finned and four-legged beings such as mother earth, brother deer and grandmother spider.

By far the most important role for women was that of arbitrator of justice — the *Ghigau* kept the peace and maintained the social justice within each village of the entire Cherokee nation. The interaction with and treatment of each other in Cherokee society was crucial but tenuous because "Wrong actions could disturb the balance" (Mankiller and Wallis 1993: 20). Unfortunately, oppression at the hand of the white man led to imbalance and the beginnings of forcibly induced assimilation into the colonizers' worldview.

## THE COLONIZERS

It is said that the Cherokee's first encounter with the Europeans occurred with the de Soto Spanish expedition in AD 1540 in what is now the Southeastern United States. The next 150 years saw a gradual increase of "first contacts," but by 1700 there was a steady stream of European colonizers hungry for land and the resources of what were our original homelands in the Allegheny regions of North and South Carolina, Kentucky, Tennessee, Georgia, Alabama, Virginia and West Virginia. It is said amongst my people that upon initial contact with the white Europeans, the Cherokee enclave asked, "Where are your women?" The European patriarchy and the absence of women in their parties were confusing to the Cherokee and strained their interactions with the whites from the very beginning. The increasing contact with the Europeans amplified tensions between the Cherokee and the Europeans due to these cultural dichotomies. However, the introduction of trade goods and the convenience of European tools led to the development of trade and political alliances. These formal and informal interactions were particularly encouraged by European and colonial governments, who did so all the while looking down their noses at the Cherokee way of life.

From the very beginning European contact affected the lives of Cherokee women. Perdue explains, "Euro-Americans shared a host of beliefs about the proper role of women in society.... Instead of viewing men and women as balancing one another, Euro-Americans regarded gender, like the rest of creation, as hierarchical, with women subservient to men" (Perdue 1998: 62). These and other drastic differences between the patriarchal and hierarchical belief system of the European Christians and the more naturist spirituality of the Cherokee further strained the interactions between them. Many of the historical writings by immigrant traders, missionaries and explorers after contact viewed Cherokee women from the European white male hierarchical perspective. Most references were very reproachful of Cherokee men. For example, early European observers made disparaging remarks such as:

> "Among the Cherokees, the woman rules the roost," and "The Cherokees have a petticoat government." It is said that when Ada Kulkula, or Little Carpenter, attended a meeting in Charleston, South Carolina, he was astonished to find no white women present.

He even asked if it were true that "white men as well as Red men were born of women." (Mankiller and Wallis 1993: 19)

The newly imposed values of the whites, the most disruptive of which was "keeping women in their place," began a process of slowly eroding the balance and harmony between Cherokee men and women.

> [The Europeans] viewed women as emotional creatures who had to be restrained by marriage and other social roles that reinforced their subservience to men. Cherokee women presented a troubling alternative [or dichotomy] to Carolinians, who acted on their own views of appropriate female behavior in their dealings with Cherokee women. Such encounters led Cherokee women to understand that Carolinians regarded their agricultural labor, sexual autonomy, control of children, and other behavior as deviant. (Perdue 1998: 62)

European men came to the Cherokee to do business, mostly trade and war, enterprises that in their terms were conducted and accomplished by males only. It was very clear that they did not expect or welcome women at these exchanges. With the arrival of the Europeans, the position of Cherokee women as matriarchs declined and the natural order of both male and female roles of the Cherokee worldview eroded (Perdue 1998).

The social culture of balance and harmony in relation to economic and political interests between Cherokee males and females was very much intact in the early 1700s. The first European traders introduced goods such as cloth, metal tools and utensils, and weapons. The exchange of these commodities for such things as Cherokee deer hides, pottery, baskets and corn began the process of creating more frequent interactions with the colonizers. Along with the increased economic interdependence there also occurred intermarriage of Cherokee women with white males, a situation that resulted in the primary assault on and dismantling of the female-centred lineage and kinship that were central to the Cherokee way of life.

> By marrying Cherokee women, the white traders found they were accepted in the Cherokee community. There were many practical rewards. White husbands learned their wives' customs and language; the women served as interpreters in matters of commerce. All of the offspring would be considered Cherokee, since the matrilineal kinship system, like that of the Jews, maintains that the children of our women are always Cherokee despite the race of their fathers. Nonetheless, there were negative effects. Marrying white traders, for example, disturbed the traditional

Cherokee social organization because many of the wives went to live with their husbands. This was contrary to our custom of husbands residing in their wives' domicile. (Mankiller and Wallis 1993: 25–26)

Although intermarriage began to erode the balance and harmony between Cherokee male and female roles, many other factors unraveled our world and our tribe. Warfare between tribes, and against those fighting beside the white man, increased the stress on our nation. Many men were disfigured or killed. A significant number of our people, male and female, young and old, died from European infectious diseases such as smallpox, influenza and tuberculosis, against which our people had little resistance. Missionaries and their coerced conversions to Christian religions did great damage to the relationship the Cherokee had with the natural world. As well, the introduction of alcohol, often used in ways we might now characterize as substance terrorism, degraded many Cherokee with its addictive qualities.

Cherokees and other Native people no longer thought of themselves as partners in any sort of compatible liaison with the world around them. Many Native Americans felt utterly violated and compromised. It seemed as if the spiritual and social tapestry they had created for centuries was unraveling. Everything lost that sacred balance. (Mankiller and Wallis 1993: 28–29)

The imbalance and change imposed upon the Cherokee continued over the next hundred years along with the development of the colonial and then United States governments. The Cherokee attempted to adapt their traditional ways to accommodate the Europeans. The influences of forced conversion by the missionaries, the destruction due to disease and the constant battle with the military were all met by the Cherokee with an attempt to placate the colonizers without giving up too much of our own direct interest. However much we attempted to maintain our selves and our society, substantive principles were changed and the disruption to harmony and balance became increasingly evident. The classification of the Indigenous peoples of North America as wards of the government led to the disintegration of the societal infrastructure of Cherokee communities. Recognizing the vital role of women in the power structure of Cherokee society, the Europeans created policies regarding land ownership and the distribution of Indigenous populations that destroyed the function of the villages and towns within the matrilineal system.

In an attempt to maintain our culture in the face of persistent onslaughts, many Cherokee men began to assimilate the ways of western white men. As more and more Cherokee people began to convert to Christianity, the more silenced Cherokee women became. The traditional Cherokee governance of matrilineality began to fade amongst many families. In accepting the European religious and political patriarchal worldview, Cherokee men began to adopt practices that further removed control of land and the trade of essential commodities from the hands of Cherokee women. The fate of Cherokee women and their shared power was sealed as Cherokee men ceded the self-governing power of both men and women to the Europeans.

Despite the influence of the Europeans on traditional Cherokee society, beliefs and spirituality, the matrilineal nature of the family continued, albeit covertly. Even in the face of genocide and increased dominance by the federal military the Cherokee continued to acquire property, fill their grain stores and attain many holdings. Regardless of our tribes' support for the colonists against the British during the American Revolution and the numerous treaties between 1777 and 1838, we became renowned as victims of one of the greatest atrocities, the Nunna dual Tsunyi, or Trail of Tears, committed by those who were sworn to protect.

## SEXISM AND BEING "CIVILIZED"

Within the conqueror societies the quest to make the Cherokee more "civilized" was seen simply as yet another step on the path of human progress. The goal of the European religious sects was to "save the savages." In fact, in "1819, as part of the government's commitment to 'civilize' all Native people, Congress authorized an annual sum of $10,000 to the War Department to support and promote the civilization of Indians" (Mankiller and Wallis 1993: 80). The overriding factor in the civilizing process at this time was to take control of the land, as the U.S. government saw hunting as "Indian" and particularly male, with no regard to the female as ruling the land through agriculture and corn. The government's view of possessing the land was "a boon to those who succeeded in 'civilizing' their proprietors" (Perdue 1998: 112). Needless to say, the concept of Cherokee women as sharing in the power structure of the nation did not fit into the colonizer's sexist values.

Sexism degraded the traditional Cherokee families because it was a direct attack on matrilineality. This attitude was expressed by John Ridge in 1826 when he wrote, "Property belonging to the wife is not exclusively at the control and disposal of the husband, and in many respects she [wife] has exclusive and distinct control" (Perdue 1998: 152). The colonizers viewed forcing the Cherokee assimilation to European cultural beliefs and values as an intrinsic right, given the privileges they set for themselves through Manifest Destiny. It was with deliberate intent that they set out to destroy the connections to power and the locus of control of the Cherokee Nation, its women, and began passing laws and regulations related to marriage and matrimony. Matrilineality, the nexus of traditional Cherokee life, was taken underground and protected through the process of appearing compliant to European policy-makers' decisions.

Scholars and researchers who have attempted to comprehensively examine the effect of colonization on Native people often do so without taking into consideration its particular impact on Native women. For example:

> Scholarly analyses of the impact of colonization on Native communities often minimize the histories of oppression of Native women. In fact, many scholars often argue that men were disproportionately affected by colonization because the economic systems imposed on Native nations deprived men of their economic roles in the communities more so than women. By narrowing our analysis solely to the explicitly economic realm of society, we fail to account for the multiple ways women have disproportionately suffered under colonization — from sexual violence to forced sterilization. (Smith 2005: 3)

Cherokee women, in their resilience, adjusted to the new social order brought about by this cultural contamination. Even in the face of sexist attitudes, cultural and physical assault, and the loss of the balance and harmony so desperately protected, Cherokee women have continued to maintain their matrilineality, their inner power and strength to come into the twentieth and twenty-first centuries with new determination.

## CHEROKEE WOMEN AND FEMINISM

Much of the research regarding the effects of colonization, as well as that examining the process of decolonization, has found that most social issues related to Indigenous communities are a result of forced assimilation policies of the federal government. In fact, many Indigenous women researchers and activists reject the idea of feminism. In my opinion, this discourse and discussion is vital to us as Indigenous women coming full circle. Andrea Smith asserts,

> Rather, my argument is that Native women activists' theories about feminism, about the struggle against sexism both within Native communities and the society at large, and about the importance of working in coalition with non-Native women are complex and varied. These theories are not monolithic and cannot simply be reduced to the dichotomy of feminist vs non-feminist. (Smith 2005: 3, and see Chapter 5 this volume)

Models and theories of feminism generally have flexibility within them, but we must continue to unpack implicit biases and open new ways of approaching how we analyze gendered cultural constructs. Not only must we, as scholars, in our examination of any population, male, female, Indigenous or not, do so with an understanding of the specific cultural dynamics at play, we must guard against unwittingly incorporating anachronistic and ethnocentric constructs. As Andrea Smith profoundly puts it, "From our position of growing up in a patriarchal, colonial, and white supremacist world, we cannot even fully imagine how a world not based on structures of oppression could operate" (Smith 2005: 19). Part of our decolonization process, difficult as it is, must be to constantly strive to re-imagine and re-create an "oppression less" worldview.

Feminism brings much to the discussion in regard to decolonization and anti-oppression, but at the same time we must be cautious and closely examine those facets of contemporary feminism arising out of white European or western — i.e., non-Indigenous — worldviews. It is indeed ironic that a so-called democratic society, which came face to face with a matriarchal, matrilineal and matrilocal society where women had a balance of power and control of their own destiny, came so late to recognizing the merits of a truly equitable worldview. Only recently are American women struggling to gain the balance and harmony that the Cherokee *Ani yun wiya* had for thousands of years.

## A CHEROKEE WOMAN'S VIEW

In bringing this back to myself as a scholar, as a woman, as a mother and as a Cherokee, I cannot assert that I am a feminist. I can say that I am a Cherokee who left the protection of my family and community very late in life and discovered that, as a woman, I faced bias and discrimination, often the kinds that took me some time to recognize for what they were. This recognition was somewhat delayed, not because I hadn't yet entertained feminist notions, but more so because I came from a family who expected the same from me as my brother, who demonstrated that it was equally important that I be respected because of my being female. I cannot disregard the dysfunction and atrocities that I observe within Indigenous communities and societies. Leaders are observed cheating on their wives and turning a blind eye to sexual and physical abuse, and political and social oppression of the women in their communities. These conditions speak to the work, healing and decolonizing we must do in order to experience real change as Indigenous people. But, at the same time, I would venture to say that white people have more to learn from Indigenous people, rather than the reverse.

Indigenous women are survivors. Most importantly, as sustainers and keepers of women's knowledge, we must step up to the plate and battle sexism, though there is much more to this than simply a counteroffensive of Indigenous feminism. Smith argues that,

> It is often the case that gender justice is often articulated as being a separate issue from issues of survival for Indigenous peoples. Such an understanding presupposes that we could actually decolonize without addressing sexism, which ignores the fact that it has been precisely through gender violence that we have lost our lands in the first place. (Smith 2005: 8)

One way I synthesize my views regarding women and power is to assert that "we can't demand power until we own the innate power we have within."

## FULL CIRCLE

> We have been striving to return to the harmony we once had. It has been a difficult task. The odds against us have been formidable. But despite everything that has happened to us, we have never given up and will never give up. There is an old Cherokee prophecy which instructs us that as long as the Cherokees continue traditional dances, the world will remain as it is, but when the dances stop, the world will come to an end. Everyone should hope that the Cherokees will continue to dance. (Mankiller and Wallis 1993: 28–29)

The girls are tired but happy that they had the chance to dance as we load the shawls and the cooler into the trunk of the car. As we drive down the dirt road, dodging potholes, I share with them the story of the Kiowa people, who passed the Gourd Dance to our nation as a gift. In honouring their tradition we women dance on the perimeter of the arena. We do this to support and respect the men, to remember the veterans of modern wars, but most importantly to remember the warriors, male and female, from our collective past. I remind my daughters of their importance as the matrilineal future of our nation: they are Cherokee and they are vital to the balance and harmony of the entire world. In passing on our traditional dances, heritage and identity, I ensure that yes, my daughters, you will grow up to be Cherokee women.

## REFERENCES

Herrmann, Anne C., and Abigail J. Stewart. 1994 *Theorizing Feminism*. Boulder, CO: Westview Press.

Mankiller, Wilma, and Michael Wallis. 1993. *Mankiller: A Chief and Her People.* New York: St Martin's Press.

Memmi, Albert. 1965. *The Colonizer and the Colonized.* Boston: Beacon Press.

*Native Peoples Magazine.* 1999. "Eastern Cherokee: 'War Woman.'" Available at <www.nativepeoples.com/article/articles/147/1/Eastern-Cherokee> (accessed March 2007).

Perdue, Theda. 1998. *Cherokee Women.* Lincoln, NA: University of Nebraska Press.

Smith, Andrea. 2005. "Native American Feminism, Sovereignty, and Social Change." *Feminist Studies* 31, 1.

# Chapter Twelve

# CULTURING POLITICS AND POLITICIZING CULTURE

*Shirley Bear*

## IMAGES ON WORDS

May 16 1936, my mother told me that
I was an evening child,
born around 8–8:30 p.m.,
it never used to mean very much to me.
I guess with a faint knowledge of
astronomy/astrology/Chinese calendar/horoscopes, etc.,
I am now more aware of my past life's events.
Too little too late, they say, whoever they are.
My first vivid memory: I have visual flashes of being
pulled in a sled (handmade, I assume)—straddling my
little brother—by someone with large winter boots,
we are wrapped together in a heavy wool blanket.
I see a well-travelled snow-packed path whizzing by,
blue streaked like the wind.
I feel the blades of the sled glazing on the icy pathway
beneath the blades and vibrating on my bottom.
I hear the rhythmic crunch of the sled runners
intermingle with the sound of the straggling winter boots.
In my memory, this is a romantic winter family scene;
I might have been three years old.
Every child attended the Maliseet Indian Day School,
controlled by nuns who couldn't speak our language
only the language of a white god.
I learned to read before I learned to write.
I learned to draw before I learned to talk.
I grew up with six brothers and one sister until I was 18
then nigwhus produced a brother who we all spoiled.
Soon after that I started my family, a son and a daughter.

Lance and Stephanie (Roger Belanger)

Shirley Bear, circa 1940 (Noel Bear)

Several years of learning what I wanted to be
when I grew up.
Painting, working for survival, gaining social political
knowledge learning to cope with and understanding
racism,
sexism and feminism. Living in U.S.A.
Mostly making mistakes. Lessons for tomorrow.

1967
Journal entry:
*I read the biography of Jamie Wyatt with a realization*
*that I could paint as good as he,*
*so I tore some walls down and set up a studio*
*in an abandoned stable.*
*I bought a potbelly wood stove,*
*my first art performance.*
          *"Independence"*
*My only audience was a very angry man*

1968
Journal entry:
*Take back your life, take back your name*
*reclaim, reclaim.*
*March 2,*
*Today I signed my painting with my birth name.*

1969
Journal entry:
*Received a grant from the Ford foundation,*
*Will travel. Research Indian art.*

1971
Journal entry;
*Working with T.R.I.B.E. in Bar Harbor, Maine.*
*Developing an alternative art program.*

1974
Journal entry:
*Freedom from emotional oppression*
*Official divorce*

1975
Journal entry:
*Married Peter J. Clair*

1976
Journal entry:
*Returned to painting, photography, and completed*
*a log house, studio and planted a garden with Peter.*

1977
Journal entry;
*My third child Ramona Kjibusk Clair is born*

Ramona Kjibusk Clair (Shirley Bear)

1979
Journal entry:
*Sandra Nicholas Lovelace and the Tobique Women's
Group walk a hundred miles in protest of discrimination
against Aboriginal women. A Canadian law which states
that an Indian woman who marries a man who does not
have Indian status as defined by the Indian Act and is no
longer an Indian.*

> *Oka to Ottawa*
> *backs burning*
> *sneakers wearing out*
> *feet blistering*
> *children crying*
> *having to be carried*
> *some complaints*
> *what's it all for?*

*heat exhaustion*
*new walkers join*

*back home I hope*
that all goes well and that they
will make it *for all the women*
who lost their status

A Question of Status Mixed media painting (Shirley Bear)

1980
Journal entry;
*First Provincial Aboriginal Women's conference
is held in Fredericton N.B.*

*I joined the Tobique Women's Group.*


1985
The Tobique Women's Group launch a book.
Feminism and social justice declaration has its price,
the past five years were grueling and in the end there
were only a few Aboriginal women in the social political
lobby.
The events of those years are chronicled in the book
*Enough is Enough: Aboriginal Women Speak Out*
as told to Janet Sillman and published by the Toronto
Women's Press. Toronto Ontario, Canada

I started exhibiting in Massachusetts and New
Hampshire, U.S., in 1964 with a group of artists who
painted and set up their work in a public park. We were
students of Ann Schecter who was a resident instructor
at the Whistler House Gallery in Lowell Mass.

In 1974, I took a painting to show a curator, at a
well known gallery in Halifax, with the hope for some
encouraging feedback but was distressed by the remark
that I already knew to identify as racial bias. This was
the first of many curators who did not look at my art
without being influenced by my race, colour and sex.
The title of "artist" is foreign to my community.

Identification words such as Nucisunhigat, or
Nud'oqwosawet are used for the respected position of
the creator of designs, paintings, carvings and other
work. It was unusual to isolate drawings and paintings
as separate entities without their being part of clothing
and other utilities used by the community. The creators
of this work were honoured with the assurance that they
would always have shelter, food and other comforts for
life.

This was true for men and women as there is no
real evidence in the separation of who actually did the

*Lintoteneh*
*In nomia matre et filia et spiritus sanctus*
Art performance at Walter Philips Gallery Banff Centre for the Arts, Banff
Alberta, 1995, media services, Banff Centre for the Arts, Banff Alberta

art. A separate sexual reality on this theory is
perpetuated by historians who are mostly male.

Our community has adopted the myth of sexual
separatism when it comes to Art and Spirituality.
Similarly we have bought into too many other theories
such as the infamous Bering Strait Crossing and women

who may not conduct or participate in spiritual activities during their menses, lactation or pregnancies. There are more leniencies toward wife abuse, sexual exploitation, devaluation of women's art and employment inequity. At this writing, however, we have numerous male community leaders and spiritualists who are taking their role seriously and becoming more inclusive.

## WOMEN'S CEREMONY

Young women as in gestalt
Torn open by new truths
New power
Old grief, guilt, and now
Hurts thrown aside — healing.

"Respect yourselves, wear skirts
So that the Creator will know you."

Did the Creator not know you
When you were birthed?
Did you not come onto this earth
Unclothed?
You came by choice from a place of
Creation — unbraided, unskirted.

Wonderful thoughts from strong, loving
Knowing grandmothers.
What are they projecting?
What are they teaching you in these
Double-edged teachings?

Does the Creator know the value
Of the spirit no matter what we wear?
Does not the Creator care
For the daughters of Nokomis?
My mind does not intend
To blow ill-will, my mind simply needs
To know the truth.

Ceremony must be preserved,
Protocol for the ceremony observed.
My respect is limitless for this.

But
"You must wear skirts"???????
"You must not be on your moon"????

Give me reality.
Just speak the truth.

Do not insult my dignity,
Integrity, intelligence and love
By using metaphor that you can't explain,
By accusing me of espousing my
White sisters' rhetoric;
"Political Correctness."

Are we a product, with a necessary
Marketing package? For whom?
Speak the truth!
Tell me in a way that these
uncultured ears will understand.

To walk the way is to know,
And the more I know
The reward for this activity,
The stronger my love will be
For "Walking the Way."
Nokomis, your daughter holds
No romantic vision of "the way,"
But for all the many years
Of seeking, asking,
The answers disclaim the teachings
Of the grandmothers as in gestalt.

A blind follower may end up
With two left feet tripping.

A blind follower may never see the
Brilliant rainbow. She may never soar.
Yet a blind follower is what is
Necessary for the maintenance of
The lofty perch of the eagle.

Doesn't everyone want to be an eagle?

No one wants to be a crow?

Nokomis with your years of knowing
And growing, surely you've grown
Patient for the seeking granddaughters.
Lead with truth, gently
                    gently
                              gently
Coax as lovers—small forward moves
With truth — gently
                    gently
                              gently


    I drew at an age before recollections. I wrote
before I knew what "poetry" meant. Like most young
people, the angst of being young, thinking you are old
enough for any adult activity, made me older and too
serious for other young women in my community. I was
labelled "weird."
    For this chapter, I share some photos of my
immediate family, just some glimpses of my art, as well,
some poetry that relates to the images.
    1991 occupation of the Treatment Centre in
Kanasatake, in a province now known as Quebec, gave
Aboriginal artists an endless amount of inspiration, it
was spearheaded by a woman artist who also became the
main spokesperson for the occupation.
    Many of the activists were also visual artists,
writers and filmmakers. Kanasatake is near a town
named Oka.

Oka Warrior Silkscreen print 22" x 32", 1991 (Shirley Bear)

## FRAGILE FREEDOMS

*Fragile Freedoms* are the delicate balance acts played
by the Indian act politicians
and the government bureaucrats in the plush carpeted
offices of the inner governmental chambers. A game that
affects the original men and women who have managed
to survive since 1492–1992. These games continue
to deny the original people the right to self-
determination.

*Fragile Freedoms* is the back lash that further
denied freedom rights to the warriors at Wounded
Knee and Kanasatake.

*Fragile Freedoms* is the fragility of the paper
made from the disappearing grasses of the rain
forests of South America, and the herbal medicines
of the American continent, the air that we breathe,
the water as it drips its final drops, our skin as it
slowly
Blotches and disintegrates from the radiated
pollutants in the air that affects our whole planet.

*Fragile Freedoms* is our violence against women
and children, our racism against people of colour,
abilities and classes.

*Fragile Freedoms* is the delicate hope for the
possibility of making this time forward as a
beginning of healing.

*Wezuweptuwegwo zamagwon, yud olu kci gizahwk*
*.gigwuson Kospenah.*


## 2002

I am in Menucha
a retreat centre
in Oregon
I am hearing about the

healing strengths from
within each of us
I'm lying on a massage table
getting a treatment from an
Osteopathic healer
as he places his hands
on the nape of my neck
his thumbs behind my ears
at the base of my skull
his fingers cupping my ears
my journey begins
I've been here before
Red swirls followed by grey-white
clouds which ball up
and float from my feet to my forehead,

Birthing Myself Oil glaze over dry pigment, 2002 (Shirley Bear)

all the while
pulsating and changing shapes
and colours
From a distance a figure appears

and starts to drift up from my feet
and stops at my breasts
A rush of brown river
tumbles down the blue mountain
Large hands with red painted
fingernails
begin to spiral but not touching me
they form several circles
around each breast.
and washes over my whole body
Winds are softly
Hissing
All
Around
Me.
When I woke up
my fear of the dreaded cancer was gone.

This is going to be a long journey, this journey of
healing. I will not always be this confident nor will I adhere
to the principles of my own healing, but I will
believe that this
Is the most beneficial way for treating the pagets. I
believe that the traditional European medical treatment
is too poisonous for anyone's body. I watched my sister
-in-law die a slow devastating and debilitating death
from the radiation and chemotherapy.

The disease moved to different parts of her body as the
treatment was moved to eradicate the tumours: her
breasts, her hips, her spine and finally her brain. When I
was first diagnosed as having pagets disease, I asked the
surgeon about alternatives and her response was;

*"I don't recommend an alternative, I've buried more
women because they chose an alternative."*

Skeleton Digital photograph, 2004 (Shirley Bear)

## YESTERDAY

**Tilly Road, Tobique Reserve**
I basked in the brilliant colours of the
Maples and left old memories where
They live
In 1965 winter/spring/summer

**Five Ochre Bones**
You wrote: *Two nights ago*
*I went to snowshoe in the moonlight.*

Baqwasun, Wuli baqwasun.

I riffle through some old letters

You wrote: *I never knew of these things*
*Before I met you.*

And
I remember: God the father and his son
casting long shadows on the midnight snow
from grandmother's generous light.
A man of the cloth, a cloth of wool.

Baqwasun wuli baqwasun!

Yesterday I filled my memory eyes
with the autumn colours:
yellow, orange, red and brown.

Rte. 1-A, Houlton to Calais, Maine
I gulped down the golden spread and
burped out old memories.
In the moonlight, on your snowshoes,
god the father's son
leaving only the protruding skeletal
filigree after a warm spring and summer growth
And left the old memories where they live.

The kugh, kugh of your snowshoes,
how gently you crept
into my life,
playing gently on the ebony keys
bypassing all the ivory.
Man of cloth, cloth of wool.

Baqwasun wuli baqwasun.

The memories pan across this maple
brilliance of Lake Edwards Watercolour,
in the autumn of 1965.

The autumn lake,
the winter moon,
the spring rain,
and the summer farewell.

1972
You're in Tibet.
You write: *I'm home, I'm home.*

You've shed your cloth of wool.
The snowshoes etch prints
moonlit shadows imprinted in my memories,
Deep God the fathers' son
we leave old memories where they live.

Today, October 1995, revisiting
letters long forgotten
after a windy night.

The leaves have fallen to the ground
leaving only the protruding skeletal
filigree after a warm spring and
summer's growth.

# Chapter Thirteen

# MY HOMETOWN
# NORTHERN CANADA SOUTH AFRICA

## *Emma LaRocque*

How did they get so rich?
How did we get so poor?
My hometown Northern Canada South Africa
How did you get so rich?

We were not always poor

How did they get our blueberry meadows
our spruce and willow groves
our sun clean streams
and blue sky lakes?
How did they get
their mansions on the lake
their cobbled circle drives
with marbled heads of lions on their iron gates?

How did they get so rich?
How did we get so poor?

One sad spring
when my mother my Cree-cultured Ama
was dying
Or was it the sad summer
when my father my tall gentle Bapa
was dying
I stood on the edge
of that blue sky lake
to say goodbye
to something
so definitive
no words in Cree
no words in Métis

no words in that colonial language
no words
could ever say
I looked at my hometown
no longer a child afraid
of stares and stone-throwing words
no longer a child
made ashamed
of smoked northern pike
bannock on blueberry sauce
sprinkled with Cree

I looked at my hometown
Gripping my small brown hands
on the hard posts of those
white iron gates
looking at the safari lions
with an even glare

How did they get so rich?
How did we get so poor?

How did our blueberry meadows
turn to pasture for "Mr" Sykes' cows?
How did our spruce and willow groves
turn to "Mr" Therien's general store?
How did my Ni-mooshoom's Scrip
turn to "Mr" Hamilton's IGA store?
How did our aspen-covered hills
turn to leveled sand piles
for gas pipelines
just behind my Nokom's backyard?
How did our moss green trails
down to the beaver creek
turn to cutlines
for power lines?
How did the dancing poplar leaves
Fall before their golden time?
How did my Nokom's sons and daughters
and their sons and daughters
and their sons and daughters
Fall before their seasons?

How did my auntie Julie die?
when she was 19 she was found dead
under a pile of sawdust
long after it happened
She was last seen with a whiteman
sometime in World War II they said
There was no investigation
not even 16 years later

How did my Nokom lose her grandchildren
that she so carefully housed in her log house
made long by her widower sons?
Was it really about
a child stealing a chocolate bar from
Therien's store?
Or was it about The Town
Stealing children to make us white
Taking Uncle Ezear's Lillian Linda Violet
Taking Uncle Alex's Lottie
All they had left
after T.B. stole their mothers
in faraway places of death

How did my uncles Alex and Ezear die?
Singing sad songs on the railroad tracks
on their way home from Town
2 a.m. in the morning
Was it really by the train as the RCMP said?

When did my mother and her sisters
Catherine, Agnes, Louisa and Mary
stop singing
those haunting songs in Cree
about lost loves and aching
to find their way home?
When did they lose the songs
those songs in their steps
wasn't it when the priests the police
and all those Home and Town good boys doing bad things came
No one talks about it
My Nokom and her daughters
Singing sad songs on the railroad tracks

on their way home from Town
2 a.m. in the morning

How did we put away Pehehsoo
and Pahkak?
When did we stop laughing with Wehsakehcha?
When did we cross ourselves
to pray to Joseph and the Virgin Mary?
How did we stop speaking Cree
How did we stop being free?

How did they get so rich?
How did we get so poor?

How did my Bapa and Ama's brothers
Alex, Ezear and Victor
and my aunties' husbands Stuart and Moise
lose their traplines?
Was it really for the Cold War planes
or was it for one of those cold marbled lions?
And what war
takes my brothers' traplines today?
Some say to save the lions

My hometown Northern Canada South Africa
making marble out of lions
making headstones out of earth
turning the earth on
Nokom's sons and daughters
and their sons and daughters
and their sons and daughters
turning Nokom
into a bag lady
before she died in the Town ditch

How did they get all the stones?
Those stones in their fireplaces,
those stones around their necks,
the boulders in the whites
of their eyes
Those stony stares,
How did they get the marbled stones in their hearts?

I look at you
My hometown Northern Canada South Africa
I look at you
no longer a child afraid
of stony stares
and rockhard words
no longer a child
made ashamed
of my Cree
dipped in cranberry sauce
giggling with Wehsakehcha
I look at the paper head-dresses
you got from Hollywood
for your Pow Wow Days
Trying to feel at home
in your postcard tourist ways
Giggling with Wehsakehcha
I look at the turquoise
in your stones
I look at your pretend lions
with an even glare
Even in my dreams I see

But still
I look
From the inside out
Gripping my still-brown hands
on the hard posts
White Iron Gates

My hometown coldstone Canada South Africa

## NOTE

Published with permission of Emma LaRocque. Previously published in *Border Crossings* 11, 4 (Fall 1992), Winnipeg, Canada.

Chapter Fourteen

# ABORIGINAL FEMINIST ACTION ON VIOLENCE AGAINST WOMEN

## Tina Beads with Rauna Kuokkanen

*Tina Beads is an Aboriginal feminist who has been an activist in Aboriginal women's organizations, notably the Aboriginal Women's Action Network in Vancouver; and in the Vancouver Rape Relief and Women's Shelter. Beads was motivated to both insist on the inclusion of Aboriginal women's voices and needs, and on the incorporation of Aboriginal feminist analysis, in the organizations in which she was involved. But her greatest energy was devoted to confronting and eliminating social wrongs like sexism, racism and poverty; and, as a rape crisis counsellor, to healing those who were wounded especially by male sexual violence against women. Rauna Kuokkanen interviewed Tina Beads in Vancouver, August 17th, 2005.*

**Beads**: I grew up in a small town with a lot of Aboriginal people, and a lot of my friends were Aboriginal kids. We were poor and they were poor, and we all lived in the same poor part of town, and overwhelmingly, a lot of them were at some point taken away and put into foster care, either for little periods of time or whatever, and yet a lot of my white friends were getting beat up at home by their parents. A lot of my Aboriginal friends who were getting taken away weren't. So, you know, clearly there was something that didn't quite make sense for me. Why would some get taken out of their homes? Maybe they didn't have food for a day but it was okay the next day, and they actually all loved each other. It was maybe dysfunctional, but it was a loving dysfunction. Whereas in some other families, I would see, clearly, this kid needs help or needs respite. Get this kid away from his parents for a while. And yet, this wasn't happening.

So I thought, why is that? Why would social workers, or ministries, or schools decide which kid they need to send in the report on and ignore what's going on in the other cases. It was really a disservice to the non-Aboriginal kids in this case, who were not getting access to the help that they needed. I think that was based on racism. Those decisions were completely racist. Everyone was expecting bad behaviour of Aboriginal people. You know the stereotypes: we were less than civilized and violence is how we resolve our conflicts and we drink too much and all that stuff.

So, it started there. I saw things as unjust. I maybe couldn't articulate it, but I knew it wasn't right. On any given day what if someone decided that I was the one that needed the "help"? And then I would get taken away for a period of time? I felt that I was lucky that my mom was white. You know, I think that kept me a little safer from being taken out of the house. So, I recognized it there, the racism part.

Then, when I was seventeen or eighteen, I had to go to court for a sexual assault. I was sexually assaulted as a kid. It wasn't until I was about sixteen that I was really mad about it, that it had happened. And I realized that all of the things that the guy had told me were not true. They were to scare me. So I went through the court system. To me it seemed so cut and dried that this needed to happen to punish him. It seemed simple to me. I was eight when I was sexually assaulted. The questions that the lawyers were able to ask me were really bizarre to ask a kid of eighteen. You know, really specific things, like was he circumcised, what did it look like, how big was it, what kind of things did he say. Things like that. Oh, and was I sexually active or had I been. None of your business first of all, and secondly, how is this relevant? How on earth does this matter? I thought what happened in that period of an hour when I was eight was the issue, not what happened in the ten years in between. And, how could that make me any less credible?

I disagreed with the judge a few times on the stand because it was just making me really angry. I would just be, like, this is an absolutely ridiculous question, your honour and he would just be so shocked. And I would be, like, I don't have to answer this, do I? And he would be like, yes, the question has been asked. And I was thinking, if this is what women have to go through just to get justice! You know, we're told it is what we should do. We call the police and they'll take care of the big bad man and everything will be good. Except they don't, they just don't do it. So, that started my interest in sexual assault issues.

## BECOMING POLITICAL

**Beads**: In 2002 I was attending the Aboriginal Feminist Symposium in Regina as an observer. I had been working for a number of years with Vancouver Rape Relief and Women's Shelter. They're a feminist collective of all races and a women's group working towards ending violence against women. I started to become worried that I was becoming tokenized as the only Aboriginal woman within the collective. So, I thought that what I needed to do was to not allow myself to be tokenized but to actually create a position that made me feel a little more comfortable. Around 1995, I insisted that I needed to be relieved from some of the crisis work. I was a rape crisis counsellor, and I needed to be relieved of some of the crisis work in order to free me up to imagine what else was going on in terms of Aboriginal women.

Many of the women that called our crisis lines were Aboriginal women.

We also had a transition house for battered women, and many of the women that stayed in that house were Aboriginal women. I didn't think that their needs were being met because they were repeat callers... they were continually coming back to the transition house. So I thought, well, something's wrong with the way we're serving Aboriginal women.

I started as a volunteer. I had two kids at home, and my partner and I had decided that daycare costs a lot and one of us would stay home, and it was me because I was making the least amount of money. By the time my youngest was about two I had had it. I wasn't going to stay home anymore; there was just no way I could do it. So I thought I would just try and do volunteer work. I was watching Oprah one day and I saw an ad that the Vancouver Rape Relief was looking for volunteers. They offered free training. I thought, maybe this will satisfy my need for that adult connection. So I went and did the training, and right from the start I was pretty pleased to see that they were recognizing that women are vulnerable to sexist violence... not only from sexism but because of racism and because of class. I think the biggest oppression facing women is sexism.

***Kuokkanen***: Aboriginal women?

***Beads***: Aboriginal women, any women. I still think that it's sexism, but I think that of course being Aboriginal and being poor or any of those other things certainly add vulnerability. So I stuck through the training and then I decided I wanted to go further and join the collective, and I became part of the Vancouver Rape Relief collective.

I do think Aboriginal women are vulnerable to assault from all men in society. I believe that men will rape or batter women in their own race/class or down. So therefore white men have access to every woman.

***Kuokkanen***: Because they know that they are more vulnerable.

***Beads***: Exactly. Aboriginal women were being preyed upon, and are still being preyed upon. And then the missing women stuff started coming up a bit, right. And the lack of outrage from society at large was really pissing me off, so that's when I decided I needed to get more organized in my political activism, and do something that complemented what I was doing at Rape Relief.

I got to go to a NAC (National Action Committee on the Status of Women) Conference in Ottawa, really early on in my work with Rape Relief. I think that one of the more senior women there had recognized that I was frustrated and didn't necessarily see much connection between women and movements in general. I didn't see that maybe feminists across Canada were also experiencing the same thing. So, she wanted me to have the opportunity to just go and see if I could comfort myself somehow, knowing that there are lots of women working on all sorts of issues. So, I went, and I sought out the Aboriginal women's caucus, and there were three of us.

NAC was an organization that claimed to represent 800 member groups. Each group is sending two or three people, you know, so there should be 1500–1600 people there. I would expect more Aboriginal women, right?

## COMBATING VIOLENCE AGAINST WOMEN

**Beads**: The other thing that I found disturbing, or alarming, or distressing, was that there weren't many Aboriginal women working within non-Aboriginal organizations. I think that many Aboriginal women who were working in sort of social service areas aren't feminists. I didn't believe that access to culture or tradition or a return to previous times, maybe pre-colonization, was actually the answer to eliminating systemic violence against women.

Some of the organizations were service-oriented. They were band-aids, right. If a woman needed a place to stay they'd find her a place, if a women needed some food, they'd find her some food. They also did some traditional teachings and some traditional activities too. I didn't see how that was doing anything to eliminate violence against women. I still lobby for more services for women, but I don't think the services are what is going to improve our condition. There needs to be policy change, there needs to be a lot of direct action, political action, protests, things like that.

So, Fay asked me if I wanted to sit in on a meeting of AWAN, which was the Aboriginal Women's Action Network. I wasn't one hundred percent convinced that I wanted to because I wasn't really convinced that they were non-traditional. Prejudgements, right. But, I went in and I was really impressed that the meeting didn't start with a prayer, it didn't start with a smudge, it didn't start with any of those things. I mean, I think there is a place and a time for ceremony. Whatever any of us to do to comfort ourselves or help ourselves or heal ourselves is fine. But, I think it's a mistake to assume that everyone of us is going to be able to relate to the same prayer or the same ceremony.

## INDIAN STATUS AND THE INDIAN ACT

Bill C-31 and the *Indian Act* is discriminatory legislation, but it doesn't affect every Aboriginal woman. When I see things brought up like Bill C-31 or matrimonial property rights and so on, I think, well that's great for some Aboriginal women, but there is such a small percentage of women who are status anyway. There are still all of the Métis women, all of the not recognized women. Changing the *Indian Act* wouldn't benefit all Aboriginal women, so I think there's not much point in really working on that issue now. I think we need to change the other conditions first, and then maybe we go back and revisit the *Indian Act*.

***Kuokkanen***: So, you wouldn't see a huge change in the lives of the women you were working with if the Act was changed tomorrow?

***Beads***: Exactly.

I noticed what was happening in Vancouver and in general, within the justice system, federally and provincially. They were looking for ways that they could save money and feel satisfied with cutting legal aid and you know, cutting all those things, and they were looking for alternatives. One of them was restorative justice. I didn't know much about restorative justice, but I was pretty sure that the white male bureaucrat wasn't going to get it right either way.

## RESTORATIVE JUSTICE AND WIFE BATTERING

***Beads***: In Vancouver they were proposing that they start an urban Aboriginal restorative justice program. There were a lot of really eager community members and I thought, well, great. This will be a good way to keep our people out of jail; the rate of Aboriginal people in jail is absolutely over- whelming. Most of those people would be there for, I'm guessing, poverty related crimes. Or maybe alcohol related violence. You know, things that really aren't a huge threat to society. I was gratified that that might be an alternative. I wasn't really sure that bureaucrats would agree that we need to decrease the incarceration of Aboriginal people, but I was willing to try. But then it went quite quickly into assumptions that this would be a good way to deal with wife battering. And then my alarms went off. So then I brought up the fact that there is a huge power imbalance that exists between men and women regardless of race.

There was a steering committee meeting of a bunch of Aboriginal organizations that wanted to support this restorative justice program. As a member of Rape Relief, I understood that they had agreed that they would also consult with women's groups to make sure that women were included in the process. So, I decided that I better bring this back to an AWAN meeting. Maybe I'm way off track? Maybe this restorative justice is the best thing on the planet? Maybe I'm wrong, right? At the time, we had one member who worked for another sexual assault organization, a woman who worked for a battered women's service, and another woman who was working for the Aboriginal transition house here. There was a lot of violence against women workers there; we all agreed that this was a problem, and we needed to slow the process down. What we wanted to do was teach ourselves, but also engage other women at the same time. There was a lot that we didn't know about the criminal justice system, the Criminal Code, all of the provincial policies that affect us, police response policies, things like that.

## EDUCATING AND EMPOWERING WOMEN

We decided we wanted to organize a sixteen-week series of workshops to educate ourselves, but we'd also invite any Aboriginal woman from the community who wanted to come in and learn with us, about restorative justice, but also about other stuff. One week we would take the "violence against women in relationships" policy and would invite a speaker for the first hour... these were four-hour classes. During the first hour we would invite, if necessary, non-Aboriginal resources people in to give us an overview. And then we would ask them to leave, and for the next three hours we would work with Aboriginal women on trying to figure this out. Where do we fit into it? And, do we fit into it? After the sixteen weeks we'd become fairly expert on matters relating to the law and also sharpened our own analysis.

## FEMINIST ANALYSIS, WOMEN'S EMPOWERMENT AND CULTURE

*Kuokkanen*: Did your analysis include feminist analysis?

*Beads*: Definitely. There was me and Fay and Mabel and Wendy. The four of us for sure were working in the field and definitely said we're feminists. We could guarantee that our own workshops were delivered with a feminist analysis in mind and speaking from a woman's perspective. And, you know, speaking from a woman's equality point of view rather than a victim's perspective. Because it's quite different, the way you think about violence when you're thinking as a victim... you're thinking as an oppressed person or group of people. Our workshops didn't do anything at all with culture. We didn't reject culture in any way, and we certainly respected anyone's culture, but we never argued for culturally appropriate anything.

We didn't agree that lack of any type of ceremony was what was causing Aboriginal women to be hurt. Then when the women went missing, for instance, we started to wonder why are Aboriginal women going missing at alarming rates? I think of the lack of opportunity, the lack of education, the lack of jobs, all of those things make women vulnerable to male violence. These are issues that affect all women, but because of racism are more harmful to Aboriginal women.

*Kuokkanen*: So, you think it is not lack of culture, but other marginalization due to race?

**Beads**: Right. If what I really needed was cultural services that wouldn't even be an option for me in Vancouver. There are no Ojibway cultural centres in Vancouver. I saw that various government agencies were bragging that they'd started up these great Aboriginal cultural programs and this was the answer for everything.

What I've heard from Aboriginal women, and what I can speak to from my own perspective, is this: I don't want to talk to a cultural group about my sexual assault, right? Cultural particularity isn't always the first priority. Some women don't want to use on-reserve transition houses, for instance, because someone's relative is the worker there, or maybe her husband's aunt runs the house. These are small communities. There needs to be some degree of privacy and anonymity when women ask for these services. I think that there is a whole other place for cultural and other healing activities, but I don't think it's at the immediate crisis place. When I'm in crisis I just need to know that I can pick up the phone and either the police will respond, or the autonomous women's group will respond, or the courts with respond. Later if what I decide I really need is to do some intensive spiritual work, then fine, that should be there too. But, I think that that is secondary to the need for safety and so on.

It's women's equality that I want to improve upon. Aboriginal women are always on my mind. If I'm thinking of myself, my relatives and my friends in relation to the things that I'm recommending, I think, "Is that going to help them"? And if it is, if it's going to improve their lives, well, then I think I have done Aboriginal feminist work.

**Kuokkanen**: Do you think there is a need to increase anti-racism work amongst the police force?

**Beads**: I support that, but I really don't think it's the answer to Aboriginal women's problems.

**Kuokkanen**: Many argue that the police don't even care to reply when they know it's a part of the city where Aboriginal people are. That they don't even respond to the call in an appropriate manner because they know it's a Native woman.

**Beads**: I think that racism and sexism in our police — well actually everywhere in our justice system — is way out of control. But, on the other hand, I know from working with non-Aboriginal women that the cops didn't respond to them either. I think that police don't respond to women.

In all my years of working on the rape crisis line, seven years, I talked to hundreds of women. Through that time I was aware of thousands of women and their stories and never did any one woman manage to get her case through to conviction. I mean, despite overwhelming evidence. Even white, well-employed women who didn't have those other barriers — and not one single conviction, and many women went to court. So, while anti-racism training or cultural sensitivity training would be useful, I don't think it addresses the problem of sexism.

I had a good working relationship with one fairly new cop and I asked him what type of training they got for working with women who have been assaulted, and about women and people of a different race. He told me about all the different workshops that are offered as part of their training, and none of them are mandatory anyway. They can choose to take a workshop on cultural sensitivity or Aboriginal people and their issues (it was a two-hour workshop), but they didn't get paid for that time. There was no incentive to do it. He talked about a lot of his colleagues being pretty unwilling anyway. He said, "I can't imagine any of them agreeing to sign up for a course."

***Kuokkanen***: So that is also when your feminist analysis developed.

***Beads***: I had a huge interest in access to birth control as a younger woman. You know, I thought that all girls needed to have access to not only hormone birth control, but to condoms to keep ourselves physically safe too. Where I grew up people were quite religious. I started to realize that women are really controlled. Lots of girls got pregnant and were sent away somewhere to have their babies. Then I realized that women are really controlled. We don't have access to birth control and we're still expected to put out. Then we're the ones that are sent out of town to go have babies. I was mad about it and thought it was unfair. Being Aboriginal just magnified everything. Aboriginal women who experience sexual assault have that much more to deal with. The sexual assault sometimes isn't the only issue. It's poverty. It's trauma. It's racism. So those are the conditions that I want to improve for all women.

## JUSTICE FOR ABORIGINAL WOMEN IS A TEMPLATE FOR JUSTICE FOR ALL WOMEN

If we can use the Aboriginal woman as the model for how we're going to build our response to women, then of course all women are going to benefit from that. It's going to be really awesome for women who have very few barriers and it's going to be really good for Aboriginal women. So that's how I started thinking about things and organizing things.

***Kuokkanen***: Have you seen any change?

***Beads***: Alliance building has really helped non-Aboriginal women to understand what the realities for Aboriginal women are. It's relieved some of the pressure from us. We have support for some of our struggles. We can't afford to be fighting with each other. There's enough that we can focus on and there's enough that we can share.

I think the experience of growing up and seeing the way Aboriginal kids were treated versus non-Aboriginal kids informed me about racism, systemic racism. And then getting older and having my own experience in court, and wondering if that was abnormal. I didn't know: was this only my experience? Was I the only one treated this way, or was it because I had a legal aid lawyer instead of an expensive lawyer? I didn't know if it was poverty related, or what?

But, connecting with other women actually taught me that, no, this is actually a pretty common experience amongst women. That was reassuring in a really lousy kind of way. It's lousy to be reassured that you were treated like crap, but that's ok, because every woman is.

## CONSIDERING EQUALITY

That's what brought me to my principles of organizing and working with women. It has to be focused on gender. There is always going to be a place for anti-racism work and anti-poverty work, but I think that for women sexism is our biggest oppression and barrier right now in achieving equality. When we talk about equality, you know, I don't actually want to be equal to men. Some things I might need more of. Some things I might need less of. Equality could be based on a substantive equality model where we look at the realities. I don't just want equal wages, equal work hours, etcetera. And I think that we do need to take into consideration all of the unpaid work that women do.

**Kuokkanen**: So it goes to the deep structures of society that need to be changed?

**Beads**: Right. We need to look individually at the women that we're organizing with and who we're listening to. Are those women that can make change? In terms of our women politicians, I don't know that they are all thinking about equality. I think that a lot of them are still very much a part of the boys' club. And I don't want women to be mimicking men. A lot of women don't want to believe that really, the reason you are so oppressed, you're so far behind, you're making less money, you're so damaged in all these different ways is because of your gender. I think that it becomes overwhelming. When you're engaging in a race fight you have a lot more solidarity with your men, right, and those may be the people that may have hurt you in your private life.

**Kuokkanen**: Have you seen more Aboriginal women actually embracing or including the feminist analysis to deal with racism?

**Beads**: In small ways I think so. For example, why are there only 5 percent women chiefs in Canada? Women do realize that there is something not quite right about that. Women are starting to take courses to take care of themselves and be part of band councils and band politics and political activity in general. I don't know that all of those women would call themselves feminists. And I don't know that they are feminists, but certainly what they are taking on is also a feminist struggle. Still, I don't see a lot of Aboriginal women jumping up and declaring themselves feminist or really agreeing with me or with other feminists with whom they are speaking.

**Kuokkanen**: So they see it as a white woman's issue?

**Beads**: Definitely.

**Kuokkanen**: How do you see actual feminism in the university and in women's groups coming together?

**Beads**: The academic circle is a very tight circle sometimes. It's really hard to get in there. Certainly with the first symposium, I looked at the list of presenters and topics and I thought, why aren't I talking about this? Why isn't Mabel presenting on this? Why isn't Wendy presenting on this?

I think there is a huge need for Aboriginal academics out there. But it should be just as credible to have learned from the school of life. It almost felt like what Aboriginal women accused the feminist movement of being: a very white privileged movement. It's a bunch of privileged educated women who are going to sit around and talk about feminism, and how in touch with reality are they? It was a wonderful event though. It was a great event. I think that there is a bit of an obligation of the academy to actually figure out who is missing, who can be incorporated and who will benefit from this.

I started thinking: What is it that made me aware of who I am and aware of discrimination to actually deciding that feminism is what I need to follow. Aboriginal feminism.

## THE PERSONAL IS POLITICAL

What I'm actually doing is outlining the journey of the way I was brought into the world. I was born to an Ojibway girl who was raped by a white guy. You know, she was very young when she got pregnant. He was working on the highways for the summer. He left to go back to university and then she was faced with the pregnancy, living in one of the smallest reserves in Canada;

230

a very poor reserve. The railroad just went straight through it and wrecked the land. And, in the meantime she got taken away from her family because of course she was pregnant and they couldn't have been looking after her. And then the state apprehended me at the hospital.

I know a little about the history of her. I know that when she was in foster care her foster family said to her, if you put this baby up for adoption then we will adopt you and give you a real family. And I just thought, what a decision. That's horrible. So that was kind of the culture back then: save all of these babies from being brought up in these horrible conditions and raise them in our white families.

When she adopted me my mom was forty and she had just remarried to my dad and they didn't really qualify for adoption of a "real" baby because she was a white immigrant who married a Native man. Children's Aid Society ended up saying, look, what we'll do is give you one of our "hard to place" babies. If they don't get placed right away they just grow up in orphanages or foster care. If you're willing to take a hard to place baby then that's fine.

So my mom asked, well, what do you mean by "hard to place"? She thought that perhaps it would be a severely disabled kid and wondered if she'd be able to care for such a child. And they said, no, we mean Indian babies. Knowing that is really kind of creepy. How is it that Aboriginal people became so second place in Canada? It's always been that way obviously.

I don't think that my mom really got it. I don't think that she understood that the reason she got a "hard to place" baby was because she married a Native man. I think that she thought maybe it had to do with her age or that it had to do with other factors. She was still pretty new to Canada. She saw my dad as a good-looking guy. She was used to fair, blond men, so suddenly there's a dark-haired man and he was a good dancer, right. So, I think she was pretty naïve about what she was getting into.

I think that a lot of Aboriginal women have the same experience that I have.

I could have just as easily not done any of the things I did. Am I lucky? I'd been brought up in poverty and came from a broken home. So how is it that I suddenly decided, well, I'm going to be okay. I'm just going to do something and be an activist. I decided that I'm not going to be on the street or become an addict or any of those things. You do have choices. Although I don't think I made a choice. I'm still trying to figure out the day when it just kind of snapped and I figured out this is where I am going to go.

**Kuokkanen**: Can you name any support structures or individuals who were important to you?

**Beads**: My mom was good. She lived in Denmark as a fifteen-year-old during Germany's occupation of Denmark during World War II and she saw a lot, some of which she shared and some of which I don't think she can. But, listening to her live through that — she came out okay. She just decided that she would make different choices. So my mom was a great influence.

I used to work in different Aboriginal organizations. I worked for the Native Brotherhood for three or four years. That was my first grown-up job. I dealt with Native fishermen. We gave them loans for boats and administered their benefits. But, you know, the people were real. The job was writing cheques and filling out forms. But when the people would actually come in and say this is what is going on and this happened to my mother, wife, sister, aunt, whatever… then it became so real. The people that I met there and some of my co-workers who were dealing with so much outside of the job: suicides and deaths and crisis galore and yet they were still coming in to work every day. I thought, wow. These people are awesome. So, they were influential.

Then by the time I got to Rape Relief, it was Bonnie Agnew, who somehow gave me the freedom or permission… she would just encourage me to say things. She would reassure me that it's probably not going to be wrong and if it was she would ask me to clarify. She really encouraged me to go on and explore this. She's the one who suggested I attend that first NAC conference, recognizing that I was pretty isolated. She died suddenly, shortly after I began to know her, and that was an extreme loss, not only to me, but to the entire Canadian feminist movement.

And then it was the individual Aboriginal women. Fay was pretty good. Sharon McIvor was a massive influence in my life. I probably admire her the most of women that I know. And talk about gutsy! If she can be that public then certainly I can. I'm not a lawyer. Not much to lose here. If she can take the risk so can I. So I think that's where I get what I've got going on today.

**Kuokkanen**: What is an Aboriginal feminist to you?

**Beads**: Well… I think you have to be an Aboriginal woman. You recognize that there is an inequality between men and women and you recognize that that is compounded by race and that you're actually looking at race, gender and class in your work. You're incorporating all three of those things, and you're using that as a backdrop to the work you do when you look at policies or media or job descriptions or anything. And, you figure out why isn't this working for an Aboriginal woman. When you can sort of apply your thinking that way then I think that you can probably call yourself an Aboriginal feminist.

# Chapter Fifteen

# COLLEEN GLENN

## A Métis Feminist in Indian Rights for Indian Women, 1973–1979

### Colleen Glenn with Joyce Green

In this chapter, Colleen Glenn, a Métis feminist born and raised in Alberta, talks about her period of activism with Indian Rights for Indian Women (IRIW). IRIW was one of the first organizations dedicated solely to elimination of sex discrimination from the *Indian Act*'s membership provisions. As a Métis woman, Glenn had nothing to gain from this objective; rather, she participated as an act of principle and solidarity. Further, as a Métis woman, Glenn found herself on numerous occasions treated poorly because she was not a status or treaty Indian. She persisted in her commitment, contributing her time and talent, because she believed *as an Aboriginal feminist* in the justice of the objective and in the need for principled solidarity. Glenn's motivation, commitment and practices are characteristic of the best of feminism. This chapter is a combination of Glenn's own notes and of transcripts from an interview she did on May 28, 2003, with Joyce Green.

The year 1970 was a very good year for feminist activists. The Report of the Royal Commission on the Status of Women (RCSW) was published, making 167 recommendations for change in the patriarchal system. Many Aboriginal women and organizations had appeared before the RCSW and had made submissions to it. The process of putting briefs together for the Commission had raised our consciousness with regard to women's issues and had even radicalized some of us.

1970 was also the year that Jeannette Lavell filed her objection to losing her Indian status when she married a man who was not an Indian. This consequence of marriage would not be visited upon a male person. In fact, Indian men could marry whomever they pleased and their wives and subsequent children would be considered Indians as well. Not only did Indian women lose their status if they "married out," but the consequence of loss of status meant that one could not return home in the event of marriage breakdown or widowhood. Nor would her children would be considered Indians. She could not inherit property or be buried with her ancestors. She would no longer be entitled to payments or royalties or to government services other Indians were entitled to (see also Joyce Green,

Chapter 8, and Sharon McIvor, Chapter 16, this volume).

This had been the law for more than a hundred years. But prior to European settlement, the many nations of Turtle Island had different systems of family law (see Henning, Chapter 11). Many tribes had well-documented matrilineal and matrilocal systems. In western Canada, where the fur trade had skewed Aboriginal economic systems before any Caucasians had even turned up, there is less information about family law systems. This did not stop some Indian men throughout Canada from claiming that patriarchy was the norm.

In the hundred years of *Indian Act* domination over the lives of Indians, not once had the federal government consulted the people who would be affected about the federal laws that governed their lives. At every opportunity, many Indians had objected to the legislated exclusion of women from their communities. No one in the federal government listened.

When Jeannette Lavell objected to section 12 (1) (b) of the *Indian Act*, citing the Canadian Bill of Rights prohibition of discrimination on the basis of sex, it was unlikely that she could have foreseen the hostility that would result. After all, the 1960s were an era of increased activism of all minorities. Civil liberties, equality of persons and human rights were a major social concern in many countries. Then Prime Minister Pierre Trudeau, who later championed the Charter of Rights and Freedoms, claimed for Canada the objective of the "Just Society."

Hence, it was most surprising to encounter the hostility of some Indians to proposals to change the *Indian Act* membership provisions and to the women that advocated change. You would have thought that the women supporting Jeannette's position had come from outer space, were some other species, not their sisters, daughters and aunts. At the same time these women were vilified, the very same men would talk about how the white man didn't know how to treat family.

As a Native person, one could be a registered, status or treaty Indian, recognized by the Canadian government as an Indian person entitled to benefits; a non-status Indian, one who had once had treaty status and somehow lost it; an Inuit person, or Métis, descended from Indian and European relationships that predated the treaty era. The issue of legislative sexism, resulting in unfair treatment of registered Indian women, was more important to those whose lives were affected by it.

Glenn produced a newspaper clipping from January 9, 1973, about a panel at the University of Calgary, featuring Jeannette Lavell.

**Glenn**: This was the first time I got interested in the issue of *Indian Act* discrimination against women. I and a couple of good friends, Bev and Gloria, had gone to hear Jeannette Lavell on a panel discussion sponsored by the

University of Calgary in a series called "Canadian Indians in Contemporary Society." That's when I met Jenny Margetts, of Indian Rights for Indian Women. We all started to be invited to meetings of the National Committee of Indian Rights for Indian Women, formed by the Native Women's Association of Canada, to look into the issue of supporting Jeannette in her challenge to the *Indian Act*.

Listening to the panel, I was so taken aback at the hostility that was directed at Jeannette. I bet Jeannette thought she was doing her bit to improve the lot of Indian people in general, and she must have been just horrified at this reaction. She never said anything, none of us ever said anything in particular about it, unless you were in a very small group with two or three other women, who you could get together and talk about how horrifying it was to be treated in such a hostile fashion by these guys. If you were a non-status Indian woman you might be afraid to say anything out loud. But Jeannette I'm sure must have felt it more than anybody because she took the brunt of all the hatred. Harold Cardinal [a prominent Indian politician of the time] was the most hostile of all.

The knowledge that there was no penalty for men who married outside their ethnic group, didn't offend everyone, not even all Indian women. For example, Vicki Crowchild, a member of the Sarcee Nation (now the Tsu Tina) is quoted in the newspaper as saying that the *Indian Act* is okay with her, she could live with this. Indian women should always follow the man, she said. She admitted there was a double standard in the way that Indian men and women are treated, but she could accept it. She argued that rightful recipients of treaty benefits would be deprived if the system were changed and that these women were motivated by greed.

At the same meeting, an Indian man kept asking Jeannette if she had support from the chief of her reserve. When she replied that at the time of her initial action the chief of her reserve supported her but the current chief did not, he acted as if this was a dishonest response. This was my introduction to the opposition to women on the part of powerful Indian elites.

*Green*: After you met Jenny, what moved you to further involvement, and how long were you involved?

*Glenn*: One of my best friends had lost her status when she married a Métis. Soon after that one of my brothers married a status Indian and she lost her status. Hearing my friend and my sister-in-law being described as greedy failures who wished to deprive legitimate Indians of their inheritance made me deeply angry. Here was something that needed to be changed. The law, and the attitudes of those who supported it, were clearly and overtly racist. The rhetoric opposing women's claim to their status amounted to anti-feminist discrimination. Surely there could be no reasonable objection to the removal of this ugly sexist blot on the Canadian legislative landscape.

I was active from 1973 until 1979. I moved to Edmonton to go to law school at the University of Alberta in 1974. Most of the IRIW women were in Edmonton, and they would call me up when they had meetings. I was useful to them, I guess. So I ended up being sort of an assistant to Jenny. I took most of the minutes. Jenny was a really good organizer in keeping the issue front and centre. But there was very little effort by anyone to bring other members into the association. In fact, one of the reasons that I became uncomfortable toward the end of the 1970s was the lack of membership vitality, and the lack of transparency, accountability and good record-keeping.

One of the guys in the Native Law Student Association had seen what was going on in the organization and said to me, "try and get them to keep membership lists," but that didn't happen. At a meeting we had in Ottawa, we adopted a set of constitutional by-laws, which as far as I know never got registered. But there were the usual requirements to keep the money we got accounted for. We needed good accounting procedures; groups have to be sure that grant monies aren't mishandled. I grew to be uncomfortable about the way money was being handled. Activist groups aren't always experts in accounting, grant writing or bureaucratic procedures, but they are required to do that kind of work when they take government money.

What really seemed to work for IRIW's politics in that period of time was that there was a lot of support from the white women's organizations. We [IRIW] had support from the Advisory Council on the Status of Women and from the National Action Committee on the Status of Women (NAC), in which there were church groups, all kinds of women's groups, that knew of the issue of women being treated unequally with men in the Indian community, and they thought that it was one of the ugliest forms of discrimination against women. The ones that were least able to defend themselves. And the problem was quite easy to fix: just don't enforce those sections of the *Indian Act*. Why not do this? But no.

There seemed to be a lot of public support, and there were a lot of women's groups in Indian communities such as The Tobique Women's Group, Shirley Bear's group. The Advisory Council on the Status of Women was the one that supported the book that Kathleen Jamieson did on 12(1)(b), *Citizens Minus*. And we had some support from within the Prime Minister's Office, from some of the women bureaucrats. We got individual support from employees of organizations, both Native and non-Native. We got other kinds of support: information from secretaries and other employees came my way, confidential documents, sometimes from the wives of Indian politicians.

Media coverage helped us. The issue of Indian women's rights was kept in the public eye by articles in magazines like *Chatelaine, Branching Out* and other academic journals. The newspapers covered meetings and interviewed members of IRIW. And IRIW held public meetings from Vancouver to Halifax.

We got political support: supporters in opposition political parties would rise in question period to bring up the issue. Flora MacDonald, a Progressive Conservative MP, was particularly supportive.

Harold Cardinal's leadership, and his opposition to changing the *Indian Act*, influenced the federal government more than we women could. I remember being in a meeting we had with NAC in Ottawa. All of us women were in a room with cabinet ministers when section 12(1)(b) was brought up. And [then cabinet minister] Marc Lalonde said, "The men wanted it that way." Well, hissing and booing from the assembled women! In 1978, the National Indian Brotherhood was still refusing to accept women's participation in the *Indian Act* discussions.

When the Supreme Court of Canada delivered its judgement in the Lavell case that fall, a majority on the court found no discrimination. For a good review of the history of this issue, see *Indian Women and the Law: Citizens Minus*, a publication of the Advisory Committee on the Status of Women, written by Kathleen Jamieson at the request of the National Committee on Indian Rights for Indian Women.

The negative Supreme Court decision left no avenue open to Native women but political activism. Fortunately this was the perfect time for it.

I remember two older women from the Fishing Lake Métis settlement. We were young women then, and they said to us: "You're going to make things better for us all." You know, that makes you feel good. There were really decent things that happened. But there were really awful things that happened too. And when all this business was going on with these men objecting to Jeannette, you'd see them lecturing the white man on how he didn't know anything about the family. You know, such hypocrisy. It makes you sick. You don't ever get used to it. Makes you feel bad.

*Green*: Was the word feminism ever used?

*Glenn*: No. There weren't any feminists. I was a member of the Native Law Student Association of Canada, of the Native Students Club at the University of Alberta and the Alberta Status of Women Action Committee. For a while I sat on the board of Planned Parenthood: Aboriginal women need and use the services of Planned Parenthood. I was involved in all kinds of stuff. I was a member of the Métis Association of Alberta. So I was really a part of the feminist community, but Jenny and these other women, while they didn't mind associating themselves with these groups, they were hesitant to say they were feminists.

In a lot of these groups, too, there was some hostility between straight and lesbian women, women "of colour' and white women, and between English and French speaking women. I always went to all of NAC's meetings. I thought we were all going to work together in solidarity on various issues. In the 1980s when I was doing stuff for NAC, I noticed the divisions. But in the beginning, I remember thinking, "It's about time we all got busy and worked on these issues," and we seemed glad to do it. And there was some support: when we had meetings in Ottawa, cabinet ministers attended. This was Trudeau's government, Marc Lalonde's. They didn't have much interest in the issue, but they attended and paid attention. That was the climate of the time.

**Green**: Where did the money come from?

**Glenn**: IRIW money came from the Secretary of State, which was funding all kinds of organizations at the time. There was a big emphasis on multi-culturalism. In the province, we had to apply for grants from the provincial government to do local workshops and the meetings that we held in Alberta. We applied to Secretary of State for money to hold national meetings. I re-member there was one in Vancouver, one in Winnipeg, one in Halifax and several in Ottawa. Jenny took care of the money. She was really good at that — writing grant applications and working to get *Citizens Minus* published.

**Green**: So this was an advocacy group but not a broad-based membership group, and did not have constituted by-laws?

**Glenn**: No. It was a single-issue organization, that being *Indian Act* member-ship. I remember being at a NAC meeting in Ottawa, and a woman from Ontario came up to Nellie Carlson and said her concern was about residency on their reserve, because husbands come home drunk on the reserve and when the police go to answer domestic complaints, they remove the wife and children because the man is the one who has the residency permit, location ticket, whatever. And Nelly said, "We're not interested in that."

**Green**: They didn't see themselves as part of a broader feminist move-ment?

**Glenn**: No, apparently not. And that's the problem with not having a broad-based group. Also, any experience that members acquired in organizing, any expertise in writing grant applications, planning meetings and that kind of stuff, you lose it. People who learn how to do that go somewhere else. I spent my whole life learning how to do something that I only did once. So organizations don't have the people with the skills to be ready to move on any issue that comes up. There's no continuity. You can't build on history. You can't teach others who come along about the things you've learned.

I remember once, an African woman came through town talking to Aboriginal groups, I think she was from SWAPO [South West Africa People's Organization]. Jenny sent me to the meeting with that woman. I was interested in international issues. This woman came to try to drum up solidarity amongst Aboriginal women in Canada. It wasn't going well. I said to her, "I'm really sorry that we're not more supportive here. It's been a long time since anybody pointed guns our way. We've forgotten this isn't the way it is all over the world."

So a lot of the people who were active on single issues couldn't relate to issues from people on other Indian reserves or from across the country or from somewhere else. We were parochial. If we could just put aside our pettiness, we could make real progress. Solidarity and alliances are the only way any progress was made on the membership issue, including the support of those white women in NAC and on the Advisory Council who leaned over backwards to make sure things were done for us. Women like Monica Townsend. We dealt with her a lot. And that's how progress was made.

**Green**: Can you talk about your own identity as a feminist, what you understand that to mean, and how that shapes your political perspectives and associations?

**Glenn**: How could you not be a feminist, given the evident oppression of women? That was a no-brainer, for me. But a lot of the women's organizations that were around at the same time as IRIW were interested only in beadwork and crafts and women's auxiliary kinds of things, not about politics. I remember one year, the big deal for the Voice of Alberta Native Women was an all-girls rodeo. They didn't ever criticize men, or talk about their own standing relative to men in their own communities. It wasn't done. Maybe it's the old residential school business. Many of these people grew up in the residential schools in which the church determined their status and of course, gender roles. The Catholic Church had very definite ideas about where women's place was. Females were just not as important. So it was difficult for them to step out of that. But then, what the hell, it was difficult for all of us.

The standard introduction into feminism for people of my age was Betty Friedan's *Feminine Mystique* of 1963, in which she *defined* the problem. Why is it we weren't powerful or satisfied? Why did we feel unhappy and bored and all those things that most of us felt? In 1969 and 1970 my marriage fell apart, I went back to school and then to university, while parenting my children.

In 1973, I was a student at the University of Calgary and had some modest experience in feminist activism. I got involved in daycare struggles. The University of Calgary had no daycare centre, of course, because there had hardly been any females on campus, particularly ones with little kids. Up until this time we were supposed to be home looking after them. So me and a bunch of other women banded together to set up a daycare centre for students at the University of Calgary. And that's where I met women and got into the women's liberation movement. We had consciousness-raising groups and all that stuff. That led to being involved in other kinds of feminist activities that grew out of that issue, the daycare centre. The daycare centre involvement meant that I met other people who thought like I did and had similar life problems. We were involved in a group in the early 1970s called Women for Political Action, which was a group of women that thought women should be involved in political parties. All political parties, not just any one in particular. A national conference was organized between a Toronto group called Women For Political Action, and one in Calgary, and that, I believe, was the founding meeting of NAC. At that time I went to Toronto for this big meeting and discovered that there were thousands of other women all across Canada, all getting involved in organizing daycare centres so that they could go to school or go to work. Whatever it was they wanted to do. And having consciousness raising groups where we got together and discovered that we had similar experiences and feelings. The same things affected us. We weren't alone. It wasn't just me, being some crazy woman who was unhappy with my life. We were all in the same boat.

I was also involved in the Métis Association of Alberta. And I had friends, one of whom was Gloria, so we talked about things, and we went to this meeting when Jeannette Lavell came to town.

And Jeannette was looking after her interests, and everyone else's interests, her children's, her relatives'. The interests of the Aboriginal community, period. Anybody who thinks that removing women from the community is going to give you a stronger society has got something missing somewhere. It just doesn't work that way.

I'll never forget seeing Gloria's birth certificate. It was a long sheet of paper. Gloria, she was born in the 1940s. At the very top is this heading: "Birth of a live Indian." This is what she carried around for a birth certificate. Perhaps there's a nice long form entitled "Birth of a dead Indian."

Chapter Sixteen

# SHARON MCIVOR
## Woman of Action

### Sharon McIvor with Rauna Kuokkanen

*Sharon McIvor is a prominent Aboriginal feminist and political activist, who for many years has played a national role in Canadian constitutional change and worked for Aboriginal women's human rights. McIvor continues her work now through the Feminist Alliance for International Action (FAFIA), a Canadian based organization dedicated to advancing women's human rights internationally.[1] Rauna Kuokkanen, a Sami feminist, interviewed Sharon McIvor at Merritt, British Columbia, on August 31, 2005.*

**Kuokkanen**: Tell me about your identification as a feminist. How long have you been a feminist?

**McIvor**: I was one of the earlier Aboriginal feminists. Most of the women I know that do the kind of political work I do don't like to be identified as a feminist: you're Aboriginal. I think I've always been a feminist.

I was born in 1948, right after the war. That was a time when Aboriginal peoples were having a really difficult time in Canada — around the world actually. From the time I was very, very young my family modelled respect for individuals and individual rights. I was never one to conform to just get along, to do what I had to in order to get along, that kind of thing. I have an aunt who is eighty-three and I asked her — she was there when I was born — I asked her why, of all of my family, my extended family, my siblings, I seemed to be the only one who does the kind of political work that I do. She said from the time I started to talk I would always ask "why" or "why not." I always challenged things. I would never just accept what was going on. This is a fundamental part of my personality. And, of course, my youth spanned a time when minorities and Aboriginal women were having a difficult time because of discriminatory laws and social practices.

I was one of the only Aboriginal children going to public school when I started school in the early fifties. I would get into trouble in the classroom because I would challenge the teacher, or I wouldn't just accept everything. I can remember in grade four being told, "If you ask any more questions then you are going to have to wait in the hall." And I said, "Well, if you send me to the hall, then I am just going to go home." So the teacher sent me to the hall, and I took my coat and I went home.

My father was one in my family who did a lot of Aboriginal theory stuff. He was an Aboriginal man who had grade twelve, which was — by Aboriginal standards — well educated. He too would never accept the status quo. This was at a time when he wasn't recognized. He was Aboriginal but he wasn't recognized as being Indian because he wasn't registered. In the parlance of these things, he was "non-status."

He had a 1941 or 1942 jeep and it was a rickety old thing, barely working, but he'd get it going. And he'd take it down to the river where we do the salmon fishing, about an hour and a bit away. He would go down with his net. Fill the net and bring the fish home. Because he was not recognized as an Indian, it was illegal for him to do it, but he said I'm Aboriginal and I am going to do it. So, away he would go, usually in early June. He would set the nets and bring them home, and Mom and I would fix them and all of that.

Invariably, every year at one point — because he would make several trips — he would get caught. And so they would take his nets. They would impound his jeep. And he would be put in jail for a day or two. And then he would be let go, and he would go to court and he would be found guilty, and he would be fined. And they would confiscate the things that they took.

But the next year his jeep would be back down to the river. And in his lifetime he was never recognized as an Indian by the governments of Canada. He died in 1978. Possibly in 1985, when the *Indian Act* was changed, he may have been able to be registered. But during his lifetime he never was. Watching all of this was another part of my education.

My mom grew up on a homestead between here and Kamloops. She was very indulged by her parents… she went to grade three and then she didn't want to go to school anymore, so they didn't make her go to school. And although she only went to grade three she was very well read. She loved reading. But she grew up along the land. She met my father and they moved in together when they were sixteen. He worked in the sawmill; he worked in the logging sawmill for almost his entire working life. They brought with them knowledge and values that I think a lot of other people weren't able to get. For my mom, that freedom of being out on the land was profoundly important — and she could make a meal out of almost anything. We did a lot of traditional food gathering. My dad hunted year round, so we had a lot of wild game. And we had fish. In Mitchell Lake and Douglas Lake, which are connected by a creek, there are Kokanee… that's a land-locked Sockeye salmon… they're about two pounds. At particular times of the year they spawn, and they run down the creek… and when they are in the creek you go and you gather salmon. So, during all of my formative years that was our lifestyle.

When I was a child, what hit me particularly hard was the inequity and injustice. We lived in a community here... well, maybe about ten blocks from here. And the treatment we got from white people in the community, that my mom got in the community, was really, really bad. I've lots of memories of the kind of racist treatment as you walked down the street with my mom... and my mom had several children. There were five of us in ten years. We were all small at the same period of time. She would come to do some shopping, and we would all be trailing behind the stroller. I remember the rude comments that she would get from strangers on the street, or people on the street.

There was one store where we would go in to get our groceries, and it was the kind where you didn't go in and serve yourself. You gave your list to the proprietor and then he would select the food and whatever you were buying. And a couple of things I can remember — I must have been very young — I was probably not even in school yet because we would go during the day. We would go into the store with my mom, and she would give him the list, and then the proprietor would start filling her food order, but if anybody else came in the store, then he would stop serving her and go serve the white customer. Sometimes it would take a while to finish our shopping. And again, the kind of comments that were made were very distressing. The other thing that got me in particular is that he would look at the list she'd given him and he wouldn't allow her to buy certain things. For example, he wouldn't allow her to buy any candy. She liked to buy little treats for us, and he wouldn't let her buy any because... well... I have no idea why. She paid in cash and I know that a lot of people were on social assistance and the story owner would scrutinize what they could buy. But my mom was spending her own money. My dad worked from the time they got together when they were sixteen. The money that my mom had was the money that my dad had earned. But, the store proprietor would scrutinize her list and wouldn't allow her to buy certain things. At the time it was curious, and as I got older I realized that this was discrimination, and he thought that my mom wasn't capable of making appropriate decisions and he was entitled to make them for her.

We would walk to the movies; it was the late 1950s. It was about six blocks, but we had to be careful because from the period of time from the mid-1930s up until probably the mid- to late 1970s, if you were Aboriginal and you were assaulted, nobody would do anything about it. Aboriginal women or girls were fair game for white male predators. We had a specific route to go home. The movie ended at nine or nine thirty... and if any car lights came you headed for the bushes. Because usually it would be men driving the cars, and it wouldn't be unusual for them to try to grab you. It was something that we had to be very careful about. So, I think that all of these experiences fed into the kind of work that I do. The unfairness of those kinds of treatment. It raised questions for me. Why is my person of less value than a person of a different gender, or a person of a different race?

So, my critical consideration of social and political matters started very young. I was in my late teens. I graduated from high school and went to the University of Waterloo, which had a summer program out there for Aboriginal youth. That would be in 1967 or 1968. It just seemed like the right thing to do at the time.

Since then my activism has probably taken a more legal focus, but my impulse to activism and justice still draws on my early experiences and background.

***Kuokkanen***: Have you always worked on Aboriginal women's issues? You were the vice-president of the Native Women's Association of Canada for a number of years.

***McIvor***: Well, I've always worked on inequality issues. Aboriginal women's issues, in particular, I probably started in the early 1980s. But the inequality issues are the ones that have always had my focus. Discrimination is nonsensical to me…. I cannot make sense out of it. For example, I got an email from a friend about two years ago about an article from a newspaper in Australia. It was a story about a thirteen-year-old Aboriginal girl who was raped by a fifty-nine-year-old Aboriginal man, and the court decided that he was not guilty of rape because it was a traditional custom.

***Kuokkanen***: Yeah, I remember that story.

***McIvor***: And I looked at it and was totally outraged. In addition to being outraged, though, it affected me emotionally. It is wrong… totally wrong…. I can't understand how individuals, communities or courts can rationalize that kind of hurt. I guess the other piece of it is that whatever you do, you'll never be able to undo the hurt that happened to her. It just adds insult to injury to say — you know — not only were you hurt, not only were you violated, but it's okay because society allows that to happen. I actually did take it very personally, and I was so angry and so outraged that this had occurred. I read it and then I emailed it to a few of my other friends to get their comments. So, I think that's the other piece: violations of human rights and inequality become very, very personal for me and I guess always have. So, if you're discriminated against, I hurt too. It's never strictly an intellectual exercise for me.

***Kuokkanen***: It affects you.

*McIvor*: It affects me in a way that I... I have to work through it. I dealt with a group of women on the West Coast who were having some serious difficulties with some men in their community. They had a man who was rampantly raping women and children in the community. And, it didn't seem like law enforcement or anyone was taking it seriously. Finally a woman brought a charge against him and filed a report with the RCMP and the RCMP had charged him. And then the elders got involved and asked that he be dealt with by an elders' circle. They were consenting to that. And he had not only raped the one young woman who had come forward but also other women. He was charged, but nothing happened and during that time he had accosted his aunt and his female cousin and a male cousin when they were out gathering berries, and he had raped all three of them. Then there was an incident where he had grabbed a woman in the middle of the village and raped her on the hood of his car in front of a whole lot of people. They didn't seem to want to do anything about it.

So, what happened was — because of the profile I had because my social and political activities, I was involved with the Native Women's Association, the woman's group called and asked if I would help. And so... there's not a lot that I can do. The RCMP weren't doing anything and the leaders in the community weren't doing anything... what can you do as an outsider? But I did go in and I talked about the issues, and well, I got some media attention. And it seemed that the fact that I said it made a difference.

They ended up closing down the elders' program that allowed the guy to continue to victimize people... that kind of thing. But it takes a lot... someone has to understand what's going on, and in that particular situation the project was funded by the federal government and provincial government. And no one took the women seriously. The women were saying we don't want it—it's not serving justice, it's continuing to violate us, you're allowing him and others to perform badly and to do these bad things and get away with it by diverting them and allowing them to do two months... and they'll continue to re-offend when they're allowed to go on their way.

I take all of that personally, and I think that I have a role to play in exposing these kinds of problems. Governments tolerate the fact that there are thousands of Aboriginal women out there — who on a daily basis get violated and have no concept that it's wrong.

We intervened with a panel that's going across the country to interview people on family violence. The Native Women's Association intervened and said we wanted to be involved — we have Aboriginal women out there that have a different story to tell. It was not easy but we successfully intervened and we had an Aboriginal women's panel that went out, funded by the same group, so that when they went out to Halifax, for instance, they would advertise in the Aboriginal communities and main communities to say: we have this panel on family violence. We put out pamphlets to say these are the kind of things that are considered violence and if you want to talk to us we're trying to get things going. We also had a private session, so that if you had people that don't want to do it publicly then we had a private Aboriginal panel. So you could come in and talk only to a panel of Aboriginal women. In private. Nobody else.

In that panel we had rape victims, for instance. The youngest rape victim was three months old, and the oldest rape victim was ninety-two or ninety-three, and there were women from everything in between. A young girl, a twelve-year-old girl in the province of Quebec, had made contact with the panel to see if she could do a private session. So they arranged for a private session for her, and she came in and gave her testimony. She said that until she saw the pamphlet that described the kinds of violence and things that we were looking at, she didn't realize that having sex with her father, her brothers, her uncles and her grandfather was anything out of the ordinary.

We had all of those stories across the country. And we had people in little isolated communities that are subjected to violence on a daily basis and have no idea that that isn't normal. That's all they know. And so one of the things that we did with the Native Women... myself and my friend... we had some money and we decided to do a Native women's newspaper. I forget how many editions we got out. There weren't that many, a dozen or so. But we would put in articles about rights and interweave them with stories. Then, when we had them all printed we'd send them out to band offices across the country. So what happened at the band offices was quite predictable. Many bands and the band councils ran the band like their own little kingdoms. We knew that what happens in the band office is that they get a bundle of newspapers, and they just throw them on the table in their office. When people come in to see the chief and council, they would often have to wait and wait and wait. Some of them would read the newspaper while they waited. I had phone calls from women in rural Saskatchewan that would say, "I read your article in the newspaper and that's how I've always felt, but I didn't know that anyone else felt that way, and so I went in and talked to the chief and this is what I told him."

So, that's how we were getting the word out. There were and are communities across the country where that is the norm, where that is the life. Where women get up in the morning and they are abused, battered. There are northern communities that have fly-in RCMP services where the police come in every other Tuesday. So, if you get beat up on a Wednesday and the RCMP are not going to come in for ten days, by the time they come, the woman no longer wishes to make a complaint. The piece that I try to do is expose it, talk about it, write about it.

**Kuokkanen**: That must have been one of the first Aboriginal women's newspapers. That was the late 1980s wasn't it?

**McIvor**: In the late 1980s, yes. I don't even know if there are any copies out there anymore. We just ran out of money and we quit doing it and we went on to other things.

I also use the courts.... I'm a lawyer, one of the other things that I do is practise and research law. I have at one point probably had the most Aboriginal women cases out there, that challenged discrimination based on sex. The courts don't recognize a concept of equality that doesn't favour white men.

When we were doing the Native Women's Association of Canada case—the federal court trial division—it was just awful. It was a case where the Native Women's Association of Canada sued the federal government for not funding NWAC equally with the Assembly of First Nations, and for not giving NWAC a seat at the Constitutional table during the Charlottetown Accord[2] negotiations, to represent Aboriginal women equally with the male-dominated Aboriginal organizations.

My friend Jane was the president of the Native Women's Society in the mid-1980s. I was the vice-president. We formed a pact — as long as she wanted to be president, I would be vice-president. That way, we could operate without all of the political backstabbing that went on. So, we were talking one day in her kitchen about the fact that the Assembly of First Nations, the Métis National Council, the Inuit Taparisat and the Congress of Aboriginal Peoples all had open invitations from the federal government to talk about the Constitution. And none of them would even acknowledge that we existed, the Native Women's Association of Canada. We were thinking about what we could do to change that.

The Métis National Council (MNC) at one point was not recognized either, and MNC challenged this in a legal case. They didn't win their legal case, but they did subsequently get an invitation to the table. And the NWT government or the Yukon government did the same thing because the territories didn't have constitutional standing like the provinces... and again they were eventually invited to have input. The federal government included them even though constitutionally they didn't have to.

So, Jane and I decided that mounting a legal case might be the best route to go, strategically, to obtain an invitation to participate in constitutional discussions. I was the vice-president of NWAC at that time. I talked to the president, Gail Stacey-Moore, and she was really not keen on going into the court system, but we finally decided that that was the way we should go. We looked for a lawyer and I ended up getting Mary Eberts, who was one of the top equality rights lawyers in Canada. I talked to Mary and she agreed to act for us. We started the case saying that we wanted equal funding with the AFN and others and a seat at the table. That was our mantra: equal funding and a seat at the table.

We only sued the government of Canada, but by the time we got to trial — it wasn't very long — the Inuit, the Métis National Council and the Congress of Aboriginal People had all third-partied themselves; that is, they'd taken a position against us and obtained intervenor standing in court to argue their cases. The Canadian government had funded them to come in against us. It was really interesting to watch. They all said that they represented women, that their organizations all represented women equally. Our position was that women weren't being represented, and thus, it was essential to have NWAC participate in constitutional discussions.

We ended up in the courtroom. I can still see us in the courtroom. It was me who went — Gail would not go — and my friend Teressa, who came to support me. On one side was Mary and on the other side the lawyer for Canada. The Province of Ontario had a lawyer there as well. Because it was a Constitutional question, the provinces brought their lawyers in and then there was a lawyer for each of the Aboriginal groups. So you've got about eight male lawyers over there, Mary Eberts over here, and Teressa and I over here, and then all of the Aboriginal lawyers there. And the judge, of course: this little old judge in federal court. And he was listening, but what I noticed was that he had this comrade thing with all of these male lawyers. They would joke with each other in the middle of Mary's presentation. They were making jokes… sexist jokes… and he had a rapport with them, and it was really noticeable… it was sad. It was really sad to see that we weren't getting a fair hearing. And it was so disrespectful toward Mary, who was a full partner in a large law firm in Toronto — one of the largest law firms in the country, and they were treating her really badly. It wasn't collegial or professional. They would say things to her to put her down.

At one point we had a break and she went out to the barristers lounge, and when she came back she was just looking odd, and she said, "Do you know what [the lawyer for Ontario; I can't remember his name] said?" She said that when they were coming back, he looked at her and asked if she would sew a button on his shirt for him. And you know this is a woman who in any other circumstance would be treated as a true colleague. It was a put down. It was interesting. There was a lot of stuff like that. So anyway, she was just treated really badly, with a lot of disrespect. The judge found against NWAC, and we appealed to the federal Court of Appeal.

Of course NWAC didn't get a lot of respect either. Not only did we not get respect, but the Aboriginal groups were really upset with us, that we brought the case. I think the government might have suggested that if they had to give money to the women, then it might come from the same pot or something like that. That's only speculation. But, anyway, the talks that led up to the Charlottetown Accord were still happening in the Royal York Hotel in Toronto. And we (NWAC) couldn't get into the meetings, because only the recognized groups could get into the meetings, and they would give them passes that they would hang around their necks. Security was tight: if you had a white pass you could go to certain meetings, if you had a red pass you could go to certain meetings, and if you had a certain coloured pass you could actually get into the meetings with the ministers. But, we couldn't get any of those. I don't think we had any passes. But we could look into doors. We could peek in. We'd be outside the doors and we would look in.

But through the media, we would tell the world about the plight of the Aboriginal women. So I was walking back to the elevators and I was stopped by two members of one of the male Aboriginal groups. I was by myself so I guess they decided they could get a little aggressive. They started yelling at me. They said that the women's association had no right calling men male chauvinist pigs. And they were taller than me, and they were actually close enough that they were spitting on me while they were yelling. They were right there, and of course I wasn't going to back down. I was looking up at them. But what was going on in my mind was… you know, what I really wanted to do was cry. Because that's what I do when I get upset, I cry. But I wasn't going to do that, not in front of them, right. So, I'm looking back and forth and I'm trying to think, how am I going to get myself out of this situation, right. And they continued to yell. And my friend Teressa, she walked back to the elevator, and so I said — oh, there you are, I've been waiting for you. Sorry guys, but I have to go. And I turned and we walked into the elevator and as soon as it closed I burst into tears.

No matter where we were we got that kind of treatment, and we did get more sinister things as well. Like, on one occasion, we got back to the hotel room and it was obvious that someone had been in the hotel room. And you could tell that they wanted me to know that they'd been in the hotel room. Things had been moved. So, it was a subtle message… a not so subtle message… we can get to you wherever you are, and that kind of thing. It was bad. It was really bad.

**Kuokkanen**: And how did you handle it?

**McIvor**: Well, we would talk to each other. We would stick together because we didn't want to be in a position where we could be harassed one-on-one or a bunch-on-one. So we looked out for each other in that regard. We acted publicly as though it didn't make one bit of difference, and as if it were not having any effect on us whatsoever. We were constantly being accosted. We were constantly being harassed one way or another.

There were four of us involved, and three of us did most of the work. I was the one that did the public stuff more. I did that for a very specific reason. I had no ties to my Aboriginal community that made it possible for any politicians to influence me. I was independent. I had my own home. My children weren't dependent on the band or anything. So I was the one that they couldn't touch in that way. The others weren't that fortunate. Their bands could take something away from them in order to manipulate them. I was the one that was the public face, because I was safe. I had to worry about my political life and my personal safety, but other than that they couldn't touch my professional or financial security, or my family — the really big stuff. And I continue to do the publicity today because I'm totally independent and I have the luxury of being able to be safe and to be free without having to worry that what I say might hurt somebody.

When the federal government refused to fund us we appealed the case to the federal Court of Appeal, and we won. It was a panel of three judges and we actually got a decent hearing at that. They interacted with our lawyer and asked pertinent questions. We did have a group of feminists in Toronto that knew that we were coming in and asked if we wanted them to come into the court when the hearing was on just to give support. And we gratefully said yes. So they came in and we had a whole bunch of women in the courtroom. And we won the appeal. The court found that we were discriminated against. And then the federal government appealed to the Supreme Court of Canada, where we lost.

During that period of time, Joe Clark was the Minister Responsible for the Constitution, and he met with us, as a result of media coverage. The governments and recognized organizations were in the Parliament building having constitutional talks and NWAC wasn't allowed in, so we had the women marching in front with their placards, protesting this exclusion. We got lots of media attention. The federal people were trying to divert that so they told the media that they were going to meet with the Native women. And so we did have a meeting with Joe Clark. And he asked us, "What do you want?" We said, "equal funding and a seat at the table." And he said, "Well, I can't do that." He talked about some of the issues. Mary Eberts was there, and Clark did make a point of saying, "I see you've got your high priced lawyer here." Little did he know that Mary was contributing her expertise and not charging us anything.

So we talked about issues and he said again, "Well, what do you want?" And we said, "Well, equal funding and a seat at the table." Then we talked some more and he finally said, "Well what can I do? What can I give you? What do you want?" And we said "equal funding and a seat at the table." And he just got up so fast and so angry that his chair went toppling backwards and he said, "Well we're not going to get anywhere if you go on like a broken record." So, he got himself some coffee and he calmed down and he came and sat at the table again.

One of our board members from Winnipeg said, "Well you know, Joe," and she started telling him about the plight of the women and children and the fact that the band council and chiefs were abusing their power and about the kinds of abuses that were going on. "You know, if you sleep with me then I'll fund your daughter's education. If you give me a blow job you can have your welfare cheque." And she started telling him and he said, "Winnie, don't get onto me about women and children." Needless to say, it was not a very good session, and we did not get any money, but what they did do without our consent was that they gave half a million dollars, for our use, but not directly to NWAC. They funneled it through CAP, the Congress of Aboriginal People, and the AFN. They gave them our money, and they said, "You give it to the women." It was earmarked for NWAC, so they couldn't *not* give it to us; but it provided the illusion that they were indeed including women.

*Kuokkanen*: But why would they do that?

*McIvor*: Because then the government didn't have to recognize us as a separate group, and it appeared as though the male-dominated Aboriginal organizations were supporting Aboriginal women. We had a really rough time, because CAP and AFN wanted us to sign agreements with them in order to get our money. We had to sign a contribution agreement with them to do certain things to get our money. And we didn't want to do that and so we did a lot of negotiation. We wanted the money no strings attached. They wanted signed agreements and audits and all of that. We did have one situation where we participated on a panel. The CAP had funding to send a panel across the country to interview their members about the Constitution, about self-government and all that, and to produce a report. AFN also had a panel. And so what they invited us to do was put a member on each panel. We took that opportunity. My friend Jane went on the CAP panel and I went on the AFN panel. But Jane had expenses that were paid that had to be billed to CAP. So what did she do? She put the expenses in to get paid out of NWAC's budget and then NWAC would bill the CAP. So, the billing went in to CAP, and CAP just sat on the money. They wouldn't give it to us. Finally, we threatened to take court action. So, we finally got the money but it was long after the Charlottetown Accord had been defeated. So we never used those monies to fund our participation in the Constitutional talks. We participated but we didn't get the money to do it until probably six to eight months after the Charlottetown Accord had been defeated.

We lived on borrowed money and whatever we could. I know that when the agreements culminated in the Charlottetown Accord and the government was preparing to have a referendum on it, that's where the ten million dollars came in. There was ten million dollars that was given by the federal government to the AFN to run their "yes" campaign. We didn't get any of that money because it was caught up in the bureaucracy. So we ended up with campaign funds of about thirty thousand dollars. We made a video, one video that cost us five thousand dollars, and it took the position opposing the Charlottetown Accord, because Aboriginal women's rights were not protected by the Charlottetown Accord. The rules were that, for every "yes" video, you had to play a "no" video. So one day it went on Hockey Night in Canada because they didn't have many "no" videos to air. Then, we got a call from a TV station in Northern Ontario that services the communities up there and they asked us for our video. But they said that video would have needed to be translated into Cree, and we said, we're sorry but we can't afford to do that. So they said we can't take it. Then they phoned us back later and asked if they could have it and they would translate it.

But, several things happened during that time period. One was, I was driving from Ottawa to Toronto and I stopped at a little rest stop and there was a McDonalds there, so I went in to get a drink, and I had my Native Women Association of Canada sweatshirt on. The woman at the till said, "I'm voting 'no' because it's not a good deal for Native women." So there were some poor working women that probably recognized the plight that we were talking about.

But when the Charlottetown Accord was defeated in the referendum, there were political consequences for the male-dominated Aboriginal organizations. The AFN had promised to deliver their communities' support for the Accord. I mean, they got the ten million dollars and they promised that their communities would support it. But the Aboriginal communities did not support it. It was defeated quite heavily in the Aboriginal vote. In those same Cree communities where our video was played, it was about an eighty-five percent "no" vote. So, we're taking credit for that. I guess because there weren't that many "no" videos, ours would get played over and over and over again.

But anyway, NWAC ended up going to the Supreme Court of Canada and losing. At that point the AFN intervened against us. Ovide Mercredi, who was the Grand Chief at that time, put in an affidavit against us that was not truthful. But, it went in and because of some political manipulation by the AFN, we weren't able to cross examine on that. So, it went in unchallenged, and the Supreme Court of Canada relied on the accuracy of that affidavit to find against us.[3] So, we ended up losing, and we were surprised when the federal government prepared the next invitation to the federal-provincial-territorial-Aboriginal meeting and NWAC got an invitation. We still didn't have equal funding. We did have a seat at the table, we had some recognition, but we still didn't have equal funding.

***Kuokkanen***: Can you talk about the solidarity that you've experienced as a feminist, and in your work?

***McIvor***: Well, we don't have very many Aboriginal feminists. The Aboriginal solidarity isn't there. Even within the NWAC you won't get many women identifying themselves as feminists. You still get responses like that of my good friend Bill Wilson.... I always smile when I say that because nobody likes him, he's not very friendly to women. Anyway, one of the things he would say was that we weren't real members of the Aboriginal community, that we were more tied to those feminists in Toronto and that we were being badly influenced by the white feminists of Toronto.

***Kuokkanen***: Do you have political alliances with non-Aboriginal feminist organizations?

***McIvor***: No alliances. We get support from them off and on, on a couple of issues. Our other mantra was that all of the political institutions, all of the institutions across Canada should be 51 percent women and 49 percent men because that would reflect the population. We had several discussions with the National Action Committee on the Status of Women (NAC) during this period, and they said they would be happy with 15 percent because it would be an improvement. We insisted that we would not settle for anything less than we were entitled to. And they said, well, that's too radical for them. They thought 15 would be a good starting point. We agreed to disagree on that.

So, we made some alliances under certain circumstances but we never did have a solid alliance because we come from a different place. For women throughout Aboriginal history, we come from a place of equality. We come from a place where in certain situations we have the superior role. I know when we were talking about equality my friend Ethel Pearce, an elder, said: "I don't want equality. Why would I want to be equal to those guys?" So that's where we come from. We come from respect. We come from equality. We never belonged to anybody. We were always our own person.

Look at our traditional Aboriginal divorce. You know, you've got your husband and wife and children in a family home, and if the wife decides that she doesn't want to be married anymore, he comes home and he sees his personal belongs outside the door. He picks them up and he goes home to his mother. That's it, the divorce. There's no question about custody. There's no question about ownership of the family home. The obligation is still there for him and his family to continue to provide for the children. And there's just no question about it.

European patriarchy treated women as something that men own. Up until the late 1930s women were owned by their husbands or fathers. They didn't have any independence. Well, we never had that history. Patriarchy was introduced with colonial contact.

Aboriginal women have a history of cultural respect for our personal integrity that no one should be able to invade. And people have been doing that, and we're saying that they can't do that. So, that's why there is a difference between our expectations and those of white women. If you have nothing and if in your history you've had nothing, then anything is an improvement. For us, we won't settle for anything less than we're entitled to, and we're entitled to that personal integrity, to equality, that place in society where you belong.

I am moved to action by injustice, but I never do for somebody what they should be doing for themselves. I can assist them to do something, but I would never take over. I guess that is one thing that I always think about in organizing. You know, what is my role? What do I have to do? Why am I doing this? You know, I make enough money. I could go lie on the beach somewhere.

I always tell the story of my oldest daughter. She was about ten or eleven at the time. She and me, my younger daughter who would have been four, my elderly aunt and my cousin all went into a restaurant here in town. We went in and we were seated. And then the server went and seated another non-Aboriginal family. And then she went to serve them first. She came to my table and I just said very nicely: "You know, we were seated first but you served them first. I really hope it doesn't have anything to do with racism." And she looked at me and turned really red in the face and said, "Oh, no no no," and she left. When I said that, my ten-year-old daughter just sunk down in her seat. My elderly aunt, who had spent a lot of time being discriminated against and abused, sort of closed into herself and my cousin did as well. We got excellent service after that, the waiter was really great, and I hope that she learned a little bit. But, my daughter sat up and she said, "Mom, why do you always do that?" And I just said, "So that you won't have to."

## NOTES

1. FAFIA's website is <www.fafia-afai.org/> (accessed March 2007).
2. The Charlottetown Accord was a 1992 proposal to amend the Canadian Constitution. It was placed before Canadians in a referendum and defeated. For more discussion of the implications of the Accord for Aboriginal women, see Joyce Green, Chapter 8.
3. For a critical analysis of the SCC decision in *NWAC v. Canada*, see Mary Eberts, Sharon McIvor and Teressa Nahanee (2006) "The Women's Court Decision in the Appeal of *NWAC v. Canada*," *Canadian Journal of Women and the Law* 18.